# SAVE THE CAT!®
# GOES TO THE
# INDIES

## The Screenwriters Guide to 50 Films from the Masters

# SALVA RUBIO
## BASED ON THE BOOKS BY
# BLAKE SNYDER

Published by *Save the Cat!*® Press

Cover Design: Barry Grimes Design
Layout: Gina Mansfield Design
Editors: Cory Milles, Naomi Beaty and Brett Jay Markel

Printed by McNaughton & Gunn, Inc., Saline, Michigan
Printed on Recycled Stock

ISBN 10: 0-9841576-6-2
ISBN 13: 978-0-9841576-6-2

# TABLE OF CONTENTS

# ACKNOWLEDGEMENTS

Let me start by thanking the many friends, family, collaborators, clients and all the loyal, close people who have given me their support, faith and encouragement while I was writing this book — thankfully, you are too many to note, and as the saying goes, you know well who you are... as I tell you all the time!

Also, this book wouldn't exist without the careful, patient, meticulous, painstaking editing work by Cory Milles and Naomi Beaty! And it looks and reads great because of Gina Mansfield's talents and skills doing the layout.

There are three people whose help and encouragement made this book possible:

First of all, let me thank my friend Miguel Angel Macarrón, AKA Maca, AKA Mr. Mck for his help finding and discussing the films that would be analyzed in the book. Ex-projectionist, fellow film analyst for many years and current teacher, his encyclopedic, firsthand knowledge of the European and American indie scenes was pivotal for me. They say a friend is someone that you call just about *any time*, so thanks for those many conversations in the middle of the night!

Second, I want to give a loud, "Thanks for trusting me!" to Brett Jay Markel, primary editor of this book. You believed in my ability to accomplish this task, and I am even more thankful knowing that you are letting me keep Blake Snyder's heritage alive and, hopefully, his ability to inspire people, to help them be creative and to empower them with storytelling. Thanks for your advice, editing and for giving me this chance!

Lastly, and in a special place of honor, thanks to Blake, wherever you are. I feel blessed for having met you — you changed my life in so many ways! Your generosity teaching the craft, your ability to make everything seem so easy and your endless "focus, discipline and positive energy" inspired me to follow your path and become a professional writer. I am so glad and honored to carry on the *Cat!* flag and keep your legacy alive.

Thank you all!

# FOREWORD

I first worked with Blake Snyder in 1986 and continued to work with him — on and off — until that fateful day in 2004 when publisher Michael Wiese asked me to edit a new screenwriting book. It was called "Save the Cat." Blake had written the first draft and Michael had already come up with the cover that would soon become iconic.

At the time, Blake was busy selling scripts but wanted to "codify" what he'd first recognized when *listening* to films while commuting from his home in Santa Barbara to Los Angeles — story categories, and beats he began to identify within the stories. And so his 10 genres, 15 beats and now-popular phrases like "save the cat," "pope in the pool" and "double mumbo jumbo" were born.

As the book came closer to its publication date, Michael sagely suggested we keep our goals modest, as the screenwriting book market was oversaturated (and still is 13 years later and counting!). The thing is… none of us had a clue what was about to happen.

The book was published in May 2005, and the rest is history. As I write this Foreword to the fourth entry in the series, *Save the Cat®* has been embraced by the professional screenwriting community across the globe.

The question is… why?

I think the biggest clue is how the Blake Snyder Beat Sheet fits so many movies produced before Blake even dreamed of writing his book. You see, he didn't really invent anything — he simply made it easy to break down movies so that today's writers could learn from those scribes who preceded them.

For all those critics who bristle at "formula," Blake was trying to do no more than provide a common language to analyze and create films. That was the primary purpose of his second book, *Save the Cat!® Goes to the Movies*, which presented Beat Sheets for 50 mostly studio-produced films (5 for each of Blake's 10 genres).

And now one of his mentees, Spain's brilliant and talented screenwriter and novelist Salva Rubio, takes an exciting step, applying Blake's language to 50 independent, European and cult films in this book, *Save the Cat® Goes to the Indies* (again 5 Beat Sheets for each of Blake's 10 genres).

Discover here how Tarantino's *Pulp Fiction* and *Reservoir Dogs*, von Donnersmarck's *The Lives of Others*, The Coen Brothers' *O Brother, Where Art Thou?* and *The Big Lebowski*, Kubrick's *Paths of Glory* (co-written with Calder Willingham and Jim Thompson) and Sofia Coppola's *Lost in Translation* — along with 43 other "indie" classics — "hit the beats."

Blake would be so proud of Salva — and would also take great joy in the fact that the language he created is still being used to help writers do what they do best: write.

Brett Jay Markel
April, 2017

# INTRODUCTION

Well, for me, it was pretty normal. Another day at the office! Literally. But then I realized that for others... it was something rather odd. And it came as a surprise to them. *But how could they not see it?* I thought. *It worked so well!*

Wait! What I am talking about? You mean that... Blake Snyder's Beat Sheet and his genres, something seemingly designed for Hollywood blockbusters, could be used for indie and auteur films? *What?* Well, let me tell you a story...

When I started my film analyst, script doctor and screenwriting career, I used to work for one of Europe's most important independent distribution, exhibition and production companies. Lots of independent and auteur scripts arrived at the office, seeking distribution, co-production, international sales and financing — in many cases before the movie was shot.

Thus, I was fortunate enough to read scripts by the Coen Brothers, Eric Rohmer, Gus Van Sant, Walter Salles, Jane Campion, Christopher Hampton (whom I even met!), Amos Gitai, Marjane Satrapi, John Turturro, Larry Clark and David Cronenberg, among many other talented writers. Of course, I also read the usual less-than-good amateur proposals and literally a thousand just plain bad ones.

It was then that I realized that the best scripts — no matter how cutting-edge the director's later approach or the resulting film — were written with a classic narrative format in mind, and of course, all of them fit the Blake Snyder Beat Sheet. And I also recognized that, once these films premiered, the most successful, most awarded and most viewed also were in harmony with the Beat Sheet!

So before we go on, let me re-emphasize this point: no matter how much the resulting film was auteur-ish, indie-like, or (insert-your-*Cahiers-du-Cinema* critique here), the original script of each of these successful yet cutting-edge films was perfectly classic in its narrative approach. And thus, Blake's techniques and genres worked beautifully to create stories that resonated.

Many of these films went on to win awards at Sundance, Berlinale, Cannes and even some from the Academy. And despite their indie status, some of them were pretty big hits at the box office. I learned that sometimes, the visual narrative, montage or art direction of the resulting film doesn't let us see the script behind it... but if the film has been a success, you can bet there's a Blake Snyder Beat Sheet lurking inside.

I realized that what was so obvious for me wasn't necessarily that apparent for many others, so as a test I wrote a Beat Sheet for Michael Haneke's Academy Award®-winning drama *Amour* for the *Save the Cat!*® blog. The feedback I got was great, and I thought that I could show my fellow European, indie and worldwide auteur screenwriters that Blake's principles would be useful for them, too.

And thus, this book was born!

## BUT IT'S ME VS. HOLLYWOOD... RIGHT?

Of course, you may be scratching your head under your beanie hat or pushing your horn-rimmed glasses up your nose, or even touching your well-groomed beard in disbelief: can a bestselling method, apparently devised for writing blockbusters, help you with your $12,000 self-made independent film about your grandpa's return to rural Wisconsin from 'Nam? Isn't Hollywood the enemy? Can this get me onto the Black List? Will Sean Penn want to star in it?

I think the *Save the Cat!*® principles are for writing good stories, period.

And I can attest to that, since as a professional screenwriter, novelist, essayist and graphic-novel writer, I have used it in many genres and formats, from artsy European comic books to commercial animation series and features.

Indeed, it was the visual style, the outer finish, that gave those works the indie/auteur-ish look — the inner story was as classic as you can get.

That is why for this book we have selected a wide array of films that belong to many categories, countries, schools and styles, but practically none of them — or so we think — have been backed by what you could call the all-mighty-dollar Hollywood industry.

We have low-budget films that became international sensations like *The Blair Witch Project*, promising debuts like *Pi* by Darren Aronofsky, small films that acquired cult status like *The Texas Chain Saw Massacre*, Euro-blockbusters like *The Full Monty*, indie gems like *Before Sunrise*, textbook classics such as *The 400 Blows*... all of which seem to defy categorization! There are, of course, other higher-budget films in our book, but they still financially fit the "independent" label, like *The Impossible*, but we promise that we have kept away from big-budget, studio-driven, blockbuster-oriented, tent-pole summer bets, super-hero franchises and the like.

But is that all there is? Are scripts for the two kinds of films — auteur and commercial — really the same? As you will see, the Blake Snyder Beat Sheet and Blake's 10 genres work perfectly in the indie world, but there *are* some differences with mainstream examples.

## OUR THEME STATED: FLEXIBILITY

We offer three guarantees. In all of our chosen films:

1) All the beats are there.
2) All of them are in the proper order.
3) All of the films feature the 5-Point Finale.

Besides these, the key word for using the Blake Snyder Beat Sheet in your indie/auteur film is simply **flexibility** — especially in certain aspects of writing regarding timing.

This much is clear: most Hollywood films have a fixed duration, with scripts following a certain set of rules pertaining to beats and act-break timing. They are usually 90-110 pages long. Some beats usually fall on page 12 (Catalyst), while others are usually around pages 45-50 (Midpoint). They are three-hole-punched and held with 2 brass brads (seriously, do they still do this?). Woe to you if your script doesn't respect these rules in the blockbuster world! The dreaded agent or studio analyst might throw it, curve-ball style, to the nearest recycling bin, and there goes a great film.

Luckily for us, in this book, the beats don't have a fixed page number, but an approximate proportion in regards to the rest of the film. Thus in the indie or auteur film realm, **script or beat length** is not a set rule, and we can have really long films, such as *Dogville* (178 mins), *Brazil* (142 mins), *Boogie Nights* (155) or even the aforementioned *Amour*, whose script is about 67 pages long yet the resulting film lasts 127 minutes... and went on to win an Academy Award®! I know many executives whose heads would explode by this fact alone.

There are other ways to play around with time, like **giving extra time to certain beats and scenes** — they could be only 3 pages long, but the director might want to experiment with scene duration or the direction of the actors. This happens, for example, in Haneke's *Funny Games* where the Dark Night of the Soul beat takes about 10 minutes. And in *Blue Is the Warmest Color* (*Life of Adèle*), the Break into Three beat is just one scene that lasts 15 minutes. Isn't it awesome that some Finales can last for almost one hour, like in the Director's Cut of *Cinema Paradiso*?

Another way I discovered that indie writers play with beats is seen in **Blake's 5-Point Finale**, the best way to nail an ending. Every one of the supposedly anti-classic films we feature follow it. And it's also a nice tool to try interesting techniques structure-wise. Did you know that *The Lives of Others* has two consecutive 5-Point Finales, one for each main character? And that in *Being John Malkovich* those beats are doubled *and* simultaneous, just like in *Blue Valentine*?

There are other ways of experimenting with beats, like using **multiple Beat Sheets**. The master of this technique is, no doubt, Quentin Tarantino — *Reservoir Dogs* breaks into two Beat Sheets (albeit cleverly hiding some beats from sight) and *Pulp Fiction* breaks into three interlaced Beat Sheets (one for each major character's story). It take sheer talent to pull something like this off, but he did it... so you can too.

Of course, there are more ways of having fun (and games) with the Beat Sheet, as we will see with each analysis. Will you be the one to find out even more? Well, tell us, of course! Honoring Blake's own tradition in his books, here is my personal email. Seriously, write us: *salva@salvarubio.info*

## TO FIT OR NOT TO FIT... THAT ISN'T THE QUESTION!

As for assigning each film to a genre, the key word is, again, flexibility. Blake made it very clear in *Save the Cat!® Goes to the Movies* that your goal in writing (and in life) shouldn't be to try and find films that do not fit in any categories, if only to prove us wrong. There are better ways to waste your time!

In the indie realm, the borders among films are not only fuzzy, but many times they openly overlap — and that's a good thing, because you could even think of mixing genres or using complementary storylines to enrich your script and your themes. This is not new. In countless films, there is a Buddy Love take to its B Story regardless of its genre. So, although doubts may arise when trying to fit an indie film into a given category, use this genre flexibility to your advantage!

After all, this also happens in mainstream films. Doesn't *Big* have elements of Out of the Bottle and Fool Triumphant? And Blake himself talked about *Ghost* as an example of a genre mix, so expect it to happen much more in our rebellious independent realm. Is *Pan's Labyrinth* more of a Golden Fleece or a Superhero? And does *Cinema Paradiso* fit better in Buddy Love (because of Totó's relationship with the projectionist) or Institutionalized (regarding the themes of his belonging to his birth town)?

Is the *Ghost Writer* more of a DWAP or a Whydunit? And *O Brother, Where Art Thou?* — doesn't it have elements of both a Buddy Fleece and an Epic Fleece? What about *sex, lies, and videotape*? Yes, it could belong to the Sex Fool subgenre but a closer look shows that it may fit better with Issue Institution. Even *Boogie Nights* could be an Institutionalized, but it fits Sex Fool, too. And *The Elephant Man* could be a Fool Triumphant, but we placed it in People's Superhero, which fits as well or better. A dual-cop classic like *The French Connection* could seem to be a Professional Love story to some, but instead, our take is that it's a Cop Whydunit. Even *Lost in Translation* could easily seem a Buddy Love too, but we decided to go for the Mid Life Passage themes. Keep in mind that all this flexibility only enriches your themes!

So here's our advice: there is no point in trying to set in stone which film belongs in which genre. Simply use this tool to your advantage by "breaking a story" and don't get too worked up trying to determine what fits and what doesn't. As Blake wrote, "In cases where we are not sure what type of movie it is, the bottom line is we now have a language to talk about it [...] if you are trying to 'stump the author' by thinking up movies that don't fit the paradigm... Stop. Won't help you."

## (IF) YOU'RE NOT GETTING IT (YET)

Another reason why I wrote this book is because sometimes the *Save the Cat!*® principles are criticized by people who deem them as "formulaic," "too Hollywood-minded" and so on.

But for Cat's sake, many people don't realize that *all* of the films Blake mentioned in *Save the Cat!*® *Goes to the Movies* were released *before* he wrote the book. I don't think Blake invented something that wasn't already there, and I don't think he ever said otherwise. The beats had always been in the stories! What Blake did was figure them out, give them a name and teach us all how to use them, and we must thank him for that. (Or maybe the problem for many was that he used such an approachable language and light-hearted, made-up terms instead of academic-heavy prose. Well, guess which approach this book has used?)

If today Blake's teachings are being used in boring and non-creative ways, especially in the Hollywood realm, please don't kill the messenger. Ask the executives who greenlit those scripts, deciding that mass audiences are dumb and deserve "the same, but *not* different." Because those audiences sometimes come out in great numbers to choose smaller, fresher, more surprising films! Ask the producers of *The Blair Witch Project*, *The Artist*, *Trainspotting*, *The Full Monty* or *Little Miss Sunshine*, will ya?

So, are the *Save the Cat!*® principles a *formula*? No, because a screenplay is a *format*. There is a big difference between the two words, because they mean that screenwriting itself, and feature films as we know them, must be written with a format in mind. After all, pop songs are another format, yet nobody complains when they are good! That is what makes them incredibly popular, but when done badly, they are just plain boring and justly labelled as formulaic... just like mainstream films. So if Hollywood is "pop music," we will think like singer-songwriters who don't avoid pop structure or formats... but rather, are creative with it.

Seriously, have you heard anyone tell you that Beethoven's symphonies (hey, they're a format, too) are formulaic? Or that you should not write sonnets (another closed format used for hundreds of years) like Petrarch... or you won't be creative? Or to forget about haikus and their wonderful 17-syllable *format*? I think that screenplays are a format too, and you simply can choose to be boring or to be creative and thus more interesting. Creative people do not need to avoid format, but rather they use it cleverly to their own advantage.

Would anyone dare say, "Formulaic!" about the works of Sofía Coppola, Krzysztof Kieslowski, Danny Boyle, Darren Aronofsky, Woody Allen, Stanley Kubrick, Lars Von Trier, David Lynch, Wes Anderson, Joel and Ethan Coen, Quentin Tarantino or François Truffaut? *Huh?*

## HAVE FUN AND SUCCESS... YOUR WAY!

Not so many years ago, there was one great paradigm in the mainstream cinema industry: write a great spec, find an agent, move to Hollywood and triumph! Or be a miserable failure.

But times have a-changed, and now, there's not just *that one goal* for aspiring screenwriters, directors and actors — despite what the many books published with the word "Hollywood" in their title want you to believe.

For starters, there are many people who may dig industry films (we all love some!), but they want to make a different kind of cinema, as art school filmmakers, indie directors, European-style *realisateurs*, and global screenwriters from all over the world. Some of us do not *only* have Hollywood in mind, but rather Sundance's Program lab, the Cannes market, Berlinale Talents, the Dreamago workshop or your local short film contest. And some of us do not necessarily dream of having an Oscar® in our bedroom — our outer success is measured in BAFTAs, Golden Palms, Goyas, César awards or the dreamt prize of your choice.

It used to be expensive and hard to make films, and studios were needed. Now, if you have an iPhone, you've just ran out of excuses to shoot, produce, cast and distribute. There is Netflix, YouTube or many online platforms and apps to fund, produce, edit and show your work, launch your career and who knows — maybe even reach Hollywood, if that's your goal after all!

Many of the filmmakers that belong to this "global filmmaking" generation will not need to move to Los Angeles or ever work for a studio, and they will be able to make a living receiving commissions, crowdfunding their films, selling them through alternative distribution channels — all through the internet. And more than making a living, they can also become rather successful and, what is even more important... happy.

Films, documentaries, shorts — visual content is needed everywhere, now more than ever! And this is only the beginning! A new era of visual media has begun.

Forget being forced to rely on gatekeepers, producers and studios. You are the one to decide what kind of films you want to make, sell and see.

We have written this book to help you make them... and make it!

## BLAKE SNYDER'S STRUCTURE AND GENRE GUIDE

To make the most of this book, you should know a little more about Blake's beats and genres. Of course, we have three books' worth of information on them, so we advise you to read the former volumes of this series: *Save the Cat!®*, *Save the Cat!® Goes to the Movies!* and *Save the Cat!® Strikes Back!* For now, here is your *Cat! 101* course guide for this book!

## THE BEATS

Blake's method is structured around two main tools: the Blake Snyder Beat Sheet and his genres.

As for the first, it consists of a 15-point structure of "beats" or "moments" that happen in any well-written story or script, in a particular order. In each beat, something must happen to the main character/protagonist/hero for the maximum enjoyment of the reader or the viewer and must serve to move the story forward.

**Opening Image**: At the beginning of the story, we must give a good first impression of the "before" image of our story's world and hero. There is usually one *systemic problem* that the main character will fix (or fail to fix!) so we can have a contrasting Final Image at the end of the story.

**Theme Stated**: In the first minutes of the film, one of the characters usually utters a line, sometimes said to the main character, in which the theme is summarized — it's what the movie is about. This is one of the two "mobile" beats than can appear anywhere in the beginning of the script.

**Set-Up**: Next, there is the section of the script where we come to know the protagonist better through the *Six Things That Need Fixing*. Sometimes we will see the protagonist in his "at home," "at work" and "at play" moments. A "Save the Cat!" scene — when the hero does something that makes us like him or her — is a good thing to have here, and also a *Stasis=Death* moment to show how much the hero needs to change.

**Catalyst**: It was a normal day in the life of our main character until... kaboom! In this beat, something happens that disrupts the hero's life. From an H-Bomb exploding, to a simple call at work, to a knock on the door or a personal tragedy, nothing will ever be the same!

**Debate**: Of course, our protagonist still does not know how much the Catalyst is going to affect his life, so we need to have a few scenes debating the impact, the next steps to take, or the overall craziness of a situation he or she never thought about. Can they dodge the adventure?

**Break into Two**: Our hero "gets the case," so the story is properly set in motion. Usually, this takes the form of a symbolic gateway or a journey with "no turning back." We are about to enter the *upside-down world* of Act Two!

**B Story**: The second mobile beat, the B Story usually introduces a character who will carry the theme or love story. This beat can happen basically anywhere up to this point, and sometimes even after. Of course, we as writers will cause *A and B Stories to cross* a lot.

**Fun and Games**: The *promise of the premise*, as Blake famously put it, this is the section of the script in which the plot lightens up to let us and the main character explore the new world. Set pieces and trailer moments belong here — this is what we came to see when enticed by the poster or logline.

**Midpoint**: One of the most challenging beats, this usually takes more than one scene. In it, our character will have a *false victory* or a *false defeat*, plus a *public coming out* which indicates who he is becoming in his character arc. It is also the moment where *stakes are raised*, there is *Sex at 60*, *clocks start ticking* and *A and B Stories* usually *cross*.

**Bad Guys Close In**: The opposition of the antagonists comes with full force in this section. Our hero had miscalculated his own powers and pressure mounts, not only from the outside, but from the inside as well, as the "team starts disintegrating." "Bad guys" can be both external (plot machinations) and internal (emotions).

**All Is Lost**: This beat is crucial! The hero is "worse off than when he started" and in many cases there is a *whiff of death* that makes victory seem impossible.

**Dark Night of the Soul**: The hero dwells on his low point as he slowly realizes that he has avoided change for so long and is in dire straits because of his inaction... so now it seems like there is no solution.

**Break into Three**: A moment of realization, a spark of genius or a sudden idea makes the hero realize that maybe the story's goal can be attained after all! This possibility is usually triggered by the love interest or mentor as *A and B Stories meet*.

**Finale**: Our Act Three starts, and the film is nearing its end! Here comes one of Blake's most useful tools, the bullet-proof **5-Point Finale** to finish your story on a great note:
1. Gathering the Team: Ready for the final assault, the hero "gathers" with another character(s) to "amend hurts," to announce his plan or to "prepare the assault."

2. Executing the Plan: The "plan" is carried out as devised by the hero, and it seems to work! Victory is in sight!

3. High Tower Surprise: "It's a trap!" Unfortunately, the baddies had something in store for our hero, so the plan is not useful anymore. The main character finds himself on his own and with everything depending on him. Will he find the strength now?

4. Dig, Deep Down: The determination to win makes the protagonist "dig, deep down" inside for the courage to do what he never thought himself capable of accomplishing.

5. The Execution of the New Plan: So with that newfound strength, the hero confronts the baddies again, usually winning the battle... but sometimes losing it despite everything.

**Final Image**: As the film ends, we see a contrasting image that is often the opposite of the Opening Image. The world, our hero or his/her allies have changed forever, showing that "All Stories Are About Transformation."

## THE GENRES

This is what the book you're holding is all about. We'll get into more detail about each genre in each chapter, but let us give you some basic guidelines before we dig deeper.

Blake's **10 genres** are universal templates which every story ever written fits. Audiences know these genres, and they want to be told the same story all over again when they go to the cinema, only in a different form. They know them so well (executives included) that when the screenplay is not told by each genre's "rules," audiences are sure that something isn't working right. In fact, sometimes everyone knows but the writer, who usually is so knee-deep in the story that he doesn't realize there are problems. Strike a bell?

For this reason, it's really useful to find out what your story is in terms of genre before you even start working on it. You will then know the **three fundamental components** each genre must have and how those components work in terms of characters, structure and theme.

And what is even cooler is that each of these 10 genres have 5 subgenres of their own, further enlarging your narrative possibilities!

Knowing these genres will give you other kinds of advantages. Your movie world is about to change! Until now, you probably thought of genres in terms of comedy, drama, action, western, Wes Anderson, etc.

From now on, you'll realize that horror cult classic *The Texas Chainsaw Massacre* and German political drama *The Lives of Others* are basically the same film! And David Lynch's disturbing *The Elephant Man* and Soderbergh-directed, Julia Roberts-starred *Erin Brockovich* belong to the same genre! And *Dogville*, the obscure avant-garde piece by Danish auteur Lars Von Trier, and the charming love letter to film that is *Cinema Paradiso*, tell the same story!

And so do the enchanting *Amélie* and macho-piece *Fight Club!*

And so does a dark, violent film like *Reservoir Dogs* and a light, comedic one like *Little Miss Sunshine!*

And... stop me, will you?

Jim wakes up in eerily quiet, seemingly abandoned London. And that's the "normal world" in the Set-Up of *28 Days Later*!

# 1 MONSTER IN THE HOUSE

It should be no surprise that we start this book about "indie, auteur and European" movies with one of the most productive genres in independent cinema history: the "Monster in the House."

MITH films are one of the most primal among the 10 *Save the Cat!*® genres, and also more akin to their commercial or mainstream counterparts. This is completely logical, since many of the classics of the genre are technically independent films, even if they are now mainstream franchises, like *Halloween*, *A Nightmare on Elm Street* and *Friday the 13th*.

As we will see, some of the most literally gut-wrenching, terrifying and scary MITH films are still considered in the realm of independent cinema — even consecrated European auteurs have given it a go.

Some of these "small" (by Hollywood standards) films demonstrate how a limited budget can only boost imagination, passion and talent, turning some of the movies we are about to analyze into classics that have shaken up the conventions of genre, if not cinema history itself. Is not an "infectious" British movie (*28 Days Later*) responsible for the resurrection and (ahem) new life of the zombie genre? Did *Saw* not inspire a new, original and successful franchise? We just expect this display of creativity to follow a story as old as time — aren't we simply re-telling the Theseus, Ariadna (the first "Final Girl"), the minotaur and the labyrinth story?

So if you are a fan of horror films and want to write a MITH, what do you need, besides morbidity, a dark imagination and lots of ketchup?

The first element you need to create is what we call a **monster**. Monsters can come in all shapes and sizes but have one common component: supernatural power. Even if they are (or were) just humans, there is something in their skills, intelligence, insanity, evil or appearance that makes them superior to the average human — from zombies to the infected (*28 Days Later*), from masked evil beings chasing teenagers in slasher films (*The Texas Chain Saw Massacre*)to the super-evil and super-polite teenagers in *Funny Games*. In any case, the real menace is that that these monsters seem able to take both your body and your soul. As Blake reminded us, make your monsters powerful, or your script's possibilities will suffer accordingly!

The second element you will need is the **house**. We can mean this literally (as in *Les Diaboliques* or *Single White Female*) but the house can also be any "labyrinth" or enclosed space our heroes are trapped in with the monster — from a really small location (the boat in *Knife in the Water*) to places as big as an endless forest (*The Blair Witch Project*) to a whole quarantined country (*28 Days Later*). The houses can be metaphorical too, as the all-encompassing surveillance that unknowingly haunts our characters in *The Lives of Others*. In any case, make sure your characters can't escape!

The third element is a **sin**, because deep within all these films (unlike our "Dude with a Problem" genre, in which everything that happens to the protagonist is undeserved), the characters somehow *earned* the problem. It is a sin of some kind which makes them deserve what they are going through, which is why we see the retribution as some kind of retaliation from higher forces. Perhaps this is why in so many movies the pure, innocent girl in the group defeats evil — she was not condemned like the rest. The sin can be simply hatred (*28 Days Later*), lying (*The Lives of Others*) or disrespect to the supernatural, as in *The Blair Witch Project*. The sin is utterly necessary (except in the "Nihilist Monster" subgenre, as we will see shortly).

There is also a peculiar character whom Blake defined as the **Half Man** that tends to show up in MITH movies. This personage "knows the nature of the beast" because he seems to be in touch with the supernatural, and usually warns our protagonists about dealing with such dark powers. In some cases, he will even help them in their fight — many times suffering because of it, since he should have known better. The Half Men are damaged, flawed, often dark mentors, like the barbecue man in *The Texas Chain Saw Massacre* or Wiesler, our POV character in *The Lives of Others*, who knew better the workings of the Stasi because he was a member.

As with the rest of our 10 genres, the MITH category has five subgenres of its own, each with a different twist to better nail the movie you are analyzing or writing.

The first of them is called the **Pure Monster**, dealing with "supercharged beasts," including zombies or the infected — they are creatures with super-strength, super-animal behavior or super-killer instincts that will hunt down your characters one by one. Just remember *The Night of the Living Dead*, *Dawn of the Dead* or any of its sequels, and you will understand the blueprint.

We also can write the **Domestic Monster**, in which the beast is very much human and the story tends to happen in an everyday environment, with the "monster" being someone who may appear to be just normal or caring — even family! But wait until you incur their wrath. *The Lives of Others*, *Hard Candy* or *The Stepfather* are worthy examples.

Next, let us study the **Serial Monster** variety, which has the workings of the tried-and-true genre called the "slasher film." The independent and European realm truly have their share of this kind of monster's doings, as seen in such films as *Cold Prey*, *Halloween* or the über-terrifying (and the sexual tourist's worst nightmare) *Hostel*.

Our next subgenre is the **Super-Natural Monster**, featuring beings, creatures or entities that come from other realms or dimensions, and thus can torture, kill and maim our bodies... and our souls... for eternity! Hits like *The Ring*, *The Shining*, *The Exorcism of Emily Rose* or our chosen example, *The Blair Witch Project*, reflect our deepest fears.

Last, but not the least scary, is the **Nihilist Monster**, the exception to the "sin" requirement. Unlike the rest of the monsters, who seemingly need a provocation to attack, the Nihilist one will assault us just because! No sin is seemingly committed, although ignorance could be one — you didn't deserve it, you just happened to be passing by or were in the wrong place at the wrong time. The cruelest of our monsters will get you, like they did in *Saw*, *Cabin Fever*, *Audition* or *Funny Games*.

## DON'T BE AFRAID OF YOUR MITH

If you really want to make your characters and audiences suffer, you've found the ideal genre. Here's what you'll need:

1. A "monster" whose powers are or seem supernatural (insanity counts!). They are evil, on the prowl and looking for you!

2. A "house" or an enclosed space where your protagonists will be trapped. It can be physical or metaphorical, as small as an actual house or as big as a whole country. Just make sure your characters have no way out!

3. A "sin" your characters have committed, either in ignorance or perhaps from arrogance — regardless, the sin has really made someone in the dark angry, and now someone else has to pay!

So now that you have sharpened your writing tools, get ready to enter the darkness and prepare to defend against the monster... or to become one!

## 28 DAYS LATER (2002)

If you were alive before 2002, you will remember that the zombie genre was pretty much... dead. But just as the deceased have a tendency to rise from their graves, this British film resurrected undead apocalypse fiction, re-animating not only dozens of successful films, TV series and comic books, but turning the genre mainstream again.

Starting with a meager $8M, director Danny Boyle and writer Alex Garland exploited collective terror by portraying the usually busy and lively city of London as an eerily empty wasteland. They not only gave us an unforgettable view of the city but also struck a common chord, dealing with the fear against our fellow man and citizens in difficult times.

Many of the worldwide praise for the film also came from the fact that the formerly slow, moaning and dragging (read: boring) traditional zombies were turned into the "infected," which have very different traits: fast-moving, enraged, agile, vicious... so don't think about outrunning them! *28 Days Later* is thus an example of the "Pure Monster" genre, in which an unusually powerful beast or animal relentlessly pursues a group of survivors. And aren't the infected nothing more than "human animals"?

By supercharging them with "rage," Boyle and Garland are telling us a story about survival in a zombie apocalypse, and also about a more decisive choice — even if we are safe from the virus, can we not be as deadly as the infected when we lose our human values?

MITH Type: Pure Monster

MITH Cousins: *Night of the Living Dead*, *Attack the Block*, *The Mist*, *Dawn of the Dead*, *Dead Snow*

28 DAYS LATER
*Written by* Alex Garland
*Directed by* Danny Boyle

**Opening Image**: TV images of a world in turmoil, violence and "people killing people." Are they infected by the virus? No, but we soon find out that there is another kind of disease that is not transmitted by blood or saliva, but is equally lethal: the virus of hate, rage and violence, which is our "sin." Is it possible to live in a world without them? Our story starts with three animal rights activists setting loose some lab monkeys and unknowingly becoming the first victims of the real virus.

**Theme Stated**: The theme is stated early on, when the doctor attacked by the activists answers a question regarding the monkeys. "Infected with what?" "Rage." It can be a disease, but also an attitude — violence and hate are just as contagious as a virus, and if spread to the whole population, can it not cause the same amount of harm?

**Set-Up**: Precisely 28 days later, a naked man named Jim (Cillian Murphy), strapped to a bed much like the chimpanzee in the first scene, wakes up to find himself in an empty hospital, seeing afterwards the barren streets and deserted whole city of London. As with all good Set-Ups, this film describes the "systemic problem": humanity has disappeared off the face of the earth! And Jim seems to be the only survivor, as he wanders the empty city calling out a single word: "Hello." Jim does not seem afraid, and he is eager to find other people. He still trusts humanity.

**Catalyst**: At minute 12, Jim finds a newspaper and finally learns what happened. After the outbreak, all UK citizens were meant to be evacuated, resulting in global chaos.

**Debate**: Doubts are the foundation of every effective Debate beat. Where have the people been evacuated to? Where must he go now? The answer comes soon, when Jim seeks refuge for the night in a nearby church and is greeted by an infected priest, who shows him (and us) the real effect of the infection — people have been turned into rabid, agile, zombie-like predators who infect each other with blood and saliva. Fortunately, Jim soon finds two other non-infected people, joker Mark (Noah Huntley) and tough-gal Selena (Naomie Harris).

**B Story**: Selena is the perfect B Story Character — not only because of the obvious attraction and sexual tension between her and Mark, but also because her own humanity is at risk. She soon claims that she will kill anyone who gets infected and that "staying alive is as good as it gets." But Jim seems to know that under that rugged façade, she is a good person, one who can still be "infected" by hatred, losing her humanity. Could he end up being infected himself?

**Break into Two**: After being briefed by Mark and Selena about how the outbreak took place and how there is no government, police, army, TV, radio or electricity, Jim decides that he wants to see his family in Deptford (South East London). Mark sets two rules: to never go anywhere alone and to travel only by day.

**Fun and Games**: And so the Fun and Games beat involves getting out in the open and risking being attacked by the infected. When they finally reach Jim's home, he finds his parents dead and soon after, they are attacked. Mark gets infected, so Selena ruthlessly dispatches of him, showing that her words were true — she will show no remorse! They find two more survivors: Frank and his teenage daughter Hannah. The group can't just hide, as they are running out of water, so Frank makes them listen to a radio transmission by the army promising them help from the 42nd blockade. Selena protests, but Hannah states "We need each other." They decide to go to the blockade, ignoring the recording's warning that "We are soldiers. We are armed." On the way, Jim viciously kills an infected boy. Is his own humanity at stake?

**Midpoint**: The *false victory* comes when they arrive at Waverley Abbey, where they can spend some hours in peace without fearing for their lives. It is a "Midpoint celebration," a "campfire scene" which for them precludes salvation and fills them with hope as they see some wild horses run free. It is also time for some brief *Sex at 60*, as Selena kisses Jim "for a heartbeat." She is obviously not ready for anything more.

**Bad Guys Close In**: The next morning, they find the 42nd blockade, where supposedly salvation awaits. Not only is it deserted, Frank gets infected and is about to attack the group, when a hail of bullets kills him. Jim, Selena and Hannah are saved (or captured?) by a bunch of surviving soldiers under the command of a Major Henry West, who tries hard to be nice to them. He is also the *Half Man* of our movie, as he is keeping an infected soldier,

Mailer, chained "to learn from him." West's intentions remain unclear, military discipline is lacking everywhere and he sees the situation as normal, because "people killing people" is what has been happening before and after the infection. Isn't this the echo of the "sin of violence"? Soon after some of the infected enter the premises, the soldiers show their true plans: to force Selena and Hannah to have sex, because by doing so, "they mean a future."

**All Is Lost**: Jim grabs Selena and Hannah and tries to flee from the house, but is knocked out, ending their last chance to escape. The lights of the house go out as their hope fades.

**Dark Night of the Soul**: Jim listens to the rant of a sargeant, who thinks that the UK has been quarantined but the rest of the world is still uninfected. Is there hope?

**Break into Three**: It seems that Jim will never find out, since in the morning he is to be shot along with the sergeant. The latter provokes the soldiers, so Jim uses the confusion to escape. And then he sees something: a plane flying overhead. They may have a chance!

**Finale**:

1. Gathering the Team: Jim decides to save Selena and Hannah, and for that he must "gather the team" of soldiers so that he can dispose of them. He rings a siren, kills one of them and leaves West behind, fighting with some infected. But unexpectedly, West survives.

2. Executing the Plan: Jim — now moving, behaving and looking like an infected (*synthesis* man!) — enters the literal castle to execute his plan: to release Mailer, the infected soldier, so that other soldiers will kill and infect each other.

3. High Tower Surprise: Jim realizes that the soldier who tried to rape Selena is holding her! So from the attic (again, a literal "high tower"), he savagely attacks him as if infected.

4. Dig, Deep Down: When Selena thinks Jim has been infected, Jim "digs deep down" and lets her attack him, but she stops at the last moment, incapable of hurting him. Jim has shown Selena that she still has some humanity inside. They will be able to be together after all. There is still hope!

5. The Execution of the New Plan: The new plan involves running away from the house, which they do in the taxi they brought, while Hannah has her own revenge by letting Mailer kill West. Then unexpectedly Jim is wounded. Will they survive?

**Final Image**: 28 days yet later, Jim wakes up in a country house with Selena and Hannah. Not far away, the last of the infected are dying of starvation. When the survivors hear a plane, they display a huge sign in the green grass. Their "hell" has turned into Jim's motto: "Hello."

## THE LIVES OF OTHERS (2006)

One of 2006's film sensations, this German story earned a variety of well-deserved prizes, including an Academy Award® for Best Foreign Language Film, truly a remarkable achievement considering it was the first full-length film of director F. H. Von Donnersmark... and shot with a $2 million budget, earning $77 million by 2007!

In our post-Snowden world, can there be a better "monster" than the Stasi, the all-knowing secret police with thousands of plain citizen informants that filed every little private secret of the German Democratic Republic people before the fall of the Berlin Wall? And isn't the whole country a "house" in which citizens can be enclosed and chased by higher powers? Finally, isn't the arrogance of lying a "sin"?

It is also a good choice for this book because it breaks many expectations — it is not even a traditional horror film, but a political drama. However, all the components of a good "Domestic Monster" are here, even the *Half Man*, that damaged character who knows about the terrible consequences of dealing with the beast, who in a twist, stars in one of our two storylines. Wait, two?

Narratively, a number of very interesting decisions were made in this film, particularly the fact that there are not one but two parallel and overlapping stories, resulting in two beat sheets, one for each of the male characters, writer Georg Dreyman and Stasi agent Hauptmann Gerd Wiesler. In another creative twist, this results in two consecutive Finales, each with their own 5-point structure! As in many cases, breaking the rules can definitely get you an Oscar®.

MITH Type: Domestic Monster

MITH Cousins: *Straw Dogs*, *We Need to Talk About Kevin*, *The Devils* (*Les Diaboliques*), *Knife in the Water*, *Hard Candy*

## THE LIVES OF OTHERS (DAS LEBEN DER ANDEREN)
*Written and Directed by* Florian Henckel von Donnersmarck

**Opening Image**: It is 1984, during the tough Socialist regime in East Germany. Any citizen can be interrogated or made an informant by the talented interrogator Gerd Wiesler (Ulrich Mühe), the prototypical Stasi agent with an almost supernatural talent to recognize a liar. He is as ruthless as the State he represents, yet can someone like him become a "good man"? Soon after, we behold the Opening Image of our second protagonist, writer Georg Dreyman (Sebastian Koch), who for now is seen as non-subversive, loyal to the government and innocent about its wrongdoings — very different from the man we'll see at the end.

**Theme Stated**: "The enemies of our State are arrogant," says Wiesler to his pupils at University, defining our "sin." Is it possible for a man to lie to that all-knowing "monster" that is the secret police and get away with it? Interestingly, Wiesler also labels Dreyman on first sight as "arrogant", joining both themes. By the end of the film, we will see where that "arrogance," in reality defiance, leads both men.

**Set-Up**: Indeed, when Wiesler's lieutenant, Grubitz (Ulrich Tukur), takes him to see one of Dreyman's stage plays, Wiesler thinks there is something fishy about him... which is also, pun intended, a *Stasis = death* moment: suspecting everyone, he will never be able to change. Dreyman's own Set-Up starts in the theater (his "work scene"), then he has a "play scene" dancing with his actress girlfriend Christa (Martina Gedeck). Later we will see them in their "home scene" (also the actual "house" of our MITH).

**Catalyst**: At minute 11, Grubitz receives a mission for Wiesler from Minister Bruno Hempf (Thomas Thieme): to secretly investigate Dreyman, offering political influence and privileges in return. Unbeknownst to Dreyman, this is also the Catalyst for him, since this interest will set the plot in motion.

**Debate**: Why is Hempf interested in Dreyman, an apparently loyal writer? We start to suspect that the author's girlfriend, talented and fascinating but insecure actress Christa, is the primary reason. As Dreyman Debates with Hempf, the only way for artists to avoid blacklisting and to get work in the GDR is to be submissive to politicians, a path Christa will soon follow when coerced by Hempf. In the Wiesler beat sheet, we learn how he lives: he is a lonely man, completely devoid of any human connection or warmth — a life so different from that of Christa and Dreyman.

**Break into Two**: In this overlapping beat, following the minister's orders, a team of Stasi agents wire and bug Dreyman's house, while Wiesler prepares his listening station in the penthouse. Everything is ready for the mission to begin — there is "no turning back" for either of the characters.

**B Story**: The "love" story beat is also dual, since it not only concerns the relationship between Christa and Dreyman, but how Wiesler becomes fascinated by these particular "lives of others" — how his reactions to them are at first based in lies and mutual deceit, and later in truth and sacrifice.

**Fun and Games**: We explore the *upside-down world* of every character. In Dreyman's case, he visits Jerska (Volkmart Kleinert), his old depressed mentor who has been blacklisted by the government, a fate that would await him should he dare defy the Stasi. Dreyman lies to him, if only to give him hope. Jerska gives Dreyman a gift; sheet music for *Sonata for a Good Man*. Wiesler explores the upside-down version of his own lonely world: the full life of a dynamic couple, first discovering that Christa's and Dreyman's life together is also driven by lies, from the petty one he tells her about his ability to knot a tie to the most serious secret she hides — an addiction to pills. There is one lie that Wiesler does not tolerate. He discovers that Minister Hempf is using him to destroy Dreyman's career so that he can have Christa for himself. "Is that why we joined [the Stasi]?" asks a disappointed Wiesler. He then "helps" Dreyman discover Christa's infidelity so that they will split up and he can shut down the stakeout. But much to Wiesler's surprise, Dreyman "lies" — not revealing what he's learned, he just hugs Christa in support. Dreyman understands what it is to "bed" government officials to get work. Shaken by this unexpected show of love and protection, Wiesler decides to learn more about the couple's private lives, caring more and more for them.

**Midpoint**: A *false defeat* comes for Wiesler when he learns that Jerska has hanged himself. And the *time clock starts ticking* for Wiesler as Minister Hempf gets impatient and asks for results from the surveillance, but Dreyman has done nothing wrong. At home, he and Christa argue, and he reveals to her, *publicly coming out*, that he knows about her affair with the politician. Worried about them, Wiesler also stages his own *public coming out* (as *A and B Stories cross*), approaching Christa in a bar as if one of her theatre fans. She is kind and tells him he is a good man... but is he? Minutes later, Christa and Dreyman reconcile and have *Sex at 60*.

**Bad Guys Close In**: Angry after Jerska's suicide, and determined to be a "good man," Dreyman decides to write a denounciation. To keep his identity hidden, sympathetic friends provide an "untraceable" typewriter with red ink, an act that will attract Bad Guys. Wiesler has to face his own Bad Guys when he starts taking more risks to protect the couple, as first his associate at the wire station and then Grubitz get suspicious. When Dreyman's article is published, more Bad Guys Close In as Wiesler lies to his superiors and risks too much to protect the couple. Regardless of his efforts to keep them together, their love is fading — they start lying to each other once again.

**All Is Lost**: Tired of her continuous rejection, Minister Hempf decides to end Christa's career. All Is Lost for Dreyman when she is arrested on account of her drug addiction and confesses that he wrote the article, but she reveals nothing about the typewriter which would prove he did. With Grubitz becoming certain that Weisler is helping the couple, he summons him for his own interrogation — ironically, the worst possible scenario for a man who understands the cruel workings of the system. This is his own All Is Lost.

**Dark Night of the Soul**: Dreyman laments Christa's arrest, while the *whiff of death* is in the air as Weisler enters the interrogation offices knowing that he may be facing his own demise.

**Break into Three**: When forced to interrogate Christa (*A and B Stories cross* again), she recognizes Wiesler as the fan she met in the bar. Sensing that she can trust him — and as the actress she is — she plays along with his cues, so both of them manage to fool Grubitz. Christa then confesses to Wiesler where the typewriter has been hidden — perhaps he can save them after all, if he gets to it before the other agents.

**Finale**: As pointed out before, this film has two consecutive finales, the first concerning Wiesler.

> 1. Gathering the Team: Offscreen, Wiesler runs to Dreyman's house to get the typewriter, as Grubitz gathers his own team of Stasi policemen to raid the house.

2. Executing the Plan: Also offscreen, as we will know later, Wiesler regains the machine, missing Dreyman by seconds, but thinking that he has saved him. At the same time, Grubitz carries out his own plan of searching the house.

3. High Tower Surprise: The surprise for Grubitz is that the typewriter is not there, but the surprise for Wiesler is very different, as the unexpected happens — feeling like a traitor to her love, Christa commits suicide by jumping in front of a truck, not knowing what Weisler had done for her. Now he can do no more.

4. Dig, Deep Down: This could be a good time for Wiesler to lie or confess to save himself, but instead he "digs, deep down" when he refuses to talk to Grubitz, so he will have to suffer the consequences. Wiesler has changed — a *synthesis* character, he used to get the truth in order to condemn people but now he has learned to lie to protect them, even sacrificing himself.

5. The Execution of the New Plan: Weisler's new "plan" is a demotion he accepts for doing what he felt was right: opening letters in a cellar for 20 years. But four years later, the Berlin wall falls.

And we have our second finale, regarding the fate of Dreyman. Does it work to have two finales in a row? Well, let's see it!

1. Gathering the Team: In 1989, Dreyman is still a successful writer. He finds Hempf and he tries to "amend hurts," confirming to him that despite his naiveté, he was under surveillance the whole time.

2. Executing the Plan: The writer's plan at this point is to find out more, so he visits the Stasi archives center, where he is given the enormous file about himself.

3. High Tower Surprise: Dreyman painfully learns that Christa indeed betrayed him, but when he finds a red ink fingerprint, he also realizes that a Stasi agent protected them!

4. Dig, Deep Down: Dreyman finds Weisler in the street, but instead of confronting him verbally, he "digs deep down" to wait and tell the story, as a writer would do...

5. The Execution of the New Plan: ...and publishes a book, *Sonata for a Good Man*, dedicated to Weisler.

**Final Image:** Germany is now a free country and Weisler is struggling to survive in this new world. However, when he finds Dreyman's book in a bookstore, and sees it is dedicated to him, he knows that he made the right choices, because as its title says, he is now a "good man."

## THE TEXAS CHAIN SAW MASSACRE (1974)

Five teenage friends on a weekend trip end up being chased by a serial killer who disposes of them one by one, until just a "Final Girl" remains alive... sounds familiar, yes? But there was a pre-*Halloween* time in which the "slasher film" trope was not that well-known, and this low-budget movie not only helped set some of its "rules," but is also considered a masterpiece.

Widely studied by scholars, *The Texas Chain Saw Massacre* holds rich cultural themes about late-Vietnam America, like the end of the hippie dream and the counter-culture, and the clash between modern values and rural family lifestyle. Even today, the scandal its supposed grisliness caused still resonates, though little actual violence or gore is shown onscreen.

Story-wise, it is an interesting film to analyze because it has little characterization and a meager plot. Still, there abounds a basic trait, one that Blake mentioned as a special characteristic of MITH movies: its *primal-ness*, as only survival counts in a film in which death is present everywhere.

In the end, it doesn't matter that we know little about the characters and how barebones (literally, we could say) its structure reads — it leaves us with only our most basic narrative tools to use, namely the BS Beat Sheet. So prepare yourself for a horror feast... although this particular film may not leave you exactly hungry for more.

MITH Type: Serial Monster

MITH Cousins: *Halloween*, *Cold Prey*, *Friday the 13th*, *Hostel*, *Prom Night*

THE TEXAS CHAIN SAW MASSACRE
*Story by* Kim Henkel and Tobe Hooper
*Directed by* Tobe Hooper

**Opening Image**: After a "based on a real story" roll, gruesome flashes of decaying body parts are shown in darkness, while an eerie newscaster talks about grave robbing, sick crimes and morbid occurrences. The scene finishes with a "grisly work of art," a statue made of body parts erected under the scorching Texas sun — death is even present in broad daylight.

**Set-Up**: A classic Set-Up for a "Serial Monster" story, five hippie teenagers drive out of their usual environment for a weekend trip, although the reason is not a happy one: they must check to see if the grave of Sally and Franklin's grandfather has been desecrated. Although not much is said about the characters, we know that wheelchair-bound Franklin is quite a whiner, Jerry is the sarcastic one, Sally is quite naive, Kirk is the tough one and Pam is addicted to horoscopes — and we might note that all signs around them are ominous and evil, so their "sin" is ignoring them.

**B Story**: Our "relationship" story here is among family, as there is great tension between Franklin and Sally. They are fighting; things are sour between them. He does not seem all that welcome on the trip and behaves like a peevish brat, which makes all of them uncomfortable, and tries Sally's patience. Later, we will meet a different set of siblings that seem to get along way better, because a family that *slays* together... *stays* together! (There goes my $1 dollar joke.)

**Theme Stated:** When the group reaches the cemetery, they meet several locals, mostly drunk rednecks who can't take their eyes off Sally, and one of them utters a foreboding rant: "Things happen hereabout they don't tell about. I see things..." What are those things and why don't they talk about them?

**Catalyst:** On their way from the graveyard they find Hitchhiker, a weird young man who freaks them out by telling how his brother and grandfather used to work at the local slaughterhouse, and that his family has "always been in meat." Afterwards, he takes a knife from Franklin and slices him in the arm, also cutting his own hand! They kick him out of the vehicle, but he smears a strange symbol with his own blood on it, a new dark sign.

**Debate:** "There are moments when we cannot believe what is happening is true," says the newspaper horoscope in pure Debate fashion, and that seems to happen to the group. What must they do now? Before answering the question, they need to refuel, so they stop at a gas station, where they also inquire about Franklin's old house. The strange Old Man (Jim Siedow) warns them not to go around it, as "those things is dangerous.... You are liable to get hurt."

**Break into Two:** Still ignoring every warning, the teens go back to the road to visit the old house, with Franklin thinking about the strange hitchhiker and eating some weird-shaped barbecue.

**Fun and Games:** At last, Sally and the others can relax when they arrive at the old family house. Even though it is ramshackle and dirty, it holds great memories for Sally, and everybody's laughter fills the place, except for Franklin, who is unable to freely move around and share the good times. Even as they laugh, there are more ominous signs found in the house, but Kirk and Pam pay no attention to them as they decide to go for a bath at the creek. It's dry, and they hear a motor humming in the distance, so maybe they can get some gasoline. Unluckily, after not noticing another sign (a human tooth), Kirk gets killed by a huge strange man in a dead skin mask. Meet Leatherface (Gunnar Hansen), model for many serial killers to come, as Pam can attest after being killed in one of the most cruel and iconic deaths in cinema history.

**Midpoint**: As night begins to fall (a sign of the *ticking clock*), *stakes have been raised*. Now getting the gasoline is a matter of life and death, although the remaining friends still don't know it. While Sally utters her "public display" as a hero — "We'll protect you" — is she really capable of protecting anyone? Can she even save herself? In any case, *A and B Stories cross* as Franklin keeps whining about his lost knife, driving Sally mad, still hiding the fact that she did not want him there. Franklin wonders about the signs they have seen and Sally can only answer: "Everything means something, I guess."

**Bad Guys Close In**: A characteristic of this beat is that "the group disintegrates" even more, with Jerry leaving them to search for his friends and entering Leatherface's home. After finding Pam in a refrigerator, he is killed too. Back at the van, Franklin wants to go with Sally even if he is a physical and emotional burden for her, as they inadvertently attract the attention of Leatherface, who appears out of the dark and dispatches of Franklin with his trademark chainsaw. With the enemy as close as he can be, Sally tries to get away in the dark countryside, running among dead trees and branches, at the same time becoming one of the screen's greatest "scream queens"!

**All Is Lost**: Sally finds salvation in the gas station, where the Old Man they met at the beginning protects and comforts her. As there is not a phone, the man decides to get his truck. This might seem like like an All Is Won moment, but Sally's mistake has cost her a final chance of survival.

**Dark Night of the Soul**: In this beat, major characters "contemplate death," and that is exactly what Sally does when she is left alone in the room, watching the barbecue meat and listening to more horrible news on the radio, reminding her — and us — that the real world hides danger too.

**Break into Three**: That danger is confirmed when the Old Man returns to the room with a sack and a strange smile, revealing that his intentions are not good. After disarming and tying up Sally (temporarily depriving her of her proactivity), he puts her in the car and drives her to a home we know all too well. They find Hitchhiker on the way, revealing that he is family (some say brothers) with him and Leatherface, a dark *Moment of Clarity* for Sally.

**Finale**:

1. Gathering the Team: The Sawyers are reunited (read: gathered) for the first time in the film, including Grandpa, "the best killer in the family," who can barely move, but can definitely enjoy the blood that Hitchhiker gets from Sally's finger before she passes out.

2. Executing the Plan: Literally "executing," as when Sally wakes up, the family decides to carry out their plan to terminate her suffering by killing her, the slaughterhouse-old-school way, and let's just say it (gasp!) involves a hammer.

3. High Tower Surprise: When Hitchhiker is about to finish off Sally, he gets overconfident and she manages to free herself, jumping out of a window and finding herself on the loose at dawn.

4. Dig, Deep Down: But Sally is still not yet safe. She must "dig, deep down" and run for her life while Hitchhiker chases her, slicing her with his straight razor, while Leatherface and his chainsaw are not far behind.

5. The Execution of the New Plan: At this point, Sally's new plan is to stop a vehicle to get away, something she almost accomplishes when a cattle truck runs over Hitchhiker. Still chased by Leatherface, she jumps in the back of a pickup and barely escapes alive.

**Final Image**: A blood-soaked Sally laughs hysterically in the car, and we know for sure that after losing all her friends and experiencing so many horrors, she is not and will never be the innocent girl she was at the beginning. As for Leatherface, he is left angry and frustrated, swinging around his chainsaw in the middle of the road, showing again that some horrors still await us in broad daylight.

## THE BLAIR WITCH PROJECT (1999)

"Supra-natural Monster" films, said Blake, are among the most frightening ones, and how could they not be so, considering that not only are our lives at the stake... but our souls, too? The reason is that the "monster" in these films can "strike anywhere, haunt our dreams until we can't tell what is real — and what isn't."

Just ask Heather Donahue, Michael C. Williams and Joshua Leonard, the three filmmakers who "in October of 1994 became lost in the woods near Burkittsville, Maryland, while shooting a documentary," this film being their "found footage." Were these events real or not?

That was the question that tens of thousands of people were asking themselves all over the world because of the smart internet campaign — at the time, one of the first — that launched this film, budgeted at reportedly less than $23,000, with box-office receipts of almost $250,000,000 (and yes, we counted all those zeroes right!).

We have also chosen this film because it features some interesting creative solutions, like the use of primarily three main characters, its lack of location changes (the forest being the "house") and its visual first person narrative. Also, legend says it sprang from a

35-page outline, with its dialogue mostly improvised — yet the editing of its 19 hours of footage to 81 minutes rendered a film that neatly fits our Beat Sheet.

MITH Type: Supra-Natural Monster

MITH Cousins: *The Exorcism of Emily Rose*, *Cabin in the Woods*, *Requiem*, *The Witch*, *Paranormal Activity*

## THE BLAIR WITCH PROJECT
*Written and directed by* Daniel Myrick & Eduardo Sánchez

**Opening Image:** After an onscreen warning that our story and its characters' fates are true, the film starts, as it will finish, with a blurry image. When the focus sharpens, we meet film director Heather Donahue, whose "Blair Witch Project" is the documentary that she intends to shoot about a mysterious Maryland witch. What will she find out in the process and how will it change her and her world?

**Theme Stated:** We are shown some pre-Halloween decorations, and Heather asks her companions, and possibly herself, "Do you believe in ghosts?" Are supra natural creatures real — or not? This notion will be tested during their whole misadventure.

**Set-Up:** In *Save the Cat!® Strikes Back*, Blake gave us a tip for any Set-Up: to visit the "at home, at play and at work places" of our protagonist to know her better. So the film starts in the safety of Heather's "home," and soon we visit "work" where we meet co-worker Josh, the nice, reasonable 16mm cameraman. Enter also shy, quiet sound mixer Mike, after which they "play" buying groceries for the trip. At this point we know more about Heather and her *six things that need fixing*: she is bossy, insistent, controlling, manipulative, self-centered and everything has to be done her way. Quite a basis for a character arc!

**B Story:** Our "love story" centers on the care and respect the team must learn to feel for each other. As we will see, at first they are not that close, brought together to make the documentary. But as the movie progresses, they will be tested and face difficult circumstances, so they will need to stick up for each other. Will they be capable of that?

**Catalyst**: They begin shooting the documentary, interviewing people who more or less believe in the Witch and provide unsettling details about its legend — focusing on the story of Rustin Parr, a man who killed seven children under the Witch's command. The group also meets Mary Brown, a seemingly crazy old lady who claims she once met the Witch and lived to tell it. Well, have you had a good look at her fence door?

**Debate**: At this point, do they believe in the Witch? They keep driving, joking around, perhaps to hide their concerns, thinking that Mary was crazy. These laughs are also their "sin" — because their disrespect and disregard as they invade the Witch's territory will bring disgrace in the end. As they reach the woods, they leave their car behind and find Coffin Rock, a place where a gruesome killing took place. "That happened here," claims Heather for her documentary. But does she believe it?

**Break into Two**: The trio spends their first night camping in the woods. The next day, Josh says he heard strange noises in the darkness, a kind of cackling. They joke about that, but things get worse as they realize they are lost. What don't they realize? As must happen in an effective Break into Two, there is "no way back." The Witch is already hunting them and they may never get out of the forest — not even if they die — as their souls would be trapped forever in the woods with her. Josh asks Heather if she believes in the Witch yet. "I don't know," she answers.

**Fun and Games**: Is there something Fun in being lost in the woods searching for a cemetery? As much as I wouldn't want to experience it, the group has fun mocking each other and playfully joking around in the forest. However, they get serious after they find something strange: seven stone piles, one of which Josh accidentally knocks over. That night they hear weird noises again, and get more and more nervous as Heather continues being mean to them. Thinking that some locals are playing a prank, they decide to go back to the car, but they don't seem able to find the way. And any possible Fun ends on the third night, when they hear noises again and upon waking up, they find three more stone piles around their tent.

**Midpoint:** A *false defeat* comes when they realize they have lost the map, *raising the stakes* as it is now harder to get home. The situation becomes *public*, and violent, when Mike reveals that he threw the map away in frustration, *raising the stakes* even more. A physical fight ensues in which the worst of each character surfaces, as Heather blames Mike for everything, again not taking any responsibility. She will not even let the boys have the compass, ignoring the possibility that her changing might save them all.

**Bad Guys Close In:** One of the characteristics of this beat is that "the team disintegrates," a condition that is particularly threatening for all-controlling Heather, since she no longer has power over the others. Still they "stick" together, finding strange eerie stick men hanging from the trees. The two guys want to get out of the woods but Heather keeps filming — self-centered, the documentary still goes first for her. That night Bad Guys really do Close In, as the trio first hears terrorizing children's voices and then their tent is shaken by someone outside. The next morning, they find their stuff thrown around, and Josh's clothes are stained with a blue slime, as if marked. He, the reasonable one, gets really angry, psychologically torturing Heather by filming her.

**All Is Lost:** They realize they are in the same place in the forest where they began. How can that be possible? "There's no one to help you," repeats Josh to a crying Heather. The next day, Josh is missing and Heather and Mike can't find him no matter how much they try. They are indeed "worse off than when the story started."

**Dark Night of the Soul**: Alone, sitting among dead leaves, Heather reflects on what has happened, still ready to blame the others, as she thinks that Josh just ran away. She also laments that she will have to carry his camera.

**Break into Three**: For the first time, Heather negotiates with Mike about what to do next. Desperate, he asks "Which was worse, the wicked witch from the East or the wicked witch from the West?" They decide to go east. Do they still have a chance?

**Finale**:
1. Gathering the Team: Their new collaborative spirit works to make them, for the first time, a team, as they comfort each other joking, talking about the things they like and even, later, hugging each other for the first time.

2. Executing the Plan: As stated, their plan is to head east until they find the way out of the woods, still terrified about what they hear on the way. But night is not far away.

3. High Tower Surprise: After they hear Josh screaming in pain again during the night, in the morning they discover a strange package made of branches and their friend's shirt. Heather looks inside and finds blood, teeth and other body parts. Though scared as hell, she decides to say nothing to Mike, possibly because she now cares for him.

4. Dig, Deep Down: The next night, Heather "digs, deep down" and finds the inner strength to apologize to the camera, which she found impossible before, acknowledging how difficult it has been for the others to deal with her and for the first time conceding that everything has been her fault.

5. The Execution of the New Plan: The last night, upon hearing Josh's cries again, they decide to get out of the tent, finding a nearby house where the cries came from. Braver (or crazier)

than ever, Mike goes inside the house and is knocked over in the basement by an unseen attacker. When Heather follows him, she is attacked too, her camera rolling on the floor.

**Final Image:** The last image is a blurry one, like the feeling we have about what happened in that basement. As much as we know that the experience changed Heather and her friends forever... was the Witch's legend true in the end? Do supra-natural beings exist? What happened with the three filmmakers' bodies and souls? Do you really want to know the answer?

## FUNNY GAMES (1997)

Can you write a psychological horror film in which the sadistic "monster" knows you are watching the movie? Austrian writer-director Michael Haneke literally played games with audiences in this film with some of the most horrid home invasion tropes. It's one of the best and most terrifying "Nihilist Monster" films that you will ever behold.

This MITH subgenre deals with a cruel kind of creature, one that looks for victims whose "sin" is not clear to them, and who do not know why something so horrible and seemingly undeserved is happening. Nihilist Monsters, besides being sadistic, says Blake, play with "games of life and death" (hence, this movie's title).

Were we bad persons, bad parents, bad citizens? The Nihilist Monster does not care and will not tell you, as he will not disclose his seemingly absurd rationale for torturing people. For this reason, Haneke shot a film about the depiction of violence in media and used meta-cinema techniques to further "play" with the rules of narrative, montage and point-of-view to make his effort even more horrifying.

The result is an interesting example of how to bend many of cinema's rules, like altering traditional feature film timing with a celebrated (and nerve-chilling) 10-minute panoramic shot while keeping intact, as we will see, a completely tight structure (which was also kept in the 2007 shot-by-shot — even made in the same house — remake with Tim Roth and Naomi Watts). So, shall we press "play"... or "rewind"?

**MITH Type:** Nihilist Monster

**MITH Cousins:** *Cabin Fever*, *Cube*, *Green Room*, *Audition*, *Battle Royale*

FUNNY GAMES
*Written and directed by* Michael Haneke

**Opening Image:** A movie like this has to start with a game, of course, albeit a very innocent one. A well-to-do family heads for a vacation, while playing "who's the composer" as they listen to classical music, and the wife Anna (Susanne Lothar) is winning. Then, violent jazz-grindcore metal music by Naked City blasts in (non-diegetically) like the assault they are going to suffer. Will they be alive by the end?

**Theme Stated:** "Did daddy look?" asks Anna, inquiring if husband Georg (Ulrich Mühe) cheated. The rules of the game are our theme. But what happens if unbeknownst to the players, those rules include horror movie conventions, the same from the genre the characters are starring in? And what happens if the "monster" knows the rules and could even cheat?

**B Story:** Our "love story" refers to how Anna and Georg can keep their love alive when they are about to suffer an ordeal which will force them to endure psychological and physical torture. Can they still love each other under such terrible circumstances?

**Set-Up:** The family arrives at their country house near the lake and they "set up" their vacation, filling the fridge and getting their sailboat ready. They also have a strange encounter with their usually friendly neighbors, who act cold and uninterested, while they are accompanied by two unknown young persons dressed completely in white. Little son Georgie (Stefan Clapczynski) misses his girlfriend Sissi, and family dog Rolfi seems uneasy, especially when neighbor

Fred and one of the white-gloved youths (introduced as "the son of a business colleague") come to say hi. Another kind of Set-Up is purely visual: a knife is left forgotten in the sailing boat.

**Catalyst**: At minute 11, "flabby" Peter, the other white-gloved youth, arrives at the house, and ever so politely — as with everything they will do (including torture) — asks for some eggs for their neighbor friends, with whom they seem to be on familiar terms, so Anna does not suspect anything.

**Debate**: How crazy can a "normal" situation like this get? Well, things get slowly more weird as Peter does not know how to answer Anna's Debate questions. What do they want the eggs for? How did he get in the house? Peter tries Anna's patience when he drops the eggs, gets the home phone uselessly wet and asks for more eggs. And things get stranger as Paul, apparently the smarter one, enters the house and asks her to try their golf clubs. Outside, Georg notices Rolfi's sudden silence, and when he arrives home, he finds Anna, temper lost, trying to kick the white-clad duo out of the house.

**Break into Two**: Clueless why Anna is so mad at the duo, Georg tries to persuade the pair to leave the house, but they just confront him provocatively. So at minute 25, an angry Georg slaps Paul, setting things in motion — Peter breaks his leg with a golf club. The violence has started and there is no turning back. Let the "funny games" begin!

**Fun and Games**: What is it like to be in a home invasion with two sadistic Nihilist Monsters? Paul is seemingly eager to have Fun and play Games. Indeed, the *promise of the premise* of being in a home invasion is delivered with flair. The family is very scared as the first games begin, one being "where is the dead body of our dog?" As Anna searches for it, Paul breaks the fourth wall and winks at "us," signaling his "Nihilist Monster superpower": he knows the rules of horror narrative and will follow them or break them for our viewing "pleasure." More horrible games ensue as Georg agonizes over his broken leg and Georgie seems paralyzed by fear.

**Midpoint**: *Stakes are* (terribly) *raised* as Paul bets that in 12 hours (*the ticking clock!*), the family will be dead, and for the second time, Paul asks "us" if we think they have a chance of winning. "You are on their side, aren't you?" But the bet is rigged: "They'll lose in any case. Obviously." Unhappily for us, at Midpoint we get a whiff of *Sex at Midpoint* too: *A and B Stories cross* as loving husband Georg is forced to tell his wife to undress, or their child will suffer the consequences. Then a *false victory* ensues: as his parents fight the assailants, Georgie is able to flee from the house.

**Bad Guys Close In**: Georgie runs away, and has to dip into the lake and swim to reach the neighbors, where he expects to get help. But he sees Paul "closing in" and hides in the house. Paul playfully chases him in the empty home, and Georgie finds his dear girlfriend, Sissi, dead. He then takes a rifle and aims at ever-smiling Paul, who even advises him on how to use it... but the chambers are empty. At home, Peter chills out watching TV, when Paul arrives with Georgie and the rifle. The *clock keeps ticking* when Paul asks for the time — they must think about their bet, so they play a new game with the family: "Eeny meeny, miny, moe."

**All Is Lost**: Paul merrily goes to the kitchen to fix himself a sandwich, and a loud bang is heard. When he comes back, the TV set is splattered with blood. Can there be anything worse for a family than having their only son killed? It is also All Is Lost for Paul, who reprimands Peter — he has killed the child, so now they will not get anything from the others. So surprisingly or not... they leave the house.

**Dark Night of the Soul**: The DNOTS beat is particularly long (10 minutes!) and nerve-wracking despite its stillness (which should inspire calm). Anna silently "contemplates the death" of her child, her defeated husband and the destruction of her family.

**Break into Three**: Now that the killers have gone, Anna frees herself and Georg, trying to think what to do next. They attempt to fix the phone, but it won't work, and her husband is too hurt to escape with her. *A and B Stories cross* again as Georg asks Anna to forgive him of his "sin": not being able to protect his family. Anna kisses her husband, showing their love is intact, and off she goes for help.

**Finale:**

1. Gathering the Team: Anna tries to gather "a team" to help her, first visiting the neighbors and then stopping a car. At home, Georg does likewise trying to call someone on the phone. But unluckily for them both, the team is really gathered when Paul and Peter arrive again, this time with Anna. Has a golf ball ever been so menacing?

2. Executing the Plan: The plan is a new game, in which Anna is forced to participate, but she tries to refuse. So exactly (and we mean exactly) at the 95-minute mark, Paul complains, saying the film is not even feature length yet! "You want a real ending, with plausible plot development, don't you?" he asks us.

3. High Tower Surprise: Suddenly, Anna takes the rifle and shoots Peter in the belly, instantly killing him. Maybe she can win, after all! But her High Tower Surprise awaits: As master of the rules of this game, Paul gets the video remote and rewinds *the movie itself*, reviving Peter and preventing Anna from taking the rifle. In retaliation, they kill Georg.

4. Dig, Deep Down: The next morning, Anna is taken to the boat with the two men and they sail away. Remember the knife Haneke ostensibly set up in the beginning? Anna uses it to "dig, deep down" and try to cut her ties. But it is useless — it was just a red herring, and she is easily disarmed.

5. The Execution of the New Plan: While Peter and Paul discuss the limits of reality and fiction, he kisses Anna goodbye and drowns her in the lake. At one hour from the deadline, he has won the bet. How couldn't he?

**Final Image**: A very similar image to the beginning: Paul enters a family's property, and they ask for some eggs that Anna supposedly needs. The woman kindly complies, and boy, we know the Nihilist Monster is going to start his cycle of torture and violence again. For the last time, he looks at us from the screen, knowing that we know too… and maybe we want to watch.

 When Dwayne faces the "Dark Night of the Soul" it takes Olive, his own *Little Miss Sunshine*, to show him the way out (and into Act 3).

# 2  GOLDEN FLEECE

If there is a story as ancient as human culture (ask old Homer about that), it's a journey. Even today, in these safe, internet-driven times, no matter if we feel the backpacker's wanderlust, sign up for a typical touristic voyage to the Bahamas, do business somewhere far from home or just go on a road trip to visit relatives, we can't ignore a fundamental truth: travel is going to change us.

And that is good news, since "all stories are about transformation,"so why are you waiting to put your characters on the road?

Please "hold your horses" a little bit more while we talk about the "Golden Fleece" genre, whose classic provenance (ask old Jason and his Argonauts about it) shows us that the adventure of traveling, its troubles, dangers, challenges and obstacles are first-class narrative material — not only will we learn new things about the road, new cultures or how to overcome our fears, a Golden Fleece will also teach us about ourselves.

Of course, there are many kinds of travels, and not all of them necessarily require leaving your home! As you will discover, when a group of characters set out on a search or gather to make a plan to reach a goal (as in our "Caper Fleece" genre), they are using their strength as a team to walk a common road toward that goal... whether they actually reach it or not.

Let's consider our three main components to use as a travel guide:

The first thing you will need to have in your writer's backpack is a **team**, which will make our movie about friendship, a common theme in GFs. Besides a main character, you should choose some travel companions, who will either accompany him from home or join him on the road. The important thing is that each member of the team complements him in one way or another — our hero may be the "dull" one, with the most room to learn, while the others are his "brains," "muscles" or "soul." Remember mainstream classics like *The Wizard of Oz*, *The Guns of Navarone* or *Star Wars*?

Now, this team is so important that you should dedicate some good scenes to introduce them and set up their powers, skills or abilities — along with what Blake called their **limp and an eyepatch**, that is, something that will make them immediately recognizable. Remember *The Full Monty* and how each character has his own strengths and weaknesses? That is what we're aiming for.

Once you have your characters and know how to introduce them, we need a **road**, the metaphorical or real path that your heroes will travel toward their goal. It can be as long as a lifetime or could cross entire galaxies, but for our heroes, what matters is always the same: the encounters and adventures they will find on the way will teach them to overcome their fears and anxieties. The road can be a 317-mile journey, as in *The Straight Story*, or it can just be a metaphorical road to victory, as in *Rocky* (yep, that one's an indie too!), or even the course to follow when performing a mission, caper or robbery, as in *Reservoir Dogs*.

Finally, you must include a **prize**, that is, the sacred object, mythical treasure or golden dream the team is chasing: things like victory, jewels or a dear one who awaits at the end of the path. The search for this prize, and the desire to go on the road, must ideally be propelled by something primal, like family, survival or love. Doesn't Rocky just want respect when training to fight Apollo? Doesn't Alvin Straight just want to find his long-estranged brother? Isn't *Reservoir Dogs* really about betrayed friendship?

Ironically, many of the times, the prize itself is not what our heroes will find at the end of their path! As you know, the MacGuffin is an object or goal designed to keep the plot and our characters moving toward it, but that object doesn't really matter that much. Often our protagonists will suddenly find a **road apple**, something that destroys their plans when victory was within sight. In many stories (but not all), the road apple will appear in the All Is Lost beat or the High Tower Surprise section of the Finale.

The goal is to remind our characters that, just like Dorothy and her companions in *The Wizard of Oz*, it doesn't matter that the Wiz can give them the characteristics they were longing for. The road itself, the adventure and the experience they gained travelling on it, has bestowed those goods on them — without the need of a divine hand or a sacred object. In the mainstream world, ask Indiana Jones! In our indie realm, the stars of films like *O Brother, Where Art Thou?* and *Little Miss Sunshine* know about this firsthand.

How many kinds of journeys can our heroes take? As always, we will define five, the first of which we'll call the **Sports Fleece**, referring to all those movies in which a "team" must compete with others to gain some kind of token, cup or victory itself. The Sports Fleece applies not only to literal sports teams, but to any story in which a bunch of characters will have to learn to work as a team (dancing, cooking or playing music). Think of this when writing your film: the real goal — even if your characters still don't realize it — is self-respect, not external awards.

Let's also examine the **Buddy Fleece**, whose signature mark is that it's lighter in tone. No matter the prize or MacGuffin, the real thematic lesson our heroes will have to learn pertains to friendship and love. Such is the case of indie smash *Little Miss Sunshine*, Mexican hit *Y Tu Mamá También*, *Motorcycle Diaries*, Antonioni's *L'Avventura* or the adaptation of Kerouac's *On the Road*.

Next comes the **Epic Fleece**, whose name takes us directly to its Greek antecedents. These films are sometimes more dramatic, with more difficult trials for our characters to endure, just like the almost-literal "Odyssey" of *Kon-Tiki*, *The Wages of Fear*, *Apocalypse Now* or *The Three Burials of Melquiades Estrada*.

We noted before that the road may be just a robbery, and that is what our **Caper Fleece** consists of, but that's not all — everything that involves a plan and a scheme, like prison escapes or war infiltration missions, belong here, as is the case in *Reservoir Dogs*, *Snatch* or *Rififi*.

Finally, we have the **Solo Fleece**, where, as its name implies, the team is composed of one person and the road can be a physical journey or simply the person's actual life and struggles to achieve success. Look at *The Straight Story*, *Broken Flowers* or *Into the Wild* and you will know what we mean. If not, ask old Ulysses!

## GETTING ALL MYTHICAL ON YOUR FLEECE

If your film idea involves a group of quirky characters getting ready to go somewhere, you should also make sure to give them:

1. A "team," a person or a group that will complement each other and, while passing through many trials and tribulations, will learn something deeper, such as the importance of friendship.

2. A "road" that may be physical, like the ones you see on maps, or metaphorical, like a heist, robbery or a life goal. What's important is its stages.

3. A "prize," something primal that sets the trip in motion and is the only thing on our characters' minds — although by the end of their journey, they will probably realize it actually wasn't that important.

So if you think you are ready, fill your writer's backpack with your laptop, this book and some food, and wake up at dawn to start your trip. You'll return a changed person, we promise!

## THE FULL MONTY (1997)

Back in 1997, the cinematic oceans of the world seemed to be dominated by the looming, enormous shape of a transatlantic Goliath called *Titanic*... but as if to illustrate the theme of our book, not far behind, there was a lighter vessel that, with a much smaller $3.5 million budget, made no less than $258 million at the box office. Top it off with four Academy Award® nominations (Film, Director, Screenplay) and one win (Best Original Score), and it's clear that we've got our own British David!

*The Full Monty* is our chosen film for the "Sports Fleece" sub-genre, because even though there are no obvious "sports" in this movie, many "coach and team" films are GFs too! Consider the frequent thematic jokes about soccer and you'll see we are in parody territory here, and compare it to such films as *The Damned United*, *Break Point* or *The Finishers* to see the flexibility of the genre.

Let's confirm that in this Golden Fleece story we have the main components. First, we have a "road" to success, in this case, the dancing abilities that the heroes must learn to be able to gain victory in their final showdown in front of a big audience (check). Also, we have a "team," each of the individuals with a particular skill, but also with insecurities to overcome (check).

And finally, we have a "prize," that is, the money the team must earn to make a better living or, in our main character's own search, to keep his son in joint custody (check). As in every good GF, what the team will find at the end of the road is not merely "gold," but something better: self-confidence and dignity. So crank up some sexy music and let's strip down this Beat Sheet!

GF Type: Sports Fleece

GF Cousins: *The Damned United*, *Redbelt*, *Ride*, *Break Point*, *Foxcatcher*

THE FULL MONTY
*Written by* Simon Beaufoy
*Directed by* Peter Cattaneo

**Opening Image**: Vintage newsreel footage shows us that back in the day, the then red-hot industrial city of Sheffield was boosted by tough men and steel. Fast cut to 25 years later and meet "Gaz" Schofield (Robert Carlyle) and Dave (Mark Addy), the latter stealing scrap metal in a derelict factory to barely pay for his son Nathan's (William Snape) child support. Scavenging metal isn't quite a dignified thing to do, of course. But these men don't see any other way to keep going.

**Theme Stated**: "Can't we do normal things sometimes?" asks Nathan. He is ashamed of his father and doesn't recognize how hard his father is trying to keep him close. They will all learn that sometimes "normal things" do not work, so thinking "outside of the clothes" may be a good way to solve their problems.

**Set-Up**: We discover the everyday world of the men who used to run the city with their hard work and who now deal with unemployment and the subsequent mid-life crises. When Gaz spots a long queue of women waiting to see a male strip act, he sneaks inside what was once a working man's club and sees how the venue is filling up. We also get the Set-Up for Dave, who feels he is too fat to be liked, even by his wiser, loving wife Jean. A clear *Stasis=Death* moment comes when Gaz takes Nathan to school and promises to take him to the Sheffield vs. Manchester soccer game… something he doesn't have the money for. If he doesn't find a way to get the needed cash, he could lose his son forever.

**B Story**: As you can imagine, our primary B Story Character is Nathan. At the beginning, he wants his dad to stop trying weird things and feels ashamed of him, but little by little, he will become much more supporting and genuinely proud of his father. There are secondary B Stories for other team members, such as Dave's relationship with Jerry.

**Catalyst**: At the Job Club (an employment agency), Gaz and his mates play cards, complaining about how the male gender is doomed to be "extincto" in a few years when they realize how much money the Chippendales are getting for stripping in front of the ladies. "It's worth a thought," says Gaz, about to... you guessed it, Debate the question.

**Debate**: Crazy as it is to think that by stripping they could get money, things look bad for Gaz, as his wife attempts to take sole custody of Nathan in court. Gaz starts discussing his idea with reluctant Dave, when they find Lomper, a security guard, about to kill himself because of the loneliness of his job. The three become friends, so the "team" has a new "player." The Debate about stripping continues while Gaz tries a hilariously ridiculous strip-tease to "You Sexy Thing." We can see that what they are about to do is, indeed, really crazy. But do they have a choice?

**Break into Two**: Ashamed of his father, Nathan has run away. After Nathan is found, Gaz tells him — with some difficulty — he is "not doing it for a laugh," but to get the money that will allow them to be together. It seems that Gaz is serious after all!

**Fun and Games**: Blake said that in any "Sports Fleece," "the fun is in watching them come together as a team." And so the team recruits new "players," including the always-necessary coach, in this case their former foreman Gerald (Tom Wilkinson), who at least knows how to dance a little. In an open audition, enter Mr. Horse (Paul Barber) and the well-endowed Guy (Hugo Speer), and the team is basically complete. This is also the time and place to delve into their male insecurities: Gerald is lying to his wife about having a job, Horse seems too old, Guy can't dance... and Dave's lack of self-confidence is harming his relationship with his wife, as he thinks she may be attracted to thinner, more attractive men.

**Midpoint**: The *clock starts ticking* when Gerald tells them they only have two weeks to be as good as the performers in *Flashdance* (which we know is crazy) but they indeed enjoy a *false victory* when they are able to perform a particular move using (again) a soccer analogy. There is also a *public coming out* when they remove their clothes together in Gerald's house, using that occasion to kick some repo men out. As a team, they give us a glimpse of "what they can be, with no obligation to be it." *Stakes are raised* for Gaz when Nathan withdraws his savings from the bank to help them rent the club for the show (trusting his father, who must rise to the occasion) and the team goes further by publicly announcing their act in billboards as "Hot Metal."

**Bad Guys Close In**: But, oh pity, the internal Bad Guys of insecurity return with a vengeance when Gaz further *raises the stakes* by announcing that they will go for "the full monty," that is, they will strip totally bare. This decision causes the "team to disintegrate," so they go back to the employment office, giving us the hilarious "Hot Stuff" queue scene. There is still a chance they'll compete, but they feel "too fat, too old, or a pigeon-chested little tosser." Leather thongs don't make things easier, so Dave finally abandons the team and takes a security guard job. While the rest of the team rehearses in front of Horse's family, a policeman finds their behavior suspicious and takes them to the station for questioning. Now Social Services is after Gaz, and he could lose Nathan. Meanwhile, Gerald's wife learns about his lie and dumps him.

**All Is Lost**: Gaz is waiting for Nathan at school when his ex-wife and her new husband tell him that he is no longer allowed to see his son. Along with the *whiff of death* of the father-son relationship, the beat is given further depth when we are told that Lomper's mother has died.

**Dark Night of the Soul**: The team attends the funeral, mourning in Lomper's company, like true friends would do. This *road apple* seems to have stopped the trip cold.

**Break into Three**: In the neighborhood, everyone is expecting them to perform, but will they? Gaz gets the news that the bar has sold 200 tickets, which means more money than they expected, so he tells Dave they've got to do it, but Dave refuses. At home, Dave makes amends with Jean in a tender *A/B Story cross* in which she tells him she wants to see the act, propelling him into Act Three.

**Finale**:

1. Gathering the Team: As is typical in sports movies, our "team" gathers in the locker room, getting ready for the show/match, while the audience is filling the bar/arena. Even Gaz's ex-wife is there! Dave finally arrives, bringing Nathan with him. But Gaz looks worried and for once, he is the self-doubting one.

2. Executing the Plan: The rest of the team "executes the plan" as they go out and confront their fears onstage: "We may not be young, we may not be pretty, we may not be right good..." And they are going for the full monty!

3. High Tower Surprise: Were you missing the almost mandatory "pep talk scene" in the locker room? The High Tower Surprise for Gaz is finding that Nathan, up to now reluctant about his dad's performing, fully supports him and gives him the strength to get onstage: "They are cheering out there. You did that. Now get out there and do your stuff."

4. Dig, Deep Down: Inspired by earning his son's respect, even though stripping for money is by no means a "normal thing," Gaz decides to go for it.

5. The Execution of the New Plan: Gaz undresses with his friends while they dance to "You Can Leave Your Hat On" to the (worldwide) audience's delight. They are clearly enjoying the moment, all insecurities overcome.

**Final Image**: Naked, the team goes for the full monty, showing that, besides getting the money and being cheered on by a loud audience, they have gained something better: true friendship and self-respect.

## LITTLE MISS SUNSHINE (2006)

What is winning and what is losing? Just ask the producers and artists who made a small independent film that became one of the biggest successes of 2006! It's hard to believe that after its premiere at Sundance, the film's distribution rights were bought in one of the biggest deals in the history of the festival, and with an $8 million budget, the film earned $100.5 million internationally!

This "little" movie was nominated for four Academy Awards®, earning two — one for Best Writing, Original Screenplay for Michael Arndt, reportedly a first-time writer. For husband-wife team Jonathan Dayton and Valerie Faris, the film was their directorial debut.

What more can we say about *Little Miss Sunshine*, other than that it perfectly fits the Blake Snyder Beat Sheet? Let's consider how wisely their creators played with the themes of the "Buddy Fleece," the subgenre where, in a light tone, a "team" (in this case, a family) learns that the important thing is not winning a beauty contest (the "prize"). The real lesson, as a worthy "road" story, is that winning or losing does not matter, what counts is the family staying together.

GF Type: Buddy Fleece

GF Cousins: *On the Road*, *Transamerica*, *Y Tu Mamá También*, *The Darjeeling Limited*, *Easy Rider*

## LITTLE MISS SUNSHINE
*Written by* Michael Arndt
*Directed by* Jonathan Dayton and Valerie Faris

**Opening Image:** The crowning of Miss America (a winner!) is a proper way to start this film, especially as we then take in little Olive's (Abigail Breslin) miming the beauty queen's wave. As in any good Golden Fleece, the rest of the family is introduced in an economical and effective fashion, showing how they cope with their self-doubts: the father, Richard's (Greg Kinnear) apparent failure as a motivational speaker, and mom Sheryl's (Toni Collette) pushiness and non-stop smoking. We also meet Dwayne (Paul Dano), the troubled teenage son who tries to become a literal *Übermensch*, heroin-snorting granddad Edwin (Alan Arkin) and Sheryl's especially insecure gay brother Frank (Steve Carell), who has recently tried to kill himself. By the Final Image, will this fractured family have come together?

**Theme Stated:** The film's theme is loudly stated and restated by Richard during his speech to an almost-empty classroom: "There are two kinds of people in this world: winners and losers... at the very core of your being there is a winner waiting to be awakened." But isn't Richard — our main character and the one who needs to change most — wrong about what makes a winner?

**Set-Up:** The Set-Up is executed in an efficient and budget-conscious manner — through a family dinner. Until now, we have been introduced to the imperfect characters separately, but we soon see that they don't really work well as a family, either. Dwayne has taken a vow of silence, Grandpa is too brutally honest, Richard tries to reinforce himself by stating the "9 Steps" of his "Refuse to Lose" program over and over again. The only one who seems innocent enough is Olive, and even she is in danger because Richard puts too much pressure on her.

**B Story:** Olive is the B Story Character. As the youngest, but also because of her charming, naive personality, she sees things in a simple light and avoids the complications of the adult world, acting as a "little mentor" for the rest and continually keeping the family together, until the very end.

**Catalyst**: A message on the answering machine gives Olive great news which is not so great for the rest of the "team": she has a place in the "Little Miss Sunshine" beauty contest in California! She has prepared a lot for the role and is really excited, but her family is not that enthusiastic.

**Debate**: A bitter argument ensues debating about going to the pageant or not. Richard wants Sheryl's sister to go in their place, as he is expecting an important book deal, while Grandpa is determined to be there with Olive, since he coached her talent act. Frank is not exactly eager to go, but he cannot be left alone because of his recent suicide attempt, and Dwayne bitterly and silently complains until mom promises to fulfill his dream of attending the Air Force Academy. "But I am not going to have any fun," he writes in a notebook.

**Break into Two**: Once they have all agreed to hit the road together, Richard submits Olive to his typical pep talk, challenging her and again putting too much pressure on the child — if they are going to travel, she must win the contest. That night, Dwayne writes, "Welcome to hell."

**Fun and Games**: As in any good GF, the trip starts with a feeling of anticipation, as we first turn on to the road that will take them from Albuquerque to California. With the family squeezed into a ramshackle VW bus that speaks of hippie times, the Fun and Games of our story show how each team member reveals themselves, like when Grandpa gives "dating" advice to Dwayne, and how the family continues to come together and veer apart. Richard pressures Olive again by implying that if she eats too much ice cream she will not be able to win... but the family rallies together to make her feel good. As their van's gears fail, pushing it becomes a meaningful symbol of the family working together. Back on the road, they further face their insecurities, like when Richard's book deal is rejected and Frank bumps into the man who broke his heart. The family seems to be disjointed again, when they realize they have forgotten Olive at a gas station. They promptly return for her, stating "No one gets left behind!" Grandpa tells Richard how proud he is of his son.

**Midpoint**: The family arrives at a motel to spend the night and *ticking clocks* are set as they must arrive in California early the next day. *A and B Stories cross* as Olive tells Grandpa that she does not want to be a loser "because daddy hates losers." Sheryl's pushiness causes an argument with Richard about the book deal (giving him a *false defeat*), so applying his own motto to himself, Richard drives to the hotel where his business partner Stan Grossman (Bryan Cranston) is staying. After the deal is again rejected by Stan, Richard *comes out publicly* telling him that he will go on alone. Only losers give up, and he will not do that. But is he truly aware yet of what winning really means?

**Bad Guys Close In**: Our Bad Guys in this film — both external and internal — are anything that could prevent the family from arriving at the contest, and Grandpa dying of an overdose is a really big example! They spend some time at the hospital and the "bereavement liaison" tells them they won't make it in time to California. Richard, starting to show real care for his family, decides that they will simply steal Grandpa's body! "Winners don't give up!" he says. The whole family works together to take the body out of the hospital, and off they go. Of course, there are more obstacles on the road — not only will the van's horn not stop honking, but they are also pulled over by the police. Luckily, some of the porn magazines left behind by grandpa cause enough of a distraction to get them off the hook. Later, to entertain themselves, Olive subjects Dwayne to a sight test from a pamphlet she got at the hospital. And everything goes wrong!

**All Is Lost**: After a 9-month vow of silence, Dwayne learns that he is colorblind, so he will not be able to become a jet pilot. Completely shocked by the news, he has a panic attack and demands to be let out of the van. Once he has screamed his lungs out, he insists on remaining on the side of the road, alone, but Sheryl won't allow that. It seems that the team will never make it to the pageant in time.

**Dark Night of the Soul**: The family attempts to get Dwayne to come back, but he only insults them as they try to convince him to return.

**Break into Three**: Richard tells Olive to go and talk to her brother. The sweet little girl knows that sometimes words are not the answer, so she just hugs Dwayne, a tender enough gesture to convince him to get back in the van. (And did you spot the "United We Stand" sign?) The family is back on the road!

**Finale**:

1. Gathering the Team: The family runs to make it in time to the registration counter. There, they "gather" to try to convince the unsympathetic manager to let them participate... and she accepts. They are in! What's more, Olive learns that Miss California loves ice cream.

2. Executing the Plan: Their "plan" now is to get Olive ready for her show, but soon they realize that they are probably out of their league—the rest of the contestants seem really professional (read: grotesque), so Olive's chances to succeed are slim.

3. High Tower Surprise: Haunted by their own insecurities, Dwayne and Frank try to take Olive out of the competition, thinking that everyone is going to laugh at her. Sheryl convinces them to "let Olive be Olive"... and then they realize that the show she prepared with Grandpa is a strip-tease!

4. Dig, Deep Down: Shocked by the "scandalous" show, the manager demands it be halted, ordering Richard to take Olive off the stage. He seems to agree, but when he is onstage with her, he "digs deep down"...

5. The Execution of the New Plan: ...and starts dancing with her, becoming part of the show! The rest of the family forgets about their insecurities as they step onto the stage until all of them are dancing around Olive — regardless of what people think — as a united family.

**Final Image**: Pushing the van again, the family starts the trip back home. We know that there are many miles ahead of them, but we can bet that this return trip will be a vastly different one, as they have happily changed forever.

## O BROTHER, WHERE ART THOU? (2000)

*In Save the Cat!® Goes to the Movies*, Blake defined the "Epic Fleece" as akin to its Greek antecedent. We can follow a really close link with our example — not only do we have the Hellenic thematic connection, but this film by the Coen brothers is also an adaptation of the immortal classic, *The Odyssey*, the blueprint for thousands of future "journey back home" films.

Homer's work would not be as famous without Ulysses, "that man skilled in all the ways of contending, a wanderer, harried for years on end..." (quoting the opening title card). Also known as Odysseus, he is one of the characters who best encompasses the "endowed by the gift of gab" Trickster archetype, here wonderfully played by Kentucky-born George Clooney.

Yet another wise decision was to set the action in rural Mississippi during the Great Depression, with a score of countless bluegrass, delta blues, gospel and other kinds of local folk music — besides painstakingly working in the sepia tones of the film, which gives it a perfect nostalgic yet current look. Plus, we writing geeks get to spot all the classic references (Greek-ster eggs?) to *The Odyssey*!

So, we are playing it safe here. As you will see, this film contains all prerequisites of a good "Epic Fleece": a long, winding, adventurous "road" (which is also metaphorical), an unlikely "team" which ends as friends and a "prize" or MacGuffin which ends up being not as important as the quest itself. So harken to the bard and let old Homer start singing!

GF Type: Epic Fleece

GF Cousins: *The Wages of Fear, The Road, The Three Burials of Melquiades Estrada, Das Boot, Apocalypse Now*

O BROTHER, WHERE ARE THOU?
*Based on Homer's "The Odyssey"*
*Written by* Ethan Coen & Joel Coen
*Directed by* Joel Coen

**Opening Image**: A chain gang working in the sun: men bound with iron chains for punishment and redemption. Lo and behold, three of them are running away! Our heroes start as prisoners, probably criminals, so we feel they have a lot to redeem themselves for. Will they be different men by the Final Image?

**Theme Stated**: Early in their getaway, the trio finds an old, blind black man driving a handcar, who speaks in tongues about their future: "You will find a fortune, though it will not be the fortune you seek." And isn't that the main theme of Golden Fleeces? Remember: the prize is not the "gold" but what is learned on the road itself.

**Set-Up**: During the first steps of their flight, we get to know Ulysses Everett McGill (George Clooney), Pete Hogwallop (John Turturro) and Delmar O'Donnell (Tim Blake Nelson). They happened to be chained together, but they don't exactly seem like friends, as they fight to decide who is the leader. They have fled for freedom and are looking for a treasure (our "GreekGuffin") that Everett allegedly hid. But first, they must unshackle themselves, so they visit Pete's cousin, Wash.

**Catalyst**: Wash betrays them! And Everett repeats four times, "Damn! We are in a tight spot." Ruthless sunglasses-clad Sheriff Cooley (Daniel von Bargen) is about to burn the barn with them inside, but Wash's son saves them just in time.

**Debate**: After leaving the kid behind, their car breaks down and they have to continue on foot. In the middle of a forest, they are surprised by a gospel-singing crowd which gets baptized in the nearby river. Delmar and Pete decide to join them, feeling themselves saved and redeemed of all sin. This is our Debate beat: does it take so little to be saved? The redemption theme is further debated when they pick up a young black man at a crossroads, guitar player Tommy Johnson (Chris Thomas King), who claims he has sold his soul to the devil in exchange for playing "real good." Everett laughs at both ways of dealing with the supernatural, feet firmly planted on the ground. As we can imagine, his character arc will involve confronting his own salvation in the face of the divine.

**Break into Two**: To make a quick buck, the trio decides to record, as the Soggy Bottom Boys, the song "Man of Constant Sorrow" (did you remember the opening title card?) for a local radio station. Well, they don't realize it yet, but this proactive decision will ultimately prove to be a key one, as the song will become a hit and literally play a great part in their salvation.

**B Story**: There are still many adventures before the B Story really develops, but it involves the mythologically-named Penelope, current wife of Everett, and his six daughters. She will only stay with him if he changes from a Trickster to a bona-fide man. Can he really do that?

**Fun and Games**: Our Fun and Games section includes traveling the South while having adventures, and also exploring the world of honesty and integrity, that is, trying not to take advantage of their opportunities for crime. Soon, the trio meets bank robber George Nelson, and when he departs, he gives them his dirty money. Is it for them to keep? At the same time, we follow another important thread: that of governor Pappy O'Daniel (Charles Durning), who feels he will not win the next election. Our heroes have Fun on the road, seemingly stealing a pie but then paying for it. And since we are near our middle, a little *Sex at 60* is due when they meet the singing river sirens.

**Midpoint**: Upon waking up soon after, they suffer a *false defeat* when the team has been broken up and Delmar thinks that Pete has been turned into a toad — they are saddened to have lost their friend. Later at a restaurant, in a sort of "Midpoint defeat party," they try to behave as rich, respectable men, and we get "a glimpse of what they could be (and will ultimately be), with no obligation to be it."

**Bad Guys Close In**: In the restaurant, they meet one-eyed Big Dan (John Goodman), who gives them a serious beating and steals all of their money, and even kills "Pete," squashing the toad. Bad Guys Sheriff Cooley and his men Close In by torturing Pete and threatening him with a noose. And when Everett finally finds his daughters and wife Penelope, he also meets B Story Bad Guy Waldrip (Ray McKinnon), who is a legitimate suitor and fist fights rather well. *Clocks start ticking* as Penelope will be married the next day and *stakes are further raised* when they see Pete in a movie theatre, advising them not to seek the treasure, as it's actually an ambush. Showing true friendship, they liberate him, but the "team disintegrates" again when Everett reckons he lied — there is no treasure; Pete made it up to lure them into escaping.

**All Is Lost**: Pete and Delmar will now have to face almost lifelong sentences. Their argument comes to a halt when they spot a KKK meeting nearby... and they see that Tommy is about to get lynched, quite a literal *whiff of death*.

**Dark Night of the Soul**: They behold their friend's impending death, and Tommy himself contemplates the end as he is taken to the gallows.

**Break into Three:** Despite the risks, they get some white hoods and try to liberate him. Big Dan exposes them and they manage to escape, defeating him with a burning wooden crucifix, similar to Odysseus defeating the Cyclops some thousand years before.

**Finale:**

1. Gathering the Team: The team "gathers" together to "storm the castle," a house where a dinner is being held. Again, they argue about who is the leader and Everett "amends hurts" with them, admitting his wrongdoings. He asks them to trust him once more.

2. Executing the Plan: Their "plan" consists of getting fake beards to get onstage. While Pete and Delmar perform their act, Everett tries to convince his wife to get back with him, showing he has not really changed yet. But boy, everything does indeed change when the audience recognizes the trio as the Soggy Bottom Boys! They are pardoned of all their past wrongdoings when "deus" Pappy O'Daniel "ex machinaes" as in classic Greek pieces.

3. High Tower Surprise: Apparently redeemed by men, Everett and his friends seem to have a bright future ahead, and they only need Penny's ring for the wedding. But at their cabin, surprise! They are caught by Sheriff Cooley, who has not heard about the pardon and wants to hang them on the spot.

4. Dig, Deep Down: For the first time, Everett gets on his knees and "digs, deep down," praying for his family and friends, seeking God's help.

5. The Execution of the New Plan: Everett's "new plan" seems to work as what Delmar calls a "miracle" (an announced flood of the valley to make a hydroelectric plant) saves them. Everett shows himself again as a skeptic, but we know he has changed and all three have finally been redeemed.

**Final Image:** Everett walks with his again wife-to-be, enjoying the fact that his adventurous days are over and happily suffering her demands. And in a clever and subtle mirror of our opening scene (where men were bound by chains), Everett's lovely daughters are bound too... by the sweet string of family love. The blind seer moves on, as he has many a story to tell.

## RESERVOIR DOGS (1992)

Hailed as one of the most influential independent motion pictures in history, this wonderful film was discovered by many of us after the success of *Pulp Fiction*. And we found, in its purest form, some of the trademarks of a director who originally intended to shoot with a meager $30,000 budget: shocking bursts of violence, controversial overtones and nonlinear narrative.

Of course, the latter is exactly what interests us most when applying the Blake Snyder Beat Sheet! Because as you can guess, being a Tarantino film, things may seem complicated — as the story jumps back and forth in time to give us details of the characters and the plot — until we realize he is actually telling two stories: the caper and its aftermath.

To make it even more interesting, also consider that many details of the caper story are actually elided, that is, left out of the film (but still narrated or implied). And to make the writing more efficient, many beats are presented in just one scene. Does this make the film an un-beat-able one? No, it only means that if you have two stories, you can have two Beat Sheets!

This acclaimed film is also a good example of a "Caper Fleece" (even though the caper itself is never seen), in which the "road" is the robbery, the "goal" is the diamonds and the "team" is literally "a variety pack of oddballs" who do not really trust each other, among whom are two men with something more valuable than money at stake: true friendship.

GF Type: Caper Fleece

GF Cousins: *The Ladykillers*, *The Red Circle (Le Cercle Rouge)*, *Bottle Rocket*, *Rififi*, *Snatch*

## RESERVOIR DOGS
*Written and Directed by* Quentin Tarantino

## BEAT SHEET 1: THE CAPER

**Opening Image**: We see the "before" image of main character Freddy Newandyke (Tim Roth), an undercover cop who informs his boss Holdaway (Randy Brooks) that he has succeeded in infiltrating dangerous gangster Joe Cabot's gang.

**Theme Stated**: "Long Beach Mike is a f*** scumbag. He is selling out his amigos," says Holdaway. Can you have friends in the underworld? And isn't Freddy going to sell out his amigos, too?

**Set-Up**: In a "Caper Fleece" Set-Up, we must introduce the characters and their quirks, and this is what Tarantino does, showing Mr. White (Harvey Keitel) and Mr. Blonde (Michael Madsen) being interviewed by Joe himself and telling about their pasts.

**Catalyst**: The Catalyst is Joe's "calls to adventure" for the three men: the robbery. It is omitted but told by Freddy AKA Mr. Orange, and it is clearly shown in the case of Mr. White and Mr. Blonde during their interview with Joe.

**B Story**: The relationship story of this film is the same for both beat sheets (in fact, it is the "glue" joining them), and is partly omitted but strongly implied: the mentor-mentee relationship of Mr. White and Mr. Orange.

**Debate**: We haven't left the scene where Joe talks to each of them yet, as the economy of the film demands so. Mr. White and Mr. Blonde internally Debate whether they will join the caper, while Mr. Orange literally Debates with Holloway about how to proceed next.

**Break into Two**: Still in the same scenes, White, Blonde and Orange know they are "in."

**Fun and Games**: What is it like to work as an undercover cop? Mr. Orange rehearses the actually amusing anecdote about his drug deal, and when he meets the rest of the gangsters, they have Fun in the car talking about Christie Love and other related occurrences unsuitable for print.

**Midpoint**: Orange's *false victory* and *public coming out* are in the beginning of his telling of the commode story to Mr. White, Joe Cabot and his son, "Nice Guy" Eddie (Chris Penn).

**Bad Guys Close In**: Mr. Orange's story becomes the focus now, as he enters a men's room with a bag full of weed and he finds four sheriffs and a police dog!

**All Is Lost**: It seems that All Is Lost for Mr. Orange when the dog starts barking because it's detected the drugs. Though the narrative is non-linear, this beat is in its perfect place.

**Dark Night of the Soul**: Mr. Orange knows the cops suspect him, but he tries to conceal his nervousness by keeping as cool as he can instead of fleeing.

**Break into Three**: Mr. Orange's coolness under pressure prompts Joe to think that he is the right man for the job, setting the actual plan in motion.

**Finale**:
1. Gathering the Team: The "team" is gathered and given new names at Joe's place. Did you see the blueprint behind him? They are laying out the plan.

2. Executing the Plan: Famously, we will never see this part, but it is described in detail by Mr. White to Mr. Orange while they are sitting in a car.

3. High Tower Surprise: Of course, something goes wrong. The alarm is set off and Mr. Blonde starts shooting people. Some flee, others are killed and Mr. Pink is shown getting the diamonds. Mr. White and Mr. Orange escape, but the latter is shot in the belly.

4. Dig, Deep Down: Bleeding to death, Mr. Orange, the undercover cop, has to "dig, deep down" to endure the pain and fear so as not to blow his cover.

5. The Execution of the New Plan: At this point, his new plan is to "bleed" until Joe arrives and the rest of the cops can arrest them.

**Final Image:** Freddy is now in danger of dying, and he is very far from the security that he showed when we first met him.

## BEAT SHEET 2: THE AFTERMATH

**Opening Image:** Some men in suits are having a funny conversation about pop song meanings and the convenience of tipping in modern America. They seem relaxed and friendly. But are they really friends? Do they trust each other? We will find out.

**Set-Up:** Something has gone wrong during an armed robbery, and now Mr. Orange is bleeding to death in a car driven by Larry, Mr. White's actual name. They seem to care for each other a lot, like real friends. But are they?

**B Story:** As stated in Beat Sheet 1, our shared B Story is Mr. White and Mr. Orange's friendship, this time from the point of view of the former. In a world of crooks, he has no doubts about Orange, and that will be his fatal mistake.

**Theme Stated**: Blood-drenched Orange asks White to leave him in front of a hospital: "I won't tell them anything, man." As we know from our former Theme Stated beat, Orange is lying to his face — he indeed plans to tell everything to the cops, since he is the traitor.

**Catalyst**: Once in the warehouse where they must wait for Joe, Mr. Pink arrives with unsettling news: he thinks the robbery was a set-up and that there is a "rat" among them.

**Debate**: Mr. Pink and Mr. White are very nervous, and they argue: have they really been betrayed? If so, by whom?

**Break into Two**: "What's done is done. We need you cool," says Mr. White, taking control of the situation and prompting the always-doubting Mr. Pink to remain calm. They have to move on.

**Fun and Games**: What must have happened? The two men try to keep calm as they reminisce about what happened during the robbery. Mr. Pink reveals he stashed the diamonds and suspects everyone, even Mr. Orange. That enrages Mr. White, who defends Mr. Orange aggressively.

**Midpoint**: *Time clocks* are set as Mr. Orange could die if not taken to a hospital. But this is also Mr. White's *false victory* (as Mr. Pink agrees to take him to a doctor) and *public coming out* as he reveals that he told Mr. Orange his real name. The violent true nature of Mr. White and Mr. Pink also comes out as they fight and point guns at each other, *raising the stakes*.

**Bad Guys Close In**: Their Bad Guy, that is, the man who botched the robbery, appears: cool psychopath Mr. Blonde, who has taken a cop hostage. Also, "Nice Guy" Eddie arrives and is not happy about the situation, leaving Mr. Blonde alone with the cop, whom he starts to torture.

**All Is Lost**: With "Stuck in the Middle With You" playing, Mr. Blonde is about to burn the cop alive, when Mr. Orange blows his own cover by shooting the psycho to death.

**Dark Night of the Soul**: Mr. Orange and the ear-severed cop contemplate their impending deaths, unable to do anything about the situation.

**Break into Three**: Mr. Orange proactively tells the cop that they will wait until Joe arrives, and only then will the police be able to save them.

**Finale**:

1. Gathering the Team: The gangster "team" is gathered when Eddie, Mr. White and Mr. Pink return and find Mr. Blonde dead.

2. Executing the Plan: Eddie asks Mr. Orange for an explanation, and he fulfills his plan of trying to make them believe that Mr. Blonde was the rat.

3. High Tower Surprise: Eddie does not accept Mr. Orange's story, but Joe arrives and confirms that Orange is the traitor, so they must kill him. Not willing to believe it, Mr. White draws his gun and Eddie does too, leading to the most famous "Mexican standoff" in film history. They are all shot, but White survives, although there is another surprise for him: Orange reveals he *is* a cop, so he has betrayed him all along and does not deserve his friendship.

4. Dig, Deep Down: Disappointed, White "digs, deep down" while trying to decide if he will kill his friend.

5. The Execution of the New Plan: Regardless of the fact that he is going to die, Mr. White shoots Mr. Orange and is killed by the police.

**Final Image**: The men we met at the beginning are all dead except Mr. Pink, who is presumably arrested or shot. They never trusted each other, and the ones who did... paid for it.


## THE STRAIGHT STORY (1999)

When speaking about David Lynch, a world of disturbing darkness comes to mind — surreal images of dangerous places, characters on the verge of madness, and mystical, noir violence. That is why nothing could be more surprising that this mellow, melancholic, life-affirming film, a US/UK/French co-production.

*The Straight Story* is based on the true journey of Alvin Straight, who rode across Iowa and Wisconsin on a lawn mower to see his brother, and it is our chosen example of what Blake defined as a "Solo Fleece," in which "a single participant goes on the trip."

While the "team" is our hero himself, the rest of the elements of a classic GF remain the same: a "road" (317 miles), a "prize" (finding his brother) and many a *road apple* that threaten to stop Alvin's trip cold.

This kind of GF is also one of the toughest to write because the rule that "each stop on the way must count" is paramount. That is why with no set pieces, no guns, no chases, no gold or money... just a man who wants to do the right thing, audiences and critics hailed the film as the masterpiece it still is.

GF Type: Solo Fleece

GF Cousins: *Into the Wild, Broken Flowers, Ulysses' Gaze, Taste of Cherry, Locke*

THE STRAIGHT STORY
*Written by* John Roach & Mary Sweeney
*Directed by* David Lynch

**Opening Image**: A sky full of stars, with its traditional meanings of eternity, solemnity and divinity. By the end of the film, knowing our main character better, this very same shot will have a very different meaning: a fulfilled vision of brotherly love.

**Set-Up**: We meet Alvin Straight (Richard Farnsworth in his last role) lying on his kitchen floor, unable to get up and worrying all those around him, like neighbors, friends and his daughter Rose (Sissy Spacek). Alvin, 73 with many health problems, is a very stubborn man who is unable to drive a car and has severe mobility problems. He refuses just about everything — being operated on, using a walker, getting tests, stopping smoking, eating healthier or anything of the sort. Given his age, we know that he will not live much longer if he goes on like this. Does this not sound like a literal *Stasis=Death* moment for all of us?

**Theme Stated**: The doctor tells Alvin: "If you don't make some changes quickly, there will be some serious consequences." Our stubborn main character seems to accept this, but the changes and consequences he is thinking about do not exactly deal with his health. Alvin knows he has to fix something else before he gets worse... he has to get his family back.

**Catalyst**: Soon after, while father and daughter watch a lightning storm, the telephone rings and Alvin knows it is bad news: his estranged brother Lyle has suffered a stroke.

**Debate**: This triggers an internal Debate in Alvin, while Rose tells us that in 1988 Alvin and Lyle's relationship soured. "I don't know what he will do," she says. A bit after, Alvin announces that he plans to go on the road to see his brother, still not knowing how he will do it.

Finally, Alvin seems to have made a decision, and starts fixing an old lawn mower to go to Wisconsin, a 317-mile trip. Is this not crazy?

**Break into Two**: Alvin finishes his preparations and states he will travel alone. Alvin and Rose look at the starry sky again, and when the new day dawns, Alvin sets out for his trip.

**B Story**: Largely off-screen, the B Story, or brotherly love story, focuses on the relationship between Alvin and Lyle. Why did they grow apart? What happened between them? Can they make amends and be together again? We will learn more as Alvin gives strangers information about his brother and himself.

**Fun and Games**: As you know, a usual sign that we are in our Fun and Games section is that there is a scene with our characters on the road, driving full-speed ahead, blasting music that... oh, wait. We get the same here, but in the spirit of this quiet, mellow film. So let us explore with Alvin what it's like to travel at 5 mph and meet people on the road. The first of our *road apples* that stop the trip cold is when the old mower breaks down, forcing Alvin to go back to his village, get a new one and start all over again. On the road, he finds a grumpy young woman who has fled from home because she is pregnant, and she gets a valuable lesson in family ties from Alvin. As in any GF, each stop on the road must count and discuss our theme. Alvin has to confront other serious obstacles for a 73-year-old man, such as a storm, and will marvel when finding himself in the middle of a cyclist race — the fastest thing you will see in the movie.

**Midpoint**: At minute 55, Alvin is cheered on when he arrives at the cyclist's campsite — a *false victory* (showing that he can make it, after all) and a *public coming out* in what becomes a "party at Midpoint." Also, even in this slow-paced film, there are *ticking clocks*, as Alvin reminds everyone around that one is not always young, so they have to make the most of their lives.

**Bad Guys Close In:** Five weeks into his trip, Alvin has to confront such Bad Guys as the enormous trucks that threaten to force him off the road, and the breaking of the belt of his mower's motor, which sends the mower out of control. Running out of money when he has to get repairs adds difficulty to his task and also functions as another *ticking clock*. Luckily, he gets help from a family that also offers to drive him to his brother's, but Alvin refuses — he has to make it on his own.

**All Is Lost:** Alvin and a man his own age reminisce about their traumatic experiences in World War II and how Alvin might have accidentally killed a friend, giving us a *whiff of death*. He reveals more about his past, and how alcohol was key to the souring of his relationship with his brother. Alvin is showing "his old way of thinking dying," that is, he does not think he is right anymore, so he has to make amends — that is the real purpose of the journey.

**Dark Night of the Soul:** At night, Alvin looks at the stars again, this shot gaining more and more meaning as the film progresses. It is literally the "darkness before the dawn."

**Break into Three:** Alvin's mower is fixed and he can continue on the way. Soon after he crosses the Mississippi (a symbolic Break into Three if there ever was one), he encounters a priest who knows his brother. *A and B stories cross* as they talk about Lyle and Alvin "confesses" about what split them apart and how he wants to make peace. "Amen to that," says the padre, blessing Alvin as he walks through the doors of our Finale beat.

**Finale:**
1. Gathering the Team: Alvin stops at a service station to gather some strength, showing his *synthetic* change: he can have a beer and know he will not be angry anymore.

2. Executing the Plan: Alvin just keeps driving, as he has done for hundreds of miles, but now he is unable to control his tears. Will he be too late?

3. High Tower Surprise: His motor sputters and dies, and it seems impossible to get help on the deserted road. Fortunately, the mower comes back to life. Phew!

4. Dig, Deep Down: Alvin reaches his brother's home and finds Lyle alive. Both of them sit, unable to talk and "digging, deep down" for their feelings, as Alvin's gesture has obviously moved his brother.

5. The Execution of the New Plan: As they rest, we can imagine that they have a lot to talk about and to pardon each other for. And of course...

**Final Image**: ...our closing image, that of the starry skies, has taken a full, *synthetic* meaning. We know that, as in the times in which they loved each other, the two brothers will talk long into the night, safe under the eternal dark sky.

Theodore contemplates the loss of *Her* in his
"Dark Night of the Soul."

# 3  OUT OF THE BOTTLE

The dream of wishing for something out of the ordinary and getting it is as old as humanity, and the lesson implied is equally as ancient: be careful what you wish for!

From the story of Pandora's box, to the Tree of Knowledge of Good and Evil in the Bible, to the legend of Aladdin from which our genre takes its name, men and women have desired some kind of magical shortcut to lighten their troubles and pains: a token, spirit, object or power that can make their life easier in any regard. Tempting, isn't it? But we know it's also... cheating.

The history of story is filled with examples of characters who are granted a peculiar power that will give them an advantage over their peers, only for them to discover that the supposed blessing is a damnation in disguise. As the legend says, you can ask the devil for eternal life, only to realize a thousand years later that you forgot to ask him for eternal youth!

As Blake taught us, these kinds of stories have a deep moral: we shouldn't desire what we can't have naturally, because if the wish was granted, we would lose something very human — the ability to overcome troubles and grow. That is why our OOTB protagonists end up rejecting the gift for their own good, showing their transformation in the process.

But wait! Are we talking about magic, fantasy and legends? Doesn't this sound dangerously like mainstream territory with films like *The Nutty Professor*, *Freaky Friday* or *What Women Want* as "beat out" in *Save the Cat!*® *Goes to the Movies*? Well, as we will see, the indie, experimental and cult realm have some of the most successful films in this genre, so whether in commercial or stylized form, we all tell the same stories: the ones that have been around forever.

So, what types of OOTB subgenres will we find? First we have the **Body Switch Bottle**, in which two individuals (human or otherwise) interchange their bodies, resulting in men becoming women, animals becoming human or other creatures, youngsters becoming oldsters, or some other reversal. Our chosen film for this category is *Being John Malkovich*, written by master of the surreal Charlie Kaufman.

Blake named the second subgenre the **Thing Bottle**, where an object, artificial item or outer mechanism makes the magic, and our blessing-turned-curse comes from it. This is the case of horror pieces *Re-Animator* and *The Evil Dead* or the much lighter Spike Jonze film *Her*, in which an Operating System brings happiness to Joaquin Phoenix's life... a joy that we know won't last.

Our third OOTB subgenre is the **Angel Bottle**. Here, a magical being fulfills the wishes, although we know that many of those dreams can be turned into nightmares unless we reject the magic and take action ourselves (or be damned forever), as in *Donnie Darko* and *Looking for Eric*. Keep in mind that in these types of stories, the "angels" can be the main characters, even literal angels as in *Wings of Desire* and its sequel *Faraway, So Close!*, or French favorite *Amélie*.

The **Curse Bottle** subgenre implies that the magic that is bestowed upon our protagonist was not really asked for by him or her, but was granted anyway. Yet, by being forced to deal with the "curse," the character will exit the story as a transformed person. In wonderful films such as *Upstream Color* and *The Black Swan,* main characters face plights similar to Edward Norton confronting a "curse" named Brad Pitt in *Fight Club*.

Finally, there's the **Surreal Bottle** subgenre. In it, the hero becomes "part of a parallel universe" where "magic-like" time warps, pseudo-science, drug-induced trips or some crazy effect turn our character's world upside-down. This is the territory of *Primer*; *Midnight in Paris*; *Synecdoche, New York* or the über-successful reality vs. madness piece called *Birdman (or The Unexpected Virtue of Ignorance)* by Alejandro González Iñárritu.

If any of the above is about to happen to your character, what are the components you will need to build your story? As always, there are three fundamental ones.

Let us start with a **wish**, since magic has to be called for. You need a protagonist who knows what he wants and not what he needs (recognize anyone like that?) and whom Blake summarized in two kinds of characters: those underdogs who star in "empowerment stories" and those big shots who need life to teach them a lesson (read: spanking) in the form of a "comeuppance tale."

After the protagonist states what they *want* (let us repeat: not what they *need*), the **spell** comes into play, that is the magic occurs — always limited by some boundaries or **Rules**. That magic puts your story in motion. It could be a new Operating System (*Her*), the main character's telekinesis (*Birdman*) or a door that happens to lead into a famous actor's mind (*Being John Malkovich*). The spark of the magic can be as whimsical and surreal as you want, but The Rules must be clearly stated and followed, or your film will come apart. And beware of what Blake dubbed **Double Mumbo Jumbo**! Do not have two kinds of magic happening in your story at the same time (the usual "aliens vs. vampires" territory). That will confuse your audiences and, surely, the gatekeepers that will read (and throw away) your script.

Finally, as in all stories about transformation, your hero needs to complete his or her character change, and in this kind of story it is easy to figure out: either they learn their **lesson** or they don't. One way to accomplish this is by having the hero *learn to do it without the magic*, meaning that they can reject the supernatural aide that was supposedly helping them to do it (as they should have from the beginning) and actually accomplish their goals by themselves. This is what Amélie Poulain does when she confronts her lover without using her "magic" (subterfuge) and what Theodore Twombly does in *Her* when he lets go of his OS, Samantha. The other possible outcome implies not being able to change and thus failing to make the decision to stop using the magic, which has a negative effect on the protagonist. This is what happens to puppeteer Craig when, instead of leaving John Malkovich's head, he decides to stay inside, losing his own personality forever. Of course, you could leave the audience wondering, as the ending of *Birdman* does.

Finally, many of these movies feature a **Confidant**, that is, someone the main character trusts with his or her secret. Sometimes the Confidant will help (as in *Amélie*), while other times the Confidant will take advantage of our hero (like Maxine does with Craig in *Being John Malkovich*).

## FIND MAGIC IN THE BOTTLE... THE RIGHT WAY!

So, if you want to tell a story that teaches your character a lesson (perhaps inspired by something you yourself magically learned), make sure to include the following elements:

1. A "wish" that your hero will make or that is granted without asking, which will set the magic moving and does not need much explanation.

2. A "spell": the powers, new world, time warp or whatever our hero is going to enjoy (at first) and suffer because of (ultimately). Just make sure the spell follows "The Rules" and avoid any "Double Mumbo Jumbo"!

3. A "lesson" that the hero will learn during the adventure, one that will push him to "do it without the magic" or to surrender to its spell — usually damning him in the process. So be careful what you wish for!

Let's now open the bottle and make your filmmaking wish come true!

## BEING JOHN MALKOVICH (1999)

"Body Switch Bottle" stories have always been wildly popular, as titles like *Big*, *13 Going on 30* and *Freaky Friday* show, at least in mainstream cinema. But can a seemingly light topic like "switching bodies" become equally effective in experimental and auteur films?

Well, just ask two of today's more interesting filmmakers, acclaimed director Spike Jonze and screenwriter Charlie Kaufman! Both are famous for making films that not only defy the rules of screenwriting, but also tell stories in which the characters' minds become a playground for storytelling in which the universe of narrative itself is sometimes portrayed as meta-cinema exercises.

*Being John Malkovich* is one of those examples, starting with the crazy idea that somewhere in New York there is a portal connecting the regular world with the mind of actor John Malkovich (played by himself) and finishing with an intelligent reflection of what it means to have an identity as well as the perils of losing it in the process of chasing our dreams.

The resulting film was nominated in three categories at the Academy Awards® and received worldwide acclaim, regularly featured in "best films of all time" lists. So now, let's follow a desperate and disillusioned puppeteer to the 7½ floor as he opens a tiny door into one of the greatest films that ever took place… inside someone's head.

OOTB Type: Body Switch Bottle

OOTB Cousins: *Howl's Moving Castle*, *The Tenant*, *Source Code*, *Enemy*, *A Scanner Darkly*

BEING JOHN MALKOVICH
*Written by* Charlie Kaufman
*Directed by* Spike Jonze

**Opening Image**: A stage's curtain opens and a poetic dance unfolds under the spell of dramatic music. It's not a person who dances, but a puppet! Our main character (played by John Cusack) practices his "Craig's dance of despair and disillusionment," operating a puppet who rejects his own image in a mirror. By the end of the movie, will the real Craig have accepted himself?

**Theme Stated**: Identity is one of the main themes of our story. While Craig watches TV, a famous puppeteer moves a gigantic Belle of Amherst puppet, reading Emily Dickinson's famous poem *I Am Nobody*. "How dreary to be somebody!" she says. What is more difficult: to be oneself... or to be another person? Does being another make life easier?

**Set-Up**: First, we get to know Craig and his "family" better. He is unhappily married to pet store manager Lotte (Cameron Diaz), and they live together with many animals whose names (identity!) he does not care to remember. Lotte suggests that he find a job, but Craig is too depressed. Very soon, it is made clear that the modern world does not need many puppeteers, especially if they are obsessed with the impossible love stories this puppeteer likes to present. Craig wants to be a famous artist, but doesn't seem to be doing too much to achieve his dreams, which makes him exist in a permanent *Stasis=Death* moment. If he does not change, he will probably "die" deep down.

**Catalyst**: At minute 12 sharp, Craig is told, "You got the job." After finding an ad in which a "man with fast hands" was sought, he visits the 7½ floor of the Mertin-Flemmer building, a place with unusually low ceilings. After meeting a strange secretary and quirky, sex-obsessed manager Dr. Lester (Orson Bean), he is hired as a filer.

**Debate**: "Any questions?" asks Dr. Lester, opening our Debate section. Craig wonders why everything is so strange, but the weird orientation video does not make things clear, and he seems more interested in a mysterious woman in white. At home, he unemotionally rejects having kids with Lotte. At work, he keeps hitting on the sexy woman, figuring out her name (identity!): she is ambitious Maxine (Catherine Keener). No matter how hard Craig tries, she does not seem interested, so at home, he builds a Maxine puppet. "Why are you a puppeteer?" he makes her puppet ask. "Perhaps it's the idea of becoming someone else for a little while," he answers. In our OOTB story, that is his "wish."

**Break into Two**: Craig's desire is promptly satisfied as the "spell" unfolds. He accidentally discovers a door in his office that leads to the inside of John Malkovich's head! Craig stays in Malkovich's mind for a little while, just to know how it feels to be famous. And then... he is out! This brief experience has already changed him, so nothing can ever be the same.

**B Story**: Our "love story" pertains, of course, to Maxine, the object of desire for Craig..., and for Lotte! As we will see in time, one special feature of this film is that its double narrative will make us follow both Craig's and Lotte's efforts to win Maxine's cold heart.

**Fun and Games**: When Craig returns from Malkovich's head, he promptly explains The Rules to Maxine: there is a door in his office that takes him "inside John Malkovich, and after about 15 minutes, you are spit out into a ditch on the side of the New Jersey Turnpike." She has become his *Confidant*, a figure with whom the OOTB hero shares the secret of the new world, which sometimes, as we will see, means trouble. Craig also makes Lotte a Confidant, and after being inside Malkovich herself, she decides she wants to be a man. "I knew who I was," she says, further hammering on our identity theme. Lotte makes a strange discovery — maybe Dr. Lester knows about the portal too. Soon, Craig and Maxine are making money taking people for the Malkovich ride, and she contacts the actor directly, seducing him while Lotte is inside. "You shouldn't assume that switching bodies is gonna be the answer to your problems," says Craig. But is he paying attention to his own "lesson"?

**Midpoint**: A "Midpoint party" in which *A and B Stories cross* is held when Craig and Lotte invite Maxine over for dinner. Afterwards, they both try to get the "kiss from the girl," and while she rejects Craig, Maxine tells Lotte she is smitten by her — but only while she is in Malkovich's body. It's a *public coming out* for everyone and a *false defeat* for the couple, as they have not only been rejected, but their marriage is clearly falling apart.

**Bad Guys Close In**: Business goes great for the Malkovich ride, but Craig is depressed and in bed again. Maxine has *Sex at 60* with the actor just to be with Lotte when she is inside his mind (are you following?). Craig cannot stand the pressure, so "the team starts to disintegrate." Jealous, he kidnaps Lotte and decides to get inside Malkovich, starting to control the actor like the puppeteer he is. After seeking Charlie Sheen's hilarious advice, Malkovich decides to investigate, and as the Bad Guy, he "tightens the grip" on Maxine and Craig when he discovers the portal into his own head, finding out what a nightmare world it is to be inside oneself. As the travesty is discovered, Malkovich orders the portal to be shut. This is key, for from now own, the narrative will switch between Craig and Lotte, doubling our beats.

**All Is Lost**: With our beats duplicated, All Is Lost for Craig as he realizes, like Lotte says, that Maxine is not interested in him. He is "worse off than when he started" — he had a wife and a family, now he is penniless, jobless and loveless. For Lotte, All Is Lost comes a little later, as Maxine also rejects her when she finds out that the last time she made love to Malkovich, it was Craig who was inside his mind.

**Dark Night of the Soul:** "What have I become? What am I, some kind of monster?" reflects Craig, contemplating his further loss of identity. Lotte's Dark Night is seeing herself first caged like an animal, then out in the rain, totally alone and with no one caring for her but her chimp.

**Break into Three:** Craig returns and enters Malkovich, telling Lotte that he has discovered how to remain inside the actor and fully control him, showing off with the puppet's dance. His *Moment of Clarity* is a negative one, since he does not seem to want to "do it without the magic." At the same time, Dr. Lester tells Lotte the truth: he has been using the portal for decades to find new bodies, basically becoming immortal, and at midnight, he and his friends will enter Malkovich forever. But if one enters after midnight, one's identity is lost forever.

**Finale:**

1. Gathering the Team: *Synthesis* starts for Craig when he plans to turn Malkovich from an actor into a puppeteer. At the same time, Lotte finds her "team" in the old friends of Dr. Lester, and they offer her a place in the actor's head.

2. Executing the Plan: For several months, Craig "executes his plan" by becoming famous with Malkovich's body. He does not realize that Maxine does not pay attention to him anymore; she is playing with a puppet in the shape of Lotte, whom she misses. When he is away from home, Dr. Lester and Lotte execute their plan: to kidnap Maxine.

3. High Tower Surprise: Thus, Craig's "surprise" is the disappearance of Maxine — he is forced to leave Malkovich's body or Maxine will be killed. But Maxine tries to escape, so this is a High Tower Surprise for Lotte, who chases Maxine inside the actor's subconscious.

4. Dig, Deep Down: After being spat out of Malkovich's head, Maxine reveals that the child she is bearing is actually Lotte's, as she conceived the baby while Lotte was inside Malkovich. Then Lotte "digs, deep down" and accepts Maxine, fulfilling her dream to be both a "mother" and a "man." At the same time, to save Maxine, Craig "digs, deep down" and accepts leaving Malkovich's body.

5. The Execution of the New Plan: Dr. Lester and his friends enter Malkovich's head before midnight, but Lotte does not show up, signaling that she will "do it without the magic." Still hoping to regain Maxine, Craig shows that he has not changed, and he enters Malkovich after midnight.

**Final Image**: Seven years later, Lester/Malkovich has married his secretary and offers a bald Charlie Sheen eternal life. At the same time, Lotte and Maxine are the loving parents of their daughter Emily, inside whom there is still some of Craig's identity! He is slowly being absorbed by the child and disappearing, thus losing any remaining trace of himself, as he never learned, as OOTB heroes should, that life is good as it is.

## AMÉLIE (2001)

Say the name of this film and you will start noticing small, magical details surrounding you, probably with the accompaniment of accordions, dreamy piano pieces, saturated warm colors, the aroma of café au lait and even the sight of a Montmartre street at dusk. But can tiny details and small *plaisirs* as these change your life?

That is the promise of *Amélie*, the unforgettable and internationally successful 1999 French film ($10m budget, $173.9m box office) that tells the story of shy and charming Amélie Poulain, an "angel" who uses small, private details to make the lives of those around her happier and more fulfilled. But what about her own life?

This OOTB film fits in the "Angel Bottle" subgenre, in which "a magical being (Amélie) comes into a unique world (Montmartre) and bestows a wish on those deserving it (her neighbors)," and this means that ironically, our main character is also the "angel" of the story. But to achieve her own "wishes," does she not need an unlikely angel, too?

A little like a French Mary Poppins or Nanny McPhee, Amélie silently, sweetly and secretly cures pains, ailments and depression. And like Zorro, she leaves her loving mark on everyone that surrounds her... everyone but herself, that is. This OOTB shows us how the "wish" to help those around us can also hide the necessity of remembering to fulfill our own dreams.

OOTB Type: Angel Bottle

OOTB Cousins: *Looking for Eric*, *Ruby Sparks*, *Donnie Darko*, *Wings of Desire*, *Miracle in Milan*

## AMÉLIE (LE FABULEUX DESTIN D'AMÉLIE POULAIN)
*Written by* Guillaume Laurant and Jean-Pierre Jeunet
*Directed by* Jean-Pierre Jeunet

**Opening Image:** Petite, charming details are everywhere in the Parisian neighborhood of Montmartre, with no one apparently paying attention to them. They are so tiny and so easily unnoticed that it seems impossible that some of them could change our world, just like a newborn baby named Amélie.

**Theme Stated:** "Amélie likes..." The film opens with the everyday "likes and dislikes" of several characters, including the quirky fixations and small pleasures of Amélie's parents as well as Amélie herself. These seemingly insignificant "likes and dislikes" are the basis of our theme, because — surprisingly — they can affect our lives greatly.

**Set-Up**: During the credits sequence in which Amélie has her "fun moment," her main flaw is revealed: she plays children's games alone. The reason is soon revealed: "at home," and after we meet her perfectionist and neurotic parents, we learn that Amélie spent her childhood in isolation because they thought she had a heart condition. As a result, she developed an overactive imagination. After she grows up (having discovered her power to either make people happy or take revenge on them using their likes and dislikes), we see her now "at work" in a café. We also meet her quirky friends and co-workers (are not every of them in their own *Stasis=Death* moments?). Even if she seems happy while around them, we get the feeling that she still is alone... and lonely.

**Catalyst**: Loudly announced by the narrator, the "moment that will change her life forever" is when she hears the news of the tragic death of Lady Di. Stunned. she drops the cap of a perfume bottle, which breaks a tile, which reveals a hole where she finds a tin box full of children's toys. Is it "small" enough to change her life? Amélie decides to find the owner. If he is moved by the gesture, she will become a regular do-gooder. That is, she will become an "angel."

**Debate**: Is it really possible to think that a small treasure like this could change anyone's life? First, Amélie must find the owner, and while doing so, she discovers that many of her neighbors seem to need the intervention of an "angel" like her. By chance she meets Nino, a strange young man who collects torn, discarded pictures from photo booths. Amélie is attracted to him, but she is too shy to say anything. She then discovers that there are three possible owners of the tin box, but none of them seems to be the correct one. So, in the spirit of the Debate, what now? Time for a *double bump* and to meet our B Story Character.

**B Story**: In this case, the B Story Character is also a mentor: Mr. Dufayel, an old painter who has brittle bone disease. Soon, we will notice that he and Amélie are quite similar in many senses — both find it difficult relating to people and both are "angels" (since

Dufayel will become Amelie's). He also knows about The Rules (Amélie will not confront her protégés, always acting anonymously) and so becomes her *Confidant*.

**Break into Two**: Helped by Dufayel, Amélie finally seeks the owner of the box, Bretodeau, and she creates a way for him to find the box by himself. Immediately, Bretodeau starts crying and reflects on his life, deciding that he will make amends with his estranged daughter. "It must be my guardian angel," he says, referencing our genre and turning Amélie into a happiness-giving being.

**Fun and Games**: What a wonderful scene to start this section! Amélie walks through the neighborhood helping a blind man "see" the great little things around him. She also starts exploring her new "angel" persona, even though she is aware that she might forget about herself and end up isolated. She again encounters Nino from the photo booth and finds his lost picture album, causing her to like him even more. But she still cannot think about herself, as she has many people to help first — making hypochondriac coworker Georgette fall in love with jealous Joseph, or avenging simple-minded Lucien by making fun of obnoxious grocer Collignon. Other plans involve many more preparations to carry out, like sending off the traveling gnome stolen from her reclusive father, showing she is a master of subterfuge, reflecting her own "magic." But will she have to confront Nino to give him back the album?

**Midpoint**: This beat usually needs one *false victory* for our hero, but in this case, Amélie is granted many, like the Collignon revenge or the start of Joseph and Georgette's love affair. Is not their scandalous encounter in the *toilette* a big, loud *Sex at 60*? Lucien and Dufayel also celebrate, and Amélie starts influencing Dufavel's life with videos of miraculous little things. *A and B Stories cross* as the old man tells her: "You have to catch your chance while you can." And Amélie does her *public coming out* when she dares to find Nino at the carnival. Unfortunately, she still is not able to speak to him.

**Bad Guys Close In**: Clearly, there are not external Bad Guys in this film, but this is where we slowly see how Amelie's "old values don't work anymore." She devises another subterfuge for Nino to find the album, but it is clear that this will not bring them closer, even if Nino proactively Closes In by leaving posters all around to meet her. In contrast, Amélie continues using her time to help others and hilariously punishes Collignon. Battling her inner Bad Guys, Amelie decides to "go for broke" and leaves Nino a message to meet her at her own bar, *raising the stakes* even more.

**All Is Lost**: Nino is late, so Amélie's exaggerated imagination thinks that after a lot of misfortunes, he is in the Afghan mountains and will never come back. But he does indeed appear, and he recognizes her. Although she knows Nino is her perfect match, she chickens out and tells him she is not the girl he is looking for. Another lost chance!

**Dark Night of the Soul**: Amélie "is beaten and she knows it" when she sees Nino leave and imagines that she becomes tears, disappearing among the café's tiles.

**Break into Three**: This beat always implies some kind of reflection by the hero, during which a mentor often comes in handy. So Amélie makes *A and B Stories cross* and visits her own angel, Mr. Dufayel, who encourages her to stop using subterfuge — or she will always be a coward. Even in her imaginary world, Amélie knows that she must change or mess up her life.

**Finale**:
1. Gathering the Team: Inspired by Mr. Dufayel, Amélie "amends hurts" and decides to "gather" her own resources to try and win over Nino, devising a new plan which involves (again) a subterfuge. Hasn't she learned yet?

2. Executing the Plan: Her "plan" is to make Nino discover the answer to the mystery that haunts them both, involving the identity of a bald man in Nino's album. But when she

is about to appear, she has doubts and Nino vanishes from sight. And what is worse, Joseph implies that Nino is dating workmate Gina... who is actually testing Nino's good heart.

3. High Tower Surprise: As Amélie laments her bad decisions, Nino surprises her by showing up at her home. She pretends not to be there, and off he goes again. As part of this "surprise," Amélie discovers a video made by her angel and mentor, Mr. Dufayel: "If you let this chance go by, your heart will become as dry and brittle as my skeleton.... Go and get him."

4. Dig, Deep Down: Inspired by Mr. Dufayel's words, Amélie opens the door to chase Nino and finds him standing there. Although unable to speak, she "digs, deep down" to execute her own new plan...

5. The Execution of the New Plan: ...which involves no words, but simply being herself. Amélie lightly kisses Nino on the corner of his mouth, on his neck and on his eyelid, with him tenderly returning her small gestures. Mr. Dufayel knows everything went right at last.

**Final Image:** We behold how Amelie's little miracles have changed everyone's lives, including Bretodou and her own reclusive father, who decides to go for a trip. Even Mr. Dufayel, who is painting something new for the first time in 20 years, has been transformed. Amélie and Nino ride his bike through the streets of Montmartre, no longer alone, but happy, in love and changed forever.

## HER (2013)

The "Thing Bottle" subgenre of OOTB deals with some kind of elixir, formula, totem or object whose magic "brings about a desired transformation in one's life," as Blake said. So what if an Operating System (OS) could transform your life by fulfilling all your emotional needs? Can that love be "real" enough?

This is the theme we find in this acclaimed work by longtime *alter*-reality explorer Spike Jonze, and it is also reportedly his first solo screenplay. The film earned almost 80 nominations worldwide, with over 20 "Screenplay" wins, including the Academy Award® for Best Writing, Original Screenplay.

In the film, we meet Theodore Twombly, working as a "letter writer" in a seemingly-near future where mobile devices can have Artificial Intelligence, to the extent that people can communicate with them as if they were real individuals.

Even with these technical capabilities, can an OS like "Samantha" really care for her user, or is it all programming? And what's more, what would happen if once a device has fallen in love with a human... could it also fall out of love? And then... could we live without its "magic"?

OOTB Type: Thing Bottle

OOTB Cousins: *Re-Animator*, *The Evil Dead*, *The Babadook*, *The Jacket*, *Lars and the Real Girl*

HER
*Written and directed by* Spike Jonze

**Opening Image:** A close-up of Theodore Twombly (Joaquin Phoenix), his gaze lost in inspiration as he dictates a love letter... to someone he doesn't even know! Theodore works for a company that writes surrogate letters to their customers' loved ones. Theodore seems to enjoy expressing his own feelings in this distant way. But can he handle them with a real person?

**Theme Stated**: "They are just letters," says Theodore to his colleague Paul (Chris Pratt). He seems to be aware of the "lesson": that to truly love someone there has to be more than words or a voice, something like... well, a real person. By the end, will he have really learned this lesson?

**Set-Up**: After seeing Theodore "at work," we learn a little bit more about his life. He is depressed and sad, choosing melancholic songs to listen to. He doesn't really pay attention to his surroundings, but is still interested in women. Through flashbacks, we learn that he is recovering from a separation, something he is trying to overcome by looking for late-night company in chat rooms. But he does not always find what he is looking for, and we know that this glum state is a clear indicator of *Stasis=Death*.

**Catalyst**: Walking the streets, Theodore is intrigued by a TV ad in which people who seem panicked and unable to see each other find hope in a new intuitive Artificial-Intelligence powered Operating System (OS) that "listens to you, understands you and knows you." Isn't that what we look for in a partner?

**Debate**: Can that promise be real? Is it crazy to think that a piece of software can give us what a person sometimes can't? Intrigued, Theodore installs the OS, named Samantha (voiced by Scarlett Johansson), who states that she can grow through experiences (can you hear The Rules being explained?). Soon, Samantha learns about Theodore's past and his breakup, and she encourages him to keep dating people. "I can't believe I am having this conversation with my computer," Theodore says, summing up the "this is crazy" side of the Debate beat.

**B Story**: We meet Amy (Amy Adams) and her partner Charles (Matt Letscher), a "real" couple that seems to be happy although there is some tension in their dialogue. Is he too much of a perfectionist? Is she too laid back? In any case, Amy and Theodore will share advice, appreciation and friendship, slowly and unknowingly building their own love. But let's not get too ahead of ourselves!

**Break into Two**: Finally, Theodore starts telling Samantha about his breakup with former wife Catherine (Rooney Mara). He still hasn't signed the divorce papers and seems to dwell on how to move forward. "You don't know what it's like to lose someone you care about," he says. "I want to be as complicated as all those people," Samantha states. They soon will both have the chance to explore their *upside-down worlds* together.

**Fun and Games**: What is it like to date an AI? Is it possible to have as much fun with an OS as you'd have with a person? Can you feel understood and supported? Exploring these *promises of the premise*, Theodore and Samantha go out and enjoy life while slowly developing feelings for each other. He states his "wish" of being able to touch her; they are still aware of their limits, even as she fantasizes about having a body. But she also says, "I am becoming much more than what they programmed." Is that possible? Meanwhile, Theodore tries to date real women like Blind Date (Olivia Wilde), but things get complicated too quickly for him. Soon, he and Samantha have virtual sex, with the usual "not ready to commit" conversation the next day. Theodore also learns that Amy and Charles have broken up, and we see how much he and Amy care for each other as friends. Can a computer also make you feel this good?

**Midpoint**: Theodore starts his Midpoint *coming out* by taking Samantha to his goddaughter's birthday, and he reveals to Amy that he is dating an OS. Amy sort of understands because she has become friends with one, and this understanding leads to. the two becoming each other's *Confidants*. "Are you falling in love with her?" asks Amy in this *A/B Story cross*. "Does that make me a freak?" is his answer. Being able to fall in love again is a *false victory* for Theodore, and Amy is quite understanding. His ex-wife Catherine is not — as he meets her to sign the divorce papers, she attacks him: "It makes me sad that you can't handle real emotions."

**Bad Guys Close In:** Affected by Catherine's words, Theodore's inner Bad Guys attack. He relapses into his depression, again considering that Samantha does not have a body and how this affects their relationship. The situation is made worse when Paul introduces Theodore to his "real" girlfriend. Samantha knows something is not right and fears that their relationship could go sour, her own anxieties and internal Bad Guys coming to light. The "magic" seems not to be working that well anymore. In an attempt to fix the relationship, Samantha reveals that she has contacted a real woman to act as a surrogate body and forces Theodore to have sex with her... and it is a disaster, since Theodore is incapable of saying "I love you" to an unknown person. Having a body is not enough either. Samantha does not seem to understand what real love is.

**All Is Lost:** The next day, Theodore and Samantha have an argument. Theodore tries to accept blame, saying that signing the divorce papers affected him, but he insists that Samantha is not a person. She states that she needs time and "leaves." Theodore is "worse off than when he started"— he was trying to get over a breakup and now will likely have to overcome another one.

**Dark Night of the Soul:** Theodore walks through the city in silence, contemplating what it is like to be alone again, considering what he should do next.

**Break into Three:** Theodore seeks Amy's advice and company for comfort. They discuss his confusion and his apparent inability to handle real emotions. He is sad because he believes he hurts everyone, and asks, "Am I in this because I'm not strong enough for a real relationship?" Amy tells him to enjoy this time, which becomes Theodore's *Moment of Clarity*. But he also suspects she not a reliable advisor, since she is also in "love" with her own OS.

**Finale:**
  1. Gathering the Team: Relying on Amy's advice, Theodore apologizes to Samantha, signaling that he still does not "get

it," but wants to change. As for Samantha, she is accepting herself and her identity. Theodore still does not know what this means — it seems that they still don't understand each other.

2. Executing the Plan: Their "plan" is to remain together, so they enjoy their new time of happiness, as Amy suggested. They do a double-date with friends and Samantha is treated like a real person and continues to accept herself. They both decide to spend some holidays in the snow, but they don't realize, as the song says, that they are "a million miles away."

3. High Tower Surprise: During the holidays, Samantha tells Theodore that she has met other OSes, including philosopher Alan Watts, and that she is changing. Theodore gets the "High Tower Surprise" when she disappears for a while. It also shocks him when he discovers that she is speaking with more than 8,000 people at a time, and that she is actually in love with 641 of them! At last, Theodore realizes that her true nature as an OS makes it impossible to have the kind of personal love he wants, and she leaves.

4. Dig, Deep Down: Every OS, including Amy's, has left their owner to pursue a life of their own, so Amy and Theodore seek comfort in each other. But first, Theodore must "dig, deep down" a little more to form his new plan.

5. The Execution of the New Plan: Theodore demonstrates his change by dictating another letter, but this time a real one, about himself. He writes to Catherine, confronting his own feelings while confessing that he will always see her as a dear friend, at last overcoming his anguish.

**Final Image:** Theodore and Amy climb to the rooftop, enjoying the view of a new day over a big city. These two "real humans" have "learned to do it without the magic," and as she leans her head on his shoulder, we know that they are going to keep finding support in each other... and maybe even love.

## FIGHT CLUB (1999)

Although not exactly an "indie film" by merely economic or production standards, this fascinating and rebellious movie doesn't belong to the mainstream either. Directed by David Fincher, it failed to meet the studio's box-office expectations, as many cult films tend to do. Even so, 20 years after its release, *Fight Club* is still featured on many "best of" lists.

Aside from the exciting screenplay by Jim Huhls, adapted from Chuck Palahniuk's novel, part of the film's enduring appeal is that its themes criticize consumerism, explore male bonding issues and discuss masculinity roles in general — topics that are still relevant today — all exemplified in its unnamed main character (whom we will call "Jack").

This film is an example of the "Curse Bottle" variety, defined by Blake as the one in which "the hero may find himself saddled with magic he didn't ask for... or is cursed by it — but needs it in order to grow." And you can bet Jack never asked to meet with Tyler Durden, but Tyler will indeed change his life and our whole world, while helping Jack mature as a man.

So the "magic" in this film is merely a hallucinatory one, and unlike Fight Club (the club, not the movie), it seems to have only one rule: you can't talk about Tyler Durden. This advice didn't seem to apply to Rosie O'Donnell — or now, to us — but here is a twist-ending warning: if you haven't seen this film, watch it before you read this Beat Sheet!

OOTB Type: Curse Bottle

OOTB Cousins: *It Follows*, *The Gift*, *Carrie*, *Upstream Color*, *The Black Swan*

FIGHT CLUB
*Based on the novel by* Chuck Palahniuk
*Written by* Jim Uhls
*Directed by* David Fincher

**Opening Image:** I am Jack's brain in panic! Witness an extreme close-up of neuron flash-like "explosions," not unlike the ones we'll see in the Final Image. This Opening Image tells us that part of the story will actually happen inside Jack's mind, the first of many clues we'll get if we pay close enough attention. Will this weird location have changed in the end, when the "magic" ends? Will Jack be able to stay in reality?

**Set-Up:** We meet Jack (Edward Norton), a plain salaried employee working for a car company, who feels like a victim of our consumerist world but is incapable of escaping its temptations — something that seems to make him less of a man, as our theme is masculinity. Jack struggles with insomnia, the "curse" that will make him hallucinate: did you notice someone in those subliminal frames? Jack has a revelation when he starts attending a testicular cancer group even though he is healthy. After crying on man-boobed Bob's (Meat Loaf) chest, Jack finds inner peace and can sleep soundly. He then decides to attend several support groups for different diseases, finding comfort among the sick and the dying. Can he go on like this forever? Is this not *Stasis=Death*?

**Theme Stated:** The theme is briefly stated in the testicular cancer support group's banner: "Remaining men together." This is a film about masculine crises, so the theme makes sense. And once we meet Tyler Durden, it will make even more sense. Will Jack and Tyler have to remain together to be men?

**Catalyst:** Almost at minute 12, enter Marla Singer (Helena Bonham Carter), Jack's worst nightmare. Like him, she is a "tourist," meaning that although she is not really sick (despite her heavy smoking and her suicidal fantasies), she starts attending every group Jack is in, annoying him and making him relapse into insomnia.

**B Story**: Although Marla is the "love" story of this film, thematically there is another person who will play our B Story manly thematic side, and that is Bob. In the past, Bob tried to push his masculinity to the max using steroids, and he ruined his life and his body, a fate that may await Jack if he does not learn his lesson in time.

**Debate**: What do you do when your life has become perfect but someone screws with it? Annoyed by Marla's constant intrusions, Jack threatens to expose her, but she is not deterred. The two negotiate who will attend which sessions before parting ways. Jack does not realize it, but Marla is actually interested in him in her own way. During one of his travels, Jack meets a strange, outspoken and self-assured man named Tyler Durden (Brad Pitt) and experiences a *double bump* when he finds out that his condo has exploded. What can he do now? He tries to call Marla but he thinks twice and instead talks to Tyler. They have a conversation on masculinity, modern values and consumerism: "The things you own end up owning you." In terms of masculinity and identity, is Tyler the kind of man Jack wants to be?

**Break into Two**: At minute 32, Tyler asks Jack to hit him hard, and they end up street fighting in the bar's parking lot, feeling strangely euphoric afterwards. This beat is our threshold into Act Two, not only because Jack is about to enter into Tyler's *upside-down world*, but because — here comes a big spoiler — they are, in fact, the same person! So Jack starts experiencing the "curse" of being who he always dreamt of being. Can he ultimately "do it without the magic" and just be himself?

**Fun and Games**: The Fun and Games of a story explores the *upside-down world* of Act Two, and for Jack, this means moving in with Tyler and experiencing the *promise of the premise*. In this case, it's living a life devoid of a car, microwave or material possessions. Can he be happy this way? It seems so, because soon he forgets about every commodity he has ever had and only enjoys fighting at night with Tyler. Later, some other men join them, eventually accompanied by more. Before the men know it, they have formed a secret society, the

Fight Club, in which The Rules are very clear. Tyler and Jack seem to be the greatest friends, but soon the latter feels that the friendship could be ruined by the reappearance of Marla, who starts having scandalously loud sex with Tyler. Jack clearly shows he is not happy about this, and she (obviously) freaks out. Also, the arson division chief of police calls Jack. They suspect that the explosion at his condo was intentional.

**Midpoint**: Tyler tests Jack's resolution by giving him a painful chemical burn: "Don't deal with this the way those dead people do!" he says. Jack passes the test, his *false victory* toward being like Tyler, but also sees how radical his alter ego is becoming. Soon after, Jack delivers a death threat to his boss that equals a *public coming out* ("Tyler's words coming out of my mouth"), and he visits Marla, for the first time seeming to care for her. *A and B Stories cross* when Jack finds Bob in the street and learns that he has joined Fight Club too. Tyler's character is attracting a lot of other men... and Jack seems to not be gaining anything from it

**Bad Guys Close In**: Lou (the owner of the club) shows up, threatening the men to stop their gatherings, but it also marks how far Jack/Tyler is willing to go (and get hurt) to keep the Club. His self-destructive tendencies increase, and he seems to be testing the men by giving them "assignments," which for now are just pranks. Tyler seems to be doing more and more behind Jack's back — his games are becoming dangerous, like when he harasses a man with a gun for not finishing his degree. Jack is also tempted to tell Marla about Tyler, but Tyler will not let him. Soon after, he starts building an army for something called "Project Mayhem," about which Jack has no clue. Jack further loses Tyler's and his men's trust when he disfigures one of their faces (Jared Leto). Tyler keeps toying with self-destruction by letting his car crash, almost killing both of them. The next morning (actually some days later), Jack wakes up and finds that Tyler is gone. Around him, Project Mayhem is taking shape, but none of his men seem to want to speak to him or tell him anything about it.

**All Is Lost**: Angry, Jack rejects Marla again and experiences the *whiff of death* when Bob is killed during one of their acts, which only inflames the group of "space monkeys" to push on with Project Mayhem. The "old way of thinking has died" and Jack has to stop Tyler before more people get hurt.

**Dark Night of the Soul**: Jack flies all around the country to find Tyler, contemplating several fights and how the Fight Club / Project Mayhem has spread uncontrollably.

**Break into Three**: *A and B Stories* briefly *meet* when Bob is referred to in a bar where Jack gets quite a shock — he is called Mr. Durden! Jack meets Tyler that night and has his own *Moment of Clarity* when he realizes he has been alone all this time and that Tyler is only a projection of his subconscious. "I am free in all the ways you are not," Tyler says, but he sounds too menacing when he states that Marla knows too much.

**Finale**:
1. Gathering the Team: Jack gathers all the clues he can find to stop Project Mayhem, but it seems impossible — its members are everywhere. He decides to meet Marla to convince her to leave the city and keep her safe, showing that he cares about her.

2. Executing the Plan: Jack turns himself in to the police, telling them all about Project Mayhem so that they can stop it.

3. High Tower Surprise: Surprises await Jack. Some policemen have also joined the Project! Jack escapes before he loses a manly part of his anatomy and goes to a "high tower" for a further surprise — there are explosives in 10 buildings! Tyler's plan is to blow them up to erase the credit debt record, "restarting" the system.

4. Dig, Deep Down: Returning to the scene of the Opening Image, Jack realizes that the only way to stop Tyler is, ironically, to make the ultimate act of self-destruction. So he lets go of all logic and, after stating, "My eyes are open," he "digs, deep down"...

5. The Execution of the New Plan: ...and shoots himself in the mouth. Tyler is killed, but Jack survives, although in a sorry state. The Project Mayhem foot soldiers arrive and obey him, showing that he can command them "without the magic." He is now *Synthesis* Man.

**Final Image**: Awakened, Jack proactively takes Marla's hand as they both witness the end of civilization as we know it. The "systemic problems" of the world are fixed... well, at least in Tyler Durden's view.

## BIRDMAN (or The Unexpected Virtue of Ignorance) (2014)

Satirical black comedy? Meta-cinematic drama? Magical realism? Psychological naturalism? Humorous theater parody? You name it, because *Birdman*, Alejandro G. Iñárritu's masterpiece from 2014, is all that and *mucho más*. It is without a doubt an OOTB film, and, being more specific than all those indecisive critics, this is a "Surreal Bottle" movie.

In this subgenre, movies feel like a dream or, more exactly, like a mind trip for the main character. In addition, The Rules apply to the whole world of the film, at least from the hero's point of view, as in *Groundhog Day*, *The Butterfly Effect* or *Eternal Sunshine of the Spotless Mind*.

Starring Michael Keaton, *Birdman* earned an incredible amount of awards (including Academy Awards® for Best Picture, Best Director, Best Original Screenplay and Best Cinematography) and surprised many people with its bold approach. It appeared to be shot in one continuous take, defying the rules of the Three-Act structure with a seemingly seamless narrative. Even the ending was reportedly rewritten... during filming!

As you can guess, no matter how crazy, trippy or surreal a film seems, when it is so wildly popular and successful, you can bet that hiding behind the maze-like theatre, the Blake Snyder Beat Sheet is waiting somewhere for its cue to step onstage. Break a leg and come with us!

OOTB Type: Surreal Bottle

OOTB Cousins: *American Splendor*; *The Science of Sleep*; *Midnight in Paris*; *Primer*; *Synechdoche, New York*

BIRDMAN (or The Unexpected Virtue of Ignorance)
*Written by* Alejandro González Iñárritu & Nicolás Giacobone & Alexander Dinelaris & Armando Bo
*Directed by* Alejandro González Iñárritu

**Opening Image:** Raymond Carver's work is one of the thematic sources of this story, so the film starts with a quote, which is actually his epitaph. "To feel oneself beloved on Earth" (did you spot the word "amor"?) was his goal, and is also our protagonist's — speaking of whom, the film opens with a man in his underwear... levitating! Is he really flying? We may know at the end.

**Theme Stated:** A know-it-all critic quotes Roland Barthes: "Gods and epic sagas... are now being done... by comic strip characters." This is our theme, and the major character's dilemma. Should he go back to being a million-dollar-earning movie star doing frivolous superhero films, or should he become a respected actor in the small world of theatre? Can't he synthesize both?

**Set-Up:** "How did we end up here?" Riggan Thomson (Michael Keaton) asks himself. Famous for playing the film superhero "Birdman," he is now risking all to become a new kind of person: a respected theater actor in a play he has adapted, directed and stars. Does he have the talent? Apparently, the stressed and insomnia-ridden Riggan has other abilities, like telekinetic powers! And he can hear Birdman's demeaning voice in his head. It all adds up to create the "surreal magic" of the movie, which we will doubt constantly, such as when one of the lights falls on an actor's head during rehearsals and Riggan claims he did it. His attorney, Jake (Zach Galifianakis), doesn't believe him, and is more worried about the probable lawsuit. To make things worse, the cast is missing a key performer: "Our perfect dream actor is not going to knock on that door."

**Catalyst**: Presto! There is a knock on the door, and actress Lesley (Naomi Watts) offers to call renowned actor Mike Shiner (Edward Norton), who happens to be all that Riggan aspires to. But is he the man for the job?

**Debate**: Riggan tests Shiner, a true professional who already knows the dialogue by heart. He is talented, self-assured, a method actor, a bit of a diva, and even changes Riggan's text. He is so confident that he can get fully naked without a wink, but also is so outspoken that he gets on everyone's nerves. During one of the previews, Shiner angrily demands his gin be real so that he can get drunk onstage, and Riggan decides to fire him before Shiner is out of control.

**Break into Two**: Riggan did not expect that Jake would refuse to fire Shiner, who can draw crowds to the play, precisely what they need for it to be successful. Shiner can also please the dreaded *New York Times* theater critic whose bad review could kill the play. So Riggan is stuck with an actor he needs to make the play a success… but one who can outshine him onstage.

**B Story**: Our B Story contains what we call a *False Mentor* — in this case, Riggan's feathered alter ego Birdman. At first, he seems to be just a voice in Riggan's head, telling him to drop everything and go back to Hollywood — but his comments will become more demeaning. Riggan is having a difficult time keeping him out of mind, but could the actor learn something from Birdman?

**Fun and Games**: Our *promise of the premise* shows how a man who has bet everything (his money, career, family and love life) on a stage play that seems bigger than himself slowly gets overwhelmed. Not exactly Fun, but you get the idea. While Shiner respects Riggan in private, in the open he implies that prestige and popularity are not the same. The former Birdman has to deal with his self-destructive daughter Samantha (Emma Stone), just out of rehab, his current girlfriend/actress Laura's (Andrea Riseborough) announcement that she is pregnant, his ex-wife Sylvia (Amy Ryan) putting fatherhood pressure on him, and the risk that critic Tabitha Dickinson (Lindsay Duncan) will give him a bad review. We also begin to see the cracks of the characters: Shiner is having a masculinity crisis he can only deal with onstage ("This is hard!"), Lesley is afraid of losing her first Broadway chance, Laura is lying about the pregnancy, and Samantha starts seducing Shiner.

**Midpoint**: Can you fit the requirements of a proper Midpoint in this rule-breaking film? First, we see Riggan's *false defeat* when he finds out Shiner has made the newspaper's front page. He also *comes out in public* when telling his own tragic and false childhood story to Shiner, who believes him... showing that he can act, after all! But back in his dressing room, *A and B Stories cross* as the Birdman voice returns to tease the angry actor ("It's always we, brother"), and he ends up destroying everything around using his telekinesis. Finally, Jake appears to set a *time clock*, as the last preview before the show is happening soon, and he further *raises the stakes* by telling Riggan that, among others, Martin Scorsese is attending the premiere.

**Bad Guys Close In**: In this section of the Beat Sheet, the hero usually "loses allies" and "his team disintegrates."— and that is exactly what happens here, putting more and more pressure on Riggan. Jake seems to be losing trust in him and reveals to others that he lied about Scorsese. Lesley lies to Riggan, too, and Samantha's romance with

Shiner heats up. Riggan feels the pressure and goes in his undershorts behind the theatre to be alone, only to accidentally lock himself out. Adding insult to injury, he then has to trek to the front of the theatre on the next street through the middle of crowded Times Square, being watched and recorded by the audience that used to love him. Not only is he ridiculed in front of his fans, he also has to enter the preview almost naked and try to finish the final scene. Later, Samantha tells him he is becoming a trending topic in social media, as the video of his outside walk has gone viral. "Believe it or not, this is power," she tells him. For a man who wanted respect and admiration the old-fashioned way, Riggan has reached a very low point.

**All Is Lost**: Riggan finds critic Tabitha at the bar, and she swears that she will destroy the play, no matter how good it is, because she hates what Riggan represents: Hollywood. He steps into All Is *Really* Lost territory when he lets loose with some harsh words to the critic, making everything worse. "I am gonna kill your play," Tabitha confirms.

**Dark Night of the Soul**: Riggan walks the streets alone at night, drinking hard and lamenting his plight when he gets the *whiff of death* from an angry man reciting Shakespeare's *Macbeth*: "Life's but a walking shadow, a poor player / That struts and frets his hour upon the stage / And then is heard no more."

**Break into Three**: The next day, the Birdman voice wakes Riggan up in the street… and shows up flying behind him! Riggan is hallucinating (or is he?) while Birdman tells him to drop everything, get plastic surgery and go back to Hollywood to make billions. Things get even stranger — Riggan seems like he is about to jump from a building. Is he going to kill himself? "Yes, I know where to go," he says, having his *Moment of Clarity*. And off he flies to the theater to enter Act Three.

**Finale:**

1. Gathering the Team: Riggan enters the theatre and gathers his team of actors off screen to carry out the play, while we momentarily remain outside.

2. Executing the Plan: The play's first act ends and the audience responds enthusiastically! Riggan seems strangely calm in his dressing room and confesses to Sylvia that he tried to kill himself once.

3. High Tower Surprise: We suspect things are not really going well inside Riggan's mind, and the High Tower Surprise happens when he shoots himself in the head. Upon waking up in the hospital, Riggan learns that he actually shot his nose and has been given a new one, and that people all over the world are praying for him. He has achieved success! He is a "respected actor-celebrity" and is loved by everyone, echoing the theme and his wish.

4. Dig, Deep Down: Left alone in the room, Riggan "digs, deep down" to take off his beak-looking bandage to see his new face. He says goodbye to the Birdman, signaling that he will now "do it without the magic." But will he succeed?

5. The Execution of the New Plan: Riggan looks through the window and sees the birds singing outside. He opens the window and oh-so-happily... jumps. Was committing suicide his "new plan"?

**Final Image:** The film does not give us enough clues, but we know something surreal is still going on when Samantha looks out of the window and smiles. Is Riggan flying? We will never really know, but somehow he and the ones that love him (like Samantha) have accepted him for who he is, so he has become *Synthesis* Man, one who can "fly" freely while not being harassed any more by the Birdman.

 Sometimes *The Impossible* occurs, a "sudden event" that causes an "innocent" family to face a "life or death battle" of survival.

# 4 DUDE WITH A PROBLEM

Okay, no doubt, you are a great dude or a wonderful dudette. You walk through life minding your own business, being a good person, living your own life and feeling the bliss of being just one more individual in the crowd, with no reasons to be worried by any possibility of danger.

And, suddenly, WHAM! You wonder... why me?

This is what all of our heroes in this genre think when their lives are suddenly thrown out of balance and put into a life or death battle: *Why me*? Well, there probably isn't a logical answer for that, but there isn't any time to think about that either — you are now in the middle of big trouble that you have to solve, because your life is at the stake!

Every day, it happens to thousands of people — you try to exist as normal and problem-free as possible, but out of the blue, something horrible happens. No, you were not asking for it. But destiny, God or your fate dealer of choice just decided to put you through the test.

This is the common storyline of our "Dude with a Problem" films, and many mainstream classics probably come to your mind right now, such as blueprint examples *North by Northwest*, *Die Hard*, *Sleeping with the Enemy*, *The Bourne* series, *Deep Impact* and many others. You'll realize that many genres like disaster flicks, some spy films, domestic thrillers and such have the same kind of storyline summarized in three words: you are screwed!

But don't let their big-budget appearance mislead you, because in the indie and auteur world, there are many films dealing with people up to their armpits in trouble, chases, persecution, disease and danger. After all... it could happen to you! So what do we need to tell this type of story?

First, you need a protagonist, but not just any kind: it must be an **innocent hero**, meaning that she or he did not do anything to see themselves swept into that particular adventure. Sure, they may or may not be angels in their ordinary lives, but they weren't looking for trouble, at least consciously. So remember, these are stories of survival, not punishment for any kind of sin: our family in *The Impossible* was not perfect, but they were just on holiday, and the *Ghost Writer* is a bit greedy but just wanted to do his job. Yet they all found themselves in deep trouble.

Speaking of which, let us introduce the second component of our genre: the problem or **sudden event**. It's important that the event is unexpected, fast and dangerous, that it "comes from nowhere and our hero has to deal with it ASAP." It could be anything from the arrival of some mobsters in *A History of Violence* to the announcement that you only have seven days to live, like in *Dallas Buyers Club*, or a tsunami wave like in *The Impossible*.

As you can guess by these examples, our third element is the **life or death battle** that ensues, and we aren't kidding around! Think of your problem with consequences as dramatic as you can and you will be on the right path, if not to solve it, then at least to write it! In the aforementioned examples, the battle is for survival — the existence of an individual, group, family, society, etc. is at stake.

By now, you might have figured out that there are five situations in which your poor "dudes" may find themselves, and the names of our subgenres are indicative of the particular "problem."

Let's start with the self-explanatory **Spy Problem**. In this case, our protagonists will find themselves in some sort of state affair, spy plot or undercover operation into which they had unknowingly stepped. Chased by agency or government officials, they may even be spies themselves, but our heroes are usually clueless about why *they* are the ones being chased. But they must figure it out, pronto!

The second subgenre is the **Law Enforcement Problem**, which pertains to in-dude-viduals that find themselves in a tight spot, balancing on the thin line between both sides of the law, where both the "good guys" (police, government, etc.) and the "bad guys" (mafia, criminals, etc.) are after them. Double the enemies, double the fun! Think of the Ryan Gosling film *Drive*, in which a getaway driver will have to outrun both the police and the mobsters.

A **Domestic Problem** takes our troubles to supposedly safe places like home, family or our own local town, where we usually feel at ease — but not anymore! Films like *House of Sand and Fog*, *The Kids Are All Right* or our chosen film, Cronenberg's *A History of Violence*, teach us how to deal with the suddenness of change.

The fourth subgenre, the **Nature Problem**, involves "acts of God" that make us endangered and miserable, often in films about disease. Consider, for example, *Dancer in the Dark* (blindness), *The Diving Bell and the Butterfly* (paralysis) or our chosen movie, *Dallas Buyers Club* (AIDS), and the loneliness they imply.

Finally, beware the **Epic Problem**, in which the threat is anything that Mother Earth wants to throw at us (from plagues, to viruses, to catastrophes). In mainstream cinema, our "dudes" have to confront tornadoes, volcanoes and meteorites. But in our indie realm, these problems can be cold, hunger, drought, wild animals or any kind of survival in the outdoors. The true-life stories featured in movies like *The Impossible* and *127 Hours* serve as perfect examples.

A common beat in these films is what Blake called the **eye of the storm** moments, in which our main character finds rest and solace, usually in the arms or comfort of another character (that could be your love story or B Story). The eye of the storm allows our protagonist to take a break and discuss matters (and how to solve them) with another, caring character. In *The Ghost Writer*, Ruth is the one to console our poor fellow scribe; in *A History of Violence* it's Edie, the protagonist's wife; and in *Dallas Buyers Club*, it the transgender Rayon (much to our homophobic protagonist's dismay — and thankfully for his personal development).

## SO WHAT IS YOUR PROBLEM... DUDE?

If you want a thrilling story, fast-paced rhythm, nerve-wracked characters and your protagonist to *really* earn his or her salvation... give them hell! You'll need:

1. An "innocent hero," usually minding his own business and unaware of what is about to transpire... just like it would happen to any of us!

2. A "sudden event"— the more surprising, the better. It must shake the protagonist's world to its foundations and throw him into a world of hurt... and it's only the beginning!

3. A "life or death battle," for the drama in these situations is knowing that your existence is at stake — and possibly that of your friends, lovers, town or society.

If you want to make your characters suffer and have them rise to the challenge, this is your genre... and your problem!

## THE GHOST WRITER (2010)

"Men who know too much" are the perfect basis for what Blake called "Spy Problem" flicks. In this subgenre, our unknowing hero-to-be is an everyday schmuck who is about to be followed, harassed, chased and sometimes kidnapped by antagonists such as initial-named agencies: CIA, KGB, FDA, DEA, NSA... insert your favorite three-letter baddies here!

Even if the heyday of the genre happened after WW2 and during the Cold War, individuals and whistleblowers such as Edward Snowden and Julian Assange may confirm that the Spy Problem subgenre is alive and well, and this film by auteur Roman Polanski perfectly shows why, as we have all of our components:

First, an "ordinary man" against "extraordinary circumstances," that is, a literally anonymous, innocent ghost writer who does not have a family, who is unaware of what is about to happen to him, is lured by money and the promise of selling millions of copies of a controversial ex-Prime Minister's biography.

In this low-key film, reminiscent of the classics, you will not see big explosions or fast car chases, but you will still be glued to your seat and wondering where Robert Harris's original plot will take you and our disgraced character in this "test of survival."

DWAP Type: Spy Problem

DWAP Cousins: *A Most Wanted Man*, *Tinker Tailor Soldier Spy*, *Confessions of a Dangerous Mind*, *The Fourth Protocol*, *Army of Shadows*

THE GHOST WRITER
*Based on the novel by* Robert Harris
*Screenplay by* Robert Harris & Roman Polanski
*Directed by* Roman Polanski

**Opening Image:** The film opens with the eerie image of an abandoned car in the cold insides of a whale-like ferry. We still don't know yet (although we may have our suspicions), but this car symbolizes a recent death. An investigation starts, but will it bear any results? As we will learn, that is unlikely.

**Theme Stated:** "Do you realize I know nothing about politics?" says an unnamed ghost writer (Ewan McGregor as "The Ghost") to his agent. This is our theme: an "innocent hero" is about to get into the two-edged, two-sided, two-faced world of politics, and for that ignorance, he will have to pay a great price.

**Set-Up:** We learn a little more about the Ghost's *things that need fixing*, like his curiosity and greed, as he is about to be offered to write the memoirs of controversial former British Prime Minister Adam Lang (Pierce Brosnan), just after formerly-assigned writer (and Lang's assistant) Mike McAra has died in an accident. "It was the book that killed him," someone says. Later, despite the Ghost's insistence he knows nothing about politics, he gets the job. "There is something not quite right about this project," the editor says, finding McAra's death suspicious.

**Catalyst**: On his way home, the Ghost gets mugged by two unknowns who steal a manuscript from him, thinking that it may be Lang's memoir. The Ghost is having second thoughts about the job, but because he wants the handsome fee, he accepts the assignment.

**Debate**: In the airport, the Ghost debates internally, seeming to have "third thoughts" when he sees Lang accused by former collaborator Richard Rycart of handing terrorists to the CIA for torture and interrogation. He finally arrives at Lang's house in the U.S., where he is introduced to his team and is given McAra's manuscript, realizing the job will be harder than he initially thought. "You must be wondering what you've let yourself in for," says B Story Character Ruth, knowing well our Debate section.

**B Story**: Lang's wife Ruth (Olivia Williams) is our B Story Character, and one who seems to be very angry about the fact that her husband is openly having an affair with his assistant Amelia (Kim Cattrall). She and the Ghost will come to romantic terms, too, but she will also occasionally provide him with *eye of the storm* moments where the two discuss what is happening. Ruth seems to be the only sincere character.

**Break into Two**: Lang himself arrives at the airport with all the characters there to meet him. Remember this location, since we will come to it again in very different circumstances. Most importantly, this marks the beginning of the real job for the Ghost.

**Fun and Games**: What is a high-profile politician like in private? How detached is he from the public? How can one make him likable and attractive for a book? The Ghost explores this *upside-down world*, finding it unlikely that a man like Lang, who isn't very sharp, has ended up in politics. The Ghost will get his chance to see him in action when Lang is denounced at The Hague war criminal courts, and helps craft a press statement. Is he learning something about politics at last? The Ghost finds among McAra's belongings some old pictures that show that Lang may be lying about his past. He also discovers a strange number, and upon dialing it, learns that McAra contacted Rycart before he died. With time apart from Lang for a while, the Ghost investigates on his own, and a local old man (Eli Wallach) tells him suspicious details about the former writer's death. Should the Ghost keep investigating? Is he in trouble, too? Curiosity is a too strong a temptation.

**Midpoint**: Ruth and the Ghost meet for dinner and a "Midpoint celebration" ensues, in which he performs a *public coming out* when he confesses knowing some suspicious facts about Lang and the circumstances surrounding McAra's death. She seems distressed and calls her husband. Later in the night, she shows up at the Ghost's room and they have sex as often happens in many a Midpoint. The next morning, the Ghost achieves a *false victory* when he decides to drop the assignment and go home.

**Bad Guys Close In**: The Ghost finds McAra's last destination before his death in the car's GPS... and the internal Bad Guy of curiosity is alive and well. He travels on the same ferry in which McAra died and drives up to an estate in New York. There, he visits a man named Emmett, who claims not to know Lang, although everything points to the probability they are old friends. Before leaving, Emmett threatens the Ghost in a veiled way.

**All Is Lost**: When he exits Emmett's home, the Ghost sees two cars following him, which means all his suspicions were right — he is about to discover something big, and it is probably the same thing that got McAra killed. To avoid ending up like McAra, his only choice is to reboard the ferry on which McAra died! He escapes to land, barely eluding his pursuers.

**Dark Night of the Soul**: Alone in the empty ferry parking lot, the Ghost reflects on what to do next, contemplating his solitude and, especially, the fact that he cannot trust anyone. Or can he?

**Break into Three:** In the hotel room, the Ghost calls Rycart and decides to meet him. Before this, he researches on the internet and discovers the Lang-Emmett connection: Emmett belongs to the CIA, which indicates that Lang could have been working for them all along, including his years as PM. The Ghost discusses this with Lang, before *A and B Stories cross* when he talks again with Ruth. Our poor "Writer with a Problem" doesn't have a choice but to Break into Three.

**Finale:**

1. Gathering the Team: Rycart takes the Ghost to the airport, giving him a mission: to return with Lang and gather information that can be used against him. The Ghost is not able to renounce this, as Rycart has taped the whole conversation. The Ghost is sure that Lang will get his way. Has he finally learned something about how politics work?

2. Executing the Plan: The Ghost gets on Lang's plane and sees that he has been discovered, so he spills the whole truth: he knows about Lang and the CIA. Lang seems surprised but not a bit scared; if he had the powers of his office, he would do everything the same way again.

3. High Tower Surprise: Upon arriving at the airport, the big surprise comes: Lang is assassinated! A veteran whose son died in Afghanistan shoots him. The Ghost is interrogated but is soon allowed to go back to Europe.

4. Dig, Deep Down: The Ghost attends the release party of the book, where Ruth is making a speech. But his suspicions are triggered by something Amelia says about the original manuscript, and the Ghost "digs, deep down" to find clues in the beginning of each chapter!

5. The Execution of the New Plan: The Ghost will let Ruth know that he has learned the truth: she was the one recruited

by the CIA by Emmett when he was her teacher, and then she married Lang to control him. Ruth is devastated, and the Ghost toasts to her in victory.

**Final Image:** There is a momentary "triumph of the individual" as the Ghost leaves the party, original manuscript in hand, possibly to denounce her. But there is something about him that has not changed: he does not know anything about politics. If he did, he would have seen the car coming towards him. After a loud *screech*, the Final Image echoes the Opening Image, showing Ruth's secret as it is scattered in the air, never to be revealed... because as we know from the beginning, some murders are never investigated.

## DRIVE (2011)

"Law Enforcement Problem" films, as Blake defined them, place its dudes between the crosshairs of the bad guys *and* the police. And you can bet that even if your only job is to drive, you will ultimately find yourself chased by both, because knowing too much is indeed a problem.

Ryan Gosling stars as the Driver, a stunt-double-actor and mechanic by day, and getaway driver and street wanderer by night. Gosling is accompanied by such great supporting actors as Bryan Cranston, Albert Brooks, Ron Perlman and Carey Mulligan.

As in all DWAPs, Ryan is "minding his own business" when he finds himself in a "test of survival," having to work for the mob to protect his boss's life while trying to save his married next-door-neighbor crush (who will give him some *eye of the storm* moments). As you can imagine, things will only get harder as Bad Guys Close In on him.

Danish director Nicholas Winding Refn was behind the cameras of this super-cool, super-slick, super-sophisticated piece of cinema (and one of my personal favorites). It displays a retro feel, vintage aesthetics and clever influences from the '80s to show an unforgettable, haunting, dream-like Los Angeles — the kind that you can only discover behind the wheel.

DWAP Type: Law Enforcement Problem

DWAP Cousins: *Serpico*, *Fahrenheit 451*, *Lone Star*, *The Place Beyond the Pines*, *Sicario*

DRIVE
*Based on the book by* James Sallis
*Screenplay by* Hossein Amini
*Directed by* Nicolas Winding Refn

**Opening Image**: Los Angeles, night. A nameless laconic man, whom we will call the Driver (Ryan Gosling), talks on the phone to a prospective client about his modus operandi as a getaway driver. There is more than meets the eye in this short scene — he is a lonesome guy in a generic room carrying a bag, probably containing all his belongings. Although never stated, his loneliness and the wish for a different, warmer, family kind of life will act as a theme in the film, and the basis for comparison to our Final Image.

**Theme Stated**: There is another theme at play, delivered in the Driver's speech and confirmed by his mentor Shannon: "No one will be looking at you." The Driver does not get involved. He just drives (which implies moving around and never having a home) and disappears.

**Set-Up**: The Driver meets his mentor friend Shannon (Bryan Cranston), a retired driver and car mechanic who has seen better times. The Driver then executes a long, elegant and discreet getaway for some robbers. He is cold, taciturn, professional and detached — not looking back once the work is done. When he returns home after the sting (crossing paths with a lady we will soon know more about), he seems to have nothing to do there. Delving in the noir-poetic overtones of the film, he returns to the streets to continue driving alone. It's his *Stasis=Death* moment — is he destined to be just a driver who moves around forever?

**Catalyst**: Upon going back home again, in a very brief and fleeting moment, the Driver gets in the elevator with neighbor Irene (Carey Mulligan) and they exchange glances and light smiles. As we'll see, their relationship will take a most dramatic turn in this very same place.

**B Story**: Irene is the obvious B Story Character, the person who, through love, may change the Driver's life to relieve it from his loneliness and isolation. But can the Driver allow himself to become involved with her and her son? That question leads to the Debate.

**Debate**: We again see the Driver in his legitimate job: he is a stunt driver, doubling for stars while wearing a mask. Soon after, he runs into Irene and her child Benicio in the supermarket. Even though he tries to avoid them, so as to not get involved, he relents and takes them home. He and Benicio like each other right away, and Irene also informs the Driver that Benicio's father is in prison. This sounds like a green light for the Driver, but should he get involved when love is at play? At some point, will he actually want to settle down, ridding himself of the loneliness that plagues him? While we ponder those questions, Shannon meets with mobsters Bernie (Albert Brooks) and Nino (Ron Perlman) to ask for a loan to buy a stock car chassis and have the Driver run at the races.

**Break into Two**: Bernie meets the Driver at the race track, and even though he shows himself to be a ruthless loan shark, Shannon closes the deal. And as you know, when you deal with the Mafia, there is no turning back, which is what must happen in any Break into Two beat. But there is another "break" for the Driver — thanks to Shannon, he will be able to get to know a little more about Irene and Benicio. And when you fall in love, there is no turning back from that, either!

**Fun and Games**: The Driver takes Irene and Benicio for a ride and starts spending time with them, having literal Fun and Games. He is also exploring a world that has been banned for him until now — the *upside-down world* of security, love and attachment to a family, finding beauty even in an *eye of the storm* drain. At the same time, the mobsters seem happy with the racing plans, but Bernie makes sure to tell the Driver about Shannon's backstory, which shows they all could get in trouble if things go wrong. Soon after, their world is shaken by the re-appearance of Irene's husband, Standard (Oscar Isaac), just out of jail. He seems to be such a decent guy who cares for his family that the stoic Driver accepts the new situation. He even rejects a job, possibly signaling that he wants to change, too. But soon after, he finds out that someone has given Benicio an unused bullet as a warning and has badly beaten Standard, who owes money to a mobster named Cook.

**Midpoint:** The Driver has a meal with the family, showing him a "glimpse of what he can be, with no obligation to be it," resulting in a Midpoint party that's a *false victory*. In a parallel scene, he decides to help Standard commit a robbery so that Standard can pay his debt and live happily with his family, thus performing a *public coming out*. Also, *stakes are raised* for both *A and B Stories* (which obviously *cross* here) because the family's survival depends on the robbery.

**Bad Guys Close In:** The theft is carried out with a little help from Cook's accomplice Blanche (Christina Hendricks), but things go awry when Standard is shot dead. The Driver is chased by some unknowns in an ominous big car, but he manages to elude them, hiding in a motel with Blanche. The TV news makes the Driver think that it was all a set-up, something confirmed by the appearance of two "bad guy" hit men who kill Blanche but are quickly disposed of by the Driver. Enraged, he finds Cook and is about to literally hammer a bullet in his head when he learns that Nino is the man behind Standard's death. When the Driver tries to explain everything to Irene, she slaps him, the Bad Guys of unrequited love making their appearance — made worse by the famous elevator scene, in which he kisses her and next stomps on a hitman's head. The Driver knows it will be almost impossible to win Irene back; he can now only protect her from a distance, especially difficult because Shannon informs Bernie about her. The "team" has totally "disintegrated" and the "Bad Guys recoup and rethink their strategy" as Bernie tells Nico off and decides to deal with the Driver himself, "tightening the grip."

**All Is Lost**: Bernie visits Shannon and slashes his arm, killing the last person that seemed to care for the Driver.

**Dark Night of the Soul**: The silent Driver contemplates Shannon's dead body, mulling about what to do next.

**Break into Three**: Still near Shannon's corpse, the Driver takes his traveling bag, signaling that he is ready to move on. But first, he must cross *A and B Stories* and dispatch of the mobsters, or Irene will never be safe again.

**Finale**:

1. Gathering the Team: The Driver "gathers his tools," consisting of a prosthetic mask taken from the film set, and visits Nico's pizzeria to get ready for the showdown.

2. Executing the Plan: His "plan" is to chase Nino in the dark and to force his car off the road. Nino survives the crash, but the Driver drowns him in the ocean. Next, he calls Bernie to meet up and give him back the money, hoping that it will make Irene safe. The Driver realizes he cannot trust Bernie, and just as he is to give him the money...

3. High Tower Surprise: ...Bernie takes out a knife and stabs him. The Driver retaliates by slashing Bernie's neck, and the mobster dies.

4. Dig, Deep Down: Bleeding profusely, the Driver rests in his car, one foot out of it, as if he symbolically still could get out and go back to Irene. In a blink, the Driver starts his car again and drives off... maybe to meet Irene? Meanwhile, she knocks at his door, but no one answers.

5. The Execution of the New Plan: The Driver is shown again at the wheel in the middle of the night, having renounced love and the hope for a family, retaining his true nature.

**Final Image**: We started off with a lonesome guy and even though he has tasted love and caring for a while, just like the wandering hero of many westerns and noir pieces, the Driver remains alone — seeking new adventures and, possibly, love.

## A HISTORY OF VIOLENCE (2005)

Sometimes, a place so familiar and seemingly close as home may conceal a deep, violent, potentially lethal problem. Thus family, couples, relationships and friends are at stake in what Blake called the "Domestic Problem" category in our DWAP films.

In these kinds of stories, home is not the secure, protected-from-harm place one expects, and in this great film by duo-personalities lover David Cronenberg, the *pater familias*, the man of the house, hides a long-kept secret: he used to be a ruthless assassin.

No one can believe that Tom Stall, who owns the town diner, may have that kind of past. He seems — and in a way, is — a perfectly "innocent, ordinary man" set against the "extraordinary circumstances" dealt by mobsters who have arrived to take him back to his original home.

The "test of survival" in this film is not only a life-or-death battle by our Jekyll-defeated-Hyde main character, but something more — the family that Tom has built over the years, the wife who loves him and the children who call him Dad... now may have to call him... Joey Cusack, mob assassin.

DWAP Type: Domestic Problem

DWAP Cousins: *Frozen River, Winter's Bone, House of Sand and Fog, A Most Violent Year, The Kids Are All Right*

A HISTORY OF VIOLENCE
*Based on the graphic novel by* John Wagner and Vince Locke
*Screenplay by* John Olson
*Directed by* David Cronenberg

**Opening Image**: A family is destroyed by sudden, senseless violence when two assassins on the run kill them. Can you believe that ruthless, unmerciful men like these could ever build such a loving family for themselves?

**Theme Stated**: We're in the small-town home of Tom Stall (Viggo Mortensen) and his wife, Edie (Maria Bello). "There is no such thing as monsters," Tom's elder son Jack says to his little sister. Is he right? In this film, Jack will learn that monsters do exist — and that his own father is or has been one of them.

**Set-Up**: A scream tears through the night. Little Sarah, younger daughter of the Stall family, has been awakened by a nightmare. The rest of the family comforts her, showing how close they are, a tone further emphasized in the breakfast scene that follows. Soon, Tom goes to work at the diner he owns, listening to a thematic joke about marrying a potential killer. "Nobody's perfect, Tom," says his coworker.

**B Story**: Our B Story Character is Edie. Even though she and Tom have been together for quite a long time, they still love each other tenderly and passionately.

**Catalyst**: For the Catalyst, we take Jack's point of view: he defeats local bully Bobby during a baseball game, which prompts the latter to confront him in the locker room. However, Jack pretends to be a coward to avoid fighting. How long can he keep away from violence this way?

**Debate**: Ignorant about their son's problems, Tom and Edie take a night off to relive their teenage erotic fantasies, while she says: "You're the best man I've ever known." Would Edie still love Tom so much if she really knew his past? At the same time, Jack debates with his crush Judy about their own future as adults, while Bobby runs into the killers we met at the beginning — and we know this means trouble.

**Break into Two**: The two killers from the Opening Image enter Tom's cafe, staying even after he tells them he is about to close. Angered, the mobsters threaten the waitress, when — in a shockingly quick and effective sequence — Tom first hits one of them in the head with a coffee pot, uses that guy's gun to return the other killer's gunfire fatally, is stabbed in the foot by the first killer and shoots him dead. Were these acts too easy for Tom?

**Fun and Games**: In the hospital, Tom watches himself transform from an unknown to a celebrity as his feat is presented on various TV networks — his face seems to be all around the country. Tom is cheered on by his friends and returns home, trying to avoid journalists. It may be good news after all, since the next day his diner is full. Unexpectedly, some somber men also show up, and one of them, the one-eyed Fogarty (Ed Harris), refers to Tom as "Joey." Tom ignores them, but local sheriff Sam tells Tom's family that they are dangerous mafia men. The next morning, Tom sees the mobsters' car and thinks they are about to attack his family, so he runs home, only to frighten his son and wife. "What if you are right?" asks Jack about the mobsters' purpose. "Then we deal with it," Tom tells him enigmatically. But at a mall, Edie bumps into Fogarty, who raises doubts about Tom: "How come he's so good at killing people?"

**Midpoint**: Jack lives his own *false victory* when, inspired by his father's acts, he brutally pounds Bobby, risking a lawsuit. Tom is angered, and upon Jack's impertinent response, slaps his face, *raising the stakes*. He could lose his family! Thus begins this *public coming out*, as he is having difficulty hiding his violent alter ego Joey from his family. *A and B Stories cross* when Edie comes back from the mall and almost confesses to having her doubts about Tom's identity.

**Bad Guys Close In**: Bad Guys literally Close In when Fogarty and his men show up, having kidnapped Jack and offering him in exchange for Tom going back to Philadelphia with them to see his brother Richie, who seems to hold a grudge against him. The *public coming out* is complete when in another quick and stunning sequence, Tom/Joey kills two of the men and acknowledges being Joey just before Jack shoots Fogarty. Again at the hospital, Edie confronts Tom about Joey, and he admits his false identity and past transgressions, claiming that Joey is dead. But the shock is too great for Edie; the "team," the family, is "disintegrating." Nevertheless, there may still be hope: when the sheriff comes to interrogate Tom the next day at home, Edie defends him to protect the family.

**All Is Lost**: When the sheriff leaves, Edie gets angry and slaps Tom, who is about to slap her back, but comes to his senses. They end up having rough sex on the stairs of their home, but afterwards, Edie just leaves him behind. This is "the worst that could happen" to Tom — his wife and son have been contaminated by Joey's violence, and now he has to deal with it.

**Dark Night of the Soul**: The typical symbol of marital problems: Edie stays awake in bed alone while Tom spends the night sleeping on the sofa, both contemplating the "death" of their marriage.

**Break into Three**: The phone sounds and the voice of Richie Cusack (William Hurt) tells his brother Joey to come to see him… or he will pay a visit to Tom's family. So in the middle of the night, Tom takes a trip to Philly to settle matters once and for all with Richie and (probably) with his past persona.

**Finale:**

1. Gathering the Team: Tom arrives in Philadelphia to meet one of Richie's minions and his transformation occurs in front of our eyes. Did you see how Tom "gathered" Joey in a heartbeat?

2. Executing the Plan: Tom's enters his brother's upscale home to settle matters. Richie seems friendly at first, happy to see his brother after so many years. But slowly, his anger grows as we discover all the troubles he had to go through to get the respect of other Mafia families after Joey left town. "Tell me what I got to do to make things right," says Tom/Joey.

3. High Tower Surprise: "You could die, Joey," Richie tells him, revealing that he intended to kill his brother all along. But Tom/Joey defends himself ably as before, taking out bodyguard after bodyguard, until he shoots his own brother — it is as if Joey has taken over the soul of Tom.

4. Dig, Deep Down: The next morning, Tom "digs, deep down" by throwing the murder weapon away in the lake and washing himself of the physical and symbolical blood on his body. He is "killing Joey," but he still must "dig" some more, for his ultimate showdown is about to begin.

5. The Execution of the New Plan: Tom goes back home to try and show his family that it is him, and not Joey, who is their loving father. In a wonderful silent scene, they accept him again in the everyday little gestures of a family dinner.

**Final Image:** At the beginning we saw a family destroyed by the hateful monsters of gratuitous cruelty. At the end, through love and acceptance, another family has resisted the pull of violence, remaining alive and united.

## THE IMPOSSIBLE (2012)

Most disaster films that have been produced within Hollywood's boundaries follow the almighty lore on how to make flicks bigger, louder and stronger. But sometimes "the impossible" happens, and an "Epic Problem" film comes from a country like Spain, which is usually famous for much smaller films that deal with drama or comedy, but almost never with impressive, ambitious set pieces like this one.

This rendition of the true story of the Belón family during the tragic 2004 Indian Ocean tsunami was a successful one, acclaimed for its writing, direction and looks, along with the sensitivity in which the catastrophe itself was portrayed — not from a drown-your-senses-FX-and-action-filled piece, but from the point of view of a simple family.

This film is also a perfect example of a "Dude with a Problem." Here, each of the main characters will face the harshest conditions, where it is a miracle to survive as an individual, let alone be reunited as a family.

A "sudden event" if there ever was one, the tsunami that caught everybody by surprise is also a "test of survival" with an "innocent" family at stake, and they will all rise to the occasion to turn their lives into a "triumph of the spirit." Much like real-life character and survivor María Belón, the story has inspired thousands of people all over the world.

DWAP Type: Epic Problem

DWAP Cousins: *Blindness, 127 Hours, No Man's Land, In Darkness, Time of the Wolf*

THE IMPOSSIBLE
*Story by* María Belón
*Written by* Sergio G. Sánchez
*Directed by* J. A. Bayona

**Opening Image:** The story begins inside a plane, where a family is traveling to Khao Lak in Thailand to spend their Christmas holidays. We are introduced to Mom, Maria; Dad, Henry; oldest son Lucas; other sons, Thomas and Simon — and we will see how much they change by the Final Image.

**Theme Stated:** "I wonder who he takes after," says Lucas (Tom Holland), the one who has the most maturing to do. He is laughing about his brother's and mom's fear of turbulence. But "taking after" his mom, Maria (Naomi Watts), will soon be no laughing matter, for there will be much for him to learn from her.

**B Story:** Our love story features Maria and Henry (Ewan McGregor), a "traditional" couple in the sense that Henry feels it's his responsibility to provide for his family, and shows signs of stress when the prospect of him doing so seems in question. We will see a subtle change in Henry's attitude over the course of the story, as he realizes that — as a family — they must all take care of each other.

**Set-Up:** During the flight, we see *things that need fixing* for the main characters. Maria and Henry argue about who exited the house last and whether or not they turned on the alarm. Henry is a little bit too controlling and self-aware of his responsibilities. Maria, on the contrary, seems a little too afraid of danger. Thomas and Simon are a touch too dependent, and Lucas, as mentioned, needs to learn how to care for his brothers instead of teasing them. They all relax when they arrive at the hotel, and they enjoy their first days there. These scenes show us their "innocence" and how unaware they are of the catastrophe that looms in the sea.

**Catalyst**: With no warning except for the ominous flight of near-by birds, horror strikes at the beach resort when a massive wave hits, wiping out everything and everybody in sight, including Maria and her family.

**Debate**: Can anyone survive such a terrible experience? How many of this family of five could have possibly lived after that shock? Can a family literally scattered by tragedy come together again? We are left in the darkness for a while, and then Maria is shown alive, caught in a tree, watching Lucas dragged by the strong currents. Although she is badly hurt, Maria shows immense courage as she attempts to save him. Blake wrote that sometimes, during the Debate section, a *double bump* is needed to push the characters into Act Two, and in this story it comes in the form of a second wave that thrashes them around again. Maria and Lucas manage to escape death, but their real challenge of survival is yet to come.

**Break into Two**: Able to stand and walk, mother and son wander among tall weeds looking for a way out. When Lucas realizes how badly hurt his mom is, they have to find help for her or she may die.

**Fun and Games**: Welcome to the *upside-down world* that occurs after a catastrophe strikes! Nothing is Fun or a Game here, but you know that this is what Blake called the beat in which the *promise of the premise* is explored — you came to see this film to experience the tsunami and its aftermath, didn't you? Maria and Lucas save a lost little child and painfully climb a tree to await help. When help finally arrives, Maria is taken to the hospital, where Lucas sees more evidence of despair and destruction. At last, Maria is attended to. But is she safe? Maria asks Lucas to help other people, and he sets off to help patients search for lost relatives. Lucas is starting to change and care for others.

**Midpoint**: When he returns to where he left his mom, he finds that she has been taken away, and is mistakenly told she has died. Now he is alone. This is a *false defeat* for him. *A and B Stories cross* when we promptly leave Lucas to find out about Henry. He has managed to save Thomas and Simon, and now, *stakes are raised* for him, since he must find Maria and Lucas — if they are alive.

**Bad Guys Close In:** The impossible odds the family are up against are the Bad Guys in this film, which we see reinforced throughout the movie. In this beat, there is usually a "disintegration of the team," and if you thought that had already happened, the filmmakers make it worse when Henry must leave Thomas and Simon to look for Maria and Lucas. He witnesses this devastated world where the ugliest characteristics of people emerge, as in a man who will not let Henry use his phone to try to contact family back home. Fortunately, other people are more understanding, and another man — a father like Henry — lends him a phone so that Henry can reassure those back home of his safety. But he is terrified when told they have not heard from Maria.

**All Is Lost:** Back at the hospital, Lucas finally finds his mom... but her life is at stake.

**Dark Night of the Soul:** Henry learns that Thomas and Simon have been taken somewhere unknown — they're now lost to him.

**Break into Three:** The story gets a ray of hope to push the characters into Act Three when Lucas sees Daniel, the little boy he and Maria saved early on, now reunited with his own family. It's not impossible.

Henry arrives at the same hospital as Lucas and Maria — yet they don't know the other is there. In this chaos, is there any chance they'll find each other?

Lucas briefly spots his dad and races after, only to lose him in the crowd. Nearby, little Simon gets out of the truck which is transporting lost kids, followed by Thomas. They hear Lucas calling his dad and the boys reunite. Henry, acting on a hunch, finds them too. *A and B Stories cross* again as the reunited family heads back to the hospital to find Maria.

**Finale:**

1. Gathering the Team: The family / team is finally "gathered" at the hospital with Maria, but there is still one battle to fight: Maria must survive surgery. In her weakened condition, this doesn't seem likely.

2. Executing the Plan: Maria summons all of her strength and will to live as she's taken into surgery.

3. High Tower Surprise: "Think of something nice," says the doctor when they are about to anesthetize Maria. But she is haunted by very disturbing memories — as she is operated on, she recalls what happened to her during the tsunami, something that we had not seen until now.

4. Dig, Deep Down: During her hallucination, Maria is about to drown with countless other people, and her apparently dead body heads toward the light. Is she dying? No, she is "digging deep down" until we see her gloriously emerging from the water to life.

5. The Execution of the New Plan: Once Maria is out of surgery, the family is able to begin their journey back home, to return to their pre-tsunami lives.

**Final Image:** Again on a plane, it is clear that the family has transformed. The kids have indeed "taken after" their mom. Showing unbridled courage, the family has come together to survive. Their ordeal has been a "triumph of the spirit."

## DALLAS BUYERS CLUB (2013)

Among the many problems that a "dude" can face, there are those stories of survival against the odds of nature. We may think about wild, savage beasts and trouble in the great outdoors as "nature," but disease is perfectly natural, too, and can drown us in a literal world of hurt.

According to Blake, these kinds of "Nature Problems" are about "how alone we can feel when facing disease" and for sure, the AIDS epidemic during the '80s made thousands of people feel terribly detached, facing an incurable disease that condemned them to social exile and, for most, death.

It took someone as brave as a rodeo cowboy to confront the problem and find a solution. That man was Ron Woodroof, an AIDS patient who ignored FDA regulations and smuggled unapproved drugs that granted dignity of life longer than anyone could have expected.

This inspiring movie presents a protagonist with a "sudden event" (getting the disease) and a "test of survival," and indeed features what Blake defined as a "triumph of the spirit," with Woodroof becoming a stirring example of fighting for life, whatever it takes.

I should note that an argument can be made the film fits Blake's "Institutionalized" genre — but I've chosen to place it here, where I think it's a "natural" fit.

DWAP Type: Nature Problem

DWAP Cousins: *The Sea Inside (Mar Adentro)*, *50/50*, *Breaking the Waves*, *Dancer in the Dark*, *The Diving Bell and the Butterfly*

DALLAS BUYERS CLUB
*Written by* Craig Borten & Melisa Wallack
*Directed by* Jean-Marc Vallée

**Opening Image:** The film aptly begins with a rollicking rodeo, a place of bravery and quick-thinking — where many risks await. In the shadows, Ron Woodroof (Matthew McConaughey, Academy Award® Best Actor) has intercourse with two women, an act which does not seem out of the ordinary for him. Will this still be Ron's world by the end of the story?

**Set-Up:** We are introduced to Ron's world and the many *things that need fixing* in his life. "At play," he has unprotected sex, drinks too much, takes drugs, is homophobic and values money over friendship (even stealing from his pals). In a nutshell, he is living a life in a seemingly permanent *Stasis=Death* moment — we know that he cannot go on like this forever. However "bad" his behavior is, he demonstrates his heart in a "Save the Cat!" moment "at work" where he yells for his boss to call an ambulance for an illegal immigrant whose leg is caught in a machine. At home, Ron is so weak, he faints with no one around to help.

**Theme Stated:** After Ron says, "Gotta die somehow," his cop friend Tucker (Steve Zahn) answers him in pure Texan fashion: "Handle your business, huh? Get your s*** together." And that is what Ron will have to learn how to do: to care about himself... and, literally, to take care of his business.

**Catalyst:** After an accident at work, Ron wakes up in a hospital and is told that he has tested positive for HIV, a diagnosis he rejects. Then he gets even worse news: based on his current poor health, he only has 30 days to live. Now, that's a "problem"!

**Debate:** Ron not surprisingly refuses to believe what the docs told him, as he thinks (as many people thought wrongly at the time) that only homosexuals got the virus. So he keeps drinking, snorting and having unprotected sex, though he knows his health is deteriorating. We learn that the hospital will hold a trial for a new controversial drug called AZT, one that might harm more than heal. Dr. Eve Saks (Jennifer Garner) is skeptical about the drug. Meanwhile, Ron researches about AIDS and finds out how he got it, by having sex with a woman who used drugs intravenously. It all adds up to our Debate question: How can you fight a seemingly incurable disease?

**Break into Two:** Ending his self-doubts, Ron visits Dr. Saks, asking to become a participant in the AZT trial. He learns that the drug might not work, and he may even be given a placebo. "I am dying," he says, showing that he finally has accepted his condition and is getting ready to attack it. But how will he choose to fight?

**B Story**: The "love" story is between Ron and Dr. Saks. They couldn't be more different in their behavior, demeanor and frequency of use of the F-word, but both of them will come to respect each other, and a sexual tension is always present between them.

**Fun and Games**: The *promise of the premise* centers on what it was like to be an AIDS patient in 1980s Texas. Ron is rejected by all his ignorant friends at play and at work, being labelled a "homo." His visit to a support group doesn't go well. Then, he decides to get AZT by his own means and starts treating himself, but his condition only worsens. At the hospital, he meets Rayon (Jared Leto, Academy Award® Best Supporting Actor), a transgendered person with whom he strikes an unlikely acquaintance. At a point where Ron wants to kill himself, he gets an *eye of the storm* moment when he goes to Mexico and meets exiled license-less Dr. Sevard, who is looking for alternative treatments that may not cure AIDS, but can give patients more time to live. Ron has an idea: to smuggle the drugs to Texas and sell them.

**Midpoint**: Luckily, Rayon wants to buy meds for her and her friends, and soon she offers to be Ron's business partner. They decide to avoid legal problems by not actually selling the drugs from Mexico, but instead creating a club for others to get them "for free" while paying monthly membership dues. The Dallas Buyers Club is born! It also means a *public coming out* for them, and especially for Ron, who starts to feel at ease in gay bars and even defends Rayon against one of his homophobic ex-friends. The duo enjoys a *false victory* because their sales are steady — even their health is improving. *Stakes are raised* since, as their business grows, they're able to help more people, but that also means there's a greater chance of their scheme being exposed.

**Bad Guys Close In**: The Club attracts the attention of the authorities, especially the FDA, who start Closing In, discovering the truth of their operation when Ron suffers a heart attack, caused by his misuse of interferon. At the same time, Dr. Saks realizes that AZT is actually making her patients worse while Ron's are improving, but she is pressured by her boss to keep the experiment going. Meanwhile, Ron is worried about Rayon, since her state is deteriorating fast. Soon after, more "external" Bad Guys show up — the IRS, the FDA and the DEA confiscate all of Ron's drugs, probably tipped off by Dr. Saks's boss. At least this gives Ron the chance to have another *eye of the storm* moment with her, showing how close they are becoming, even though their love is impossible. Unbeknownst to Ron, and preparing for her own death, Rayon visits her estranged father and gets life insurance money from him, guaranteeing that the Dallas Buyers Club will be able to stay open a little longer. Later, Ron hugs Rayon for the first time, demonstrating his growth and how much their friendship has come to mean to him.

**All Is Lost:** At minute 80, Rayon coughs up blood and is taken to the hospital. She is attended by Dr. Saks but to no avail — when Ron arrives, the *whiff of death* is in the air. Rayon is already dead, and when Ron finds out, he assaults Dr. Saks's boss.

**Dark Night of the Soul:** Depressed, Ron "pays Death a visit" when he indulges himself in alcohol and a prostitute, but is too sad and weak to go on, crying alone for his friend's death. The "old ways" do not work for him anymore.

**Break into Three:** The next day, Ron shows up at the office and is told that they are really low on cash. He decides to hook up some newcomers even if they cannot pay. Our Theme Stated of "handling his business" has taken an entirely new meaning — he is now valuing people over money. *A and B Stories cross* when Dr. Saks comes to see him, and he finally convinces her about AZT's dangers, prompting her, at last, to rebel against the trial.

**Finale:**
1. Gathering the Team: For Ron, this involves "making plans for the attack" on the FDA. When he is unable to procure more of the effective but illegal meds, he instructs his counselor to file

a lawsuit against the Administration, and he prints leaflets to give the people the proper information about safe meds.

2. Executing the Plan: While the filing of a lawsuit is boring to watch, the filmmakers allow us to see Ron confronting a big pharma rep and the FDA guy during a public meeting, and Ron manages to give the crowd the necessary information.

3. High Tower Surprise: Dr. Saks is fired and she shares an intimate moment with Ron, drinking from the same bottle and showing how close they are. A classic B Story Character, she's helped Ron change... and he's helped her too. Ron talks about his dream of having a normal life: "ice-cold beer, bull ride again, take my woman dancing." In court, the judge is compassionate toward Ron and admonishes the FDA, but lacks the legal tools to do anything.

4. Dig, Deep Down: Ron feels lost, but his friends and customers cheer for him and for all that he has done for them. He is about to lose his mind, but Tucker helps him, showing that he has and will have to keep "digging, deep down" throughout the rest of his life.

5. The Execution of the New Plan: Sick and still facing a looming death, Ron sticks to his new plan of having a normal life, as he is shown bull riding again, mirroring the Opening Image. His victory is a moral one and a "triumph of the spirit," as DWAP stories require.

**Final Image**: After showing him bravely riding the bull (a symbolic representation of the disease), the closing credits tell us that the man who was given a month to live survived for seven more years. His determination and courage have helped so many others, even until today.

If they survive this life phase "Rite of Passage," they'll both grow as people — even as they grow apart in *Blue Valentine*.

# 5  RITES OF PASSAGE

If there is one genre that has more presence in auteur cinema, independent films and European dramas than it does in mainstream flicks, it is what Blake called "Rites of Passage." Perhaps this is because there are smaller set pieces, barely any explosions and virtually no car chases. Instead, you will find that the majority of the stories are character-driven, as deep as one can get. Simply put, these films are about people and their life struggles.

And are they primal! Most of the "rites" are in fact normal, unavoidable stages in life. We sure don't want to experience them! But we must, and we watch these movies to learn, for they can teach us how to overcome them.

The first subgenre is the **Mid-life Passage**, that dreaded phase in which we aren't so young anymore — though we're not at the age of retirement — and everything around us tells us we are closer to the latter. This is the time when we usually take into account what we have achieved in life (job, family, love, riches) and start to feel nervous if all the boxes are not conveniently checked. For both men and women, this may include embracing a new lifestyle to try and rejuvenate us (ask any Ferrari dealer), but most often, life doesn't work that way. If you want to know what we mean, watch films as different as Visconti's *The Leopard*, Fellini's *8½* or *Save the Tiger* (no, that's not the premium version of this book!).

We might also have to confront the **Separation Passage**, those times in life in which, voluntarily or not, we split up with someone and try to move on — easier said than done! Films like *High Fidelity*, *Blue Valentine*, *Three Colors: White* or Bergman's *Scenes from a Marriage* demonstrate this.

Our next threshold (if you want to go all-Campbell) is the **Death Passage**, which seemingly speaks for itself, although it has many permutations: the impending death of a loved one, the bereavement process, the re-adjusting to everyday life or any of the five stages that Dr. Kubler-Ross wrote about. This subgenre is evident in films such as *Amour*, *Three Colors: Blue*, *The Descendants* and a very long et cetera.

We should also refer to another aisle we all hope to never travel down, the **Addiction Passage**. As its name properly suggests, addictions come in all shapes and sizes, and getting out of them not only implies a 10-Step program, but lots of courage, support and willpower — something our characters might not have early on in their adventure. Such is the case with films like *Trainspotting*, *Requiem for a Dream* or *Drugstore Cowboy*.

Last, we have the **Adolescent Passage**, which everyone has gone through (personally, though, I'm still not sure I'm finished with it). This subgenre pertains to all the changes that we will suffer (and sometimes enjoy), including family confrontations, discovery of love, sex initiations, search for personal freedom and finding our own identity, as occurs in *The 400 Blows*, *Persepolis*, *Fish Tank* or *The Virgin Suicides*.

What do we need to tell these stories? As always, we have three fundamental components.

First, we need a **life problem** for the character to experience. Of course, defining your story by the subgenre can help you understand what kind of problem to throw at your hero. However, you could think of others, like losing your job or reaching your retirement — just mix them with any of the aforementioned issues, and you should be good to go! Think about how something like unexpectedly getting pregnant or becoming a dad could be a "problem" — if it was too early (Adolescent), too late (Mid-life) or in the middle of a breakup (Separation), each variation will bring its own set of unique circumstances. Leaving your home and going through adolescence mix well (*The 400 Blows*), as does losing your family and restarting your career (*Blue*) or having a midlife crisis while preparing for an impending breakup (*Lost* *in Translation*). And in this last case, you could cleverly set up a sequel! Great idea! I can write that! Did you hear me, Sofia? ... uh, Sofia?

Next, you need what Blake called a **wrong way**: our characters, as most of us do, will confront these problems in such a manner that will only worsen things and will make the characters feel more and more stuck, unable to solve them. They are in the "time-out chair of life" and will not be allowed out of it until they face their situation. We know each of these "life problems" invariably brings change, which we resist, and our characters will try their hardest to avoid dealing with them and the pain involved, too. Take, for instance, *Last Tango in Paris*, where Marlon Brando throws himself into a rejuvenating love story after the death of his wife, or *8½*, where a film director tries to make a movie while in a mid-life crisis (not the greatest idea). Or you could be helpless to do anything about it (*Amour*), so you can only watch your loved one suffer while trying to think of a way to ease the pain, even if it involves, well, ending her life.

After trying all possible solutions to your problem and only making things worse, you and your characters will realize that there is only one way forward: **acceptance**. As Blake told us, "Only the counterintuitive move of embracing pain will help." In the beginning, our characters may realize that the world has changed, but instead of going along with it, they refuse to acknowledge the situation. By the end, the hero must surrender to pain and honestly embrace change, accept the situation and go forward, even if it implies welcoming loss at last. Sometimes, like in *The Leopard*, we learn that something has to change for things to go on being the same. In others, as in *Blue*, we know we have a full life ahead of us. The hero will "embrace his new self" and become another person in the process since, as we must constantly remember, all stories are about transformation.

You may not know how superheroes feel, how secret agents proceed or how to escape a minotaur in a labyrinth... but you have most likely gone through one or more of our Passages. The good news is you already know the story! The bad news is you may have to accept your own change to finish it.

## THE PASSING OF THE RITE

Maybe as catharsis, or because you see a rite coming your way, you want to write a ROP — one of your best possibilities for success in the industry, since all of us can empathize. To throw your character into the pits and perils of one of life's many passages, here's what you need to do:

1. Choose a "life problem" or passage, one we will all go through at one point or another. It's best if the problem is one we really dread.

2. Choose a "wrong way" of coping with the problem, since our natural reaction to change is denial. You may get inspiration from your own life!

3. Choose a kind of "acceptance," that particular truth the hero has been fighting against throughout the film, which implies letting go of their resistance and embracing their new world.

Study this chapter and watch ROP films closely... they may save you a fortune in therapy!

## LOST IN TRANSLATION (2003)

For an actor or musician, to be "big in Japan" means to enjoy a time of success and popularity in the Asian nation. Ironically, it also can imply that the artist in question is going through a lean spell in his native country, market... or life.

This very special movie tells the story of Bob Harris, an actor who travels to Tokyo to endorse a particular brand of whiskey, but just like in his career, he is actually going through a mid-life crisis only worsened by his feeling of loneliness and detachment in a society so different from his own.

When Bob finds Charlotte, a twenty-something college graduate going through a similar phase, a window of life possibilities opens for both of them. But as in any good ROP, they approach the situation "the wrong way" and, afraid of daring to make their lives different, avoid acknowledging their mutual feelings... and risk losing each other.

Sofia Coppola managed to establish herself as a renowned filmmaker with this, her second movie. Perhaps due to its Japanese spirit, the beats of the story are subtle and even fleeting, making it a particularly good film for our study. So pay close attention, and be careful not to get lost in the translation of this beat sheet!

ROP Type: Mid-life Passage

ROP Cousins: *The Leopard, Save the Tiger, Manhattan, Sideways, 8½*

LOST IN TRANSLATION
*Written and Directed by* Sofia Coppola

**Opening Image:** After a close-up shot of, well, a certain body part of Charlotte (Scarlett Johansson), we meet actor Bob Harris (Bill Murray), newly-landed in Tokyo and sleeping in a taxi, unaware of the night lights of the city around him. Bob's sleep is the sign that he is oblivious to life and the new opportunities that this strange world may present to him. In the end, we will again see him in a taxi — a very different man.

**Set-Up**: Celebrity Bob seems eager to remain anonymous, but as he quickly discovers, it's not that easy: he is too tall to blend in, too big for the hotel robe and too famous to be unrecognized. At the same time, we meet Charlotte, a young American girl as sleepless and as out of place as he is. Both seem to be in *Stasis=Death* moments — either something must change in their lives, or they will remain like this forever.

**Theme Stated**: The theme is subtly stated in the guilt-inducing fax that Bob's wife, Lydia, sends him, complaining that he has forgotten his son's birthday. "I'm sure he'll understand," Bob says. He is detached from his family, love and career; we know that if he returns to America unchanged, his life is destined to be unhappy.

**Catalyst**: Bob and Charlotte meet in the elevator — two strangers who stand out so much from the crowd (one tall, the other a blonde) they secretly share a small glance and a shy smile.

**Debate**: Will they end up getting to know one another? That is the question to be answered while we learn more about their lives. Bob struggles with translation issues during his frustrating commercial shoot, and Charlotte feels ignored by her celebrity photographer husband John (Giovanni Ribisi). Then, Bob rejects the "premium fantasy" of a prostitute (showing he is not up for just an easy fling), while Charlotte wanders through Tokyo, frustrated at not being able to feel anything when she visits a temple. Are they both out of touch with passion?

**Break into Two**: At minute 23, just when it is supposed to happen, Charlotte and Bob acknowledge each other at the bar. No words are exchanged, but their slow mutual convergence has taken a definite advance, with no turning back for either.

**B Story**: Both Bob and Charlotte have B Stories dealing with their unsatisfactory current relationships. All that Lydia is worried about is what color Bob prefers for his carpet, and John seems to be too interested in shallow-but-sexy celebrity Kelly (Anna Faris). Neither Bob nor Charlotte seem to find the romance, understanding and attention they desire from their current partners.

**Fun and Games:** How do two sleepless, lonely strangers spend their time in Tokyo? Their separate scenes become an exploration of their searches in life: Bob tries to live healthier by exercising and swimming, while Charlotte listens to a self-help tape and practices ikebana. Finally, they happen to meet at the bar again and clearly lay their boundaries, promptly telling each other that they are married. "You are probably just having a midlife crisis," she says, acknowledging our ROP tropes. After more loneliness, insomnia and feeling out of place, when Charlotte's husband leaves her alone for a few days, she extends an offer to Bob to go out with some friends.

**Midpoint:** This excuse to go out becomes, as in any good Midpoint, a chance for their *public coming out*, that is, to behave as if they had indeed changed. They both have fun with their new friend, sing karaoke and run away from an enraged airgun-toting bar owner, finally sharing intimacy and a cigarette when Charlotte leans her head on his shoulder. With the risk of infidelity looming, the *stakes have been raised*. Minutes later, Bob takes her in his arms to her room. But while this is as much *Sex at 60* as we will get, Bob just tucks her into bed — they are not ready for something more. Back in his room, Bob talks to his wife, but again, it's all about domestic matters, not him. "That was a stupid idea," he says. Is he referring to the phone call or to imagining that he and Charlotte can be together?

**Bad Guys Close In:** The clock is ticking as both Bob's and Charlotte's time in Japan is slowly coming to an end. Have they changed after their Midpoint adventure? They should have, but haven't! Bob plays golf alone while Charlotte looks through old pictures. They also spend more time together, talking about life and hopes for the future. They sleep in the same bed, but still don't have sex — although Bob allows himself to rest his hand on her feet. "I'm stuck," she confesses. "You're not hopeless," is his answer. Bob decides to do a talk show to stay a little longer with her, but he feels ridiculous — it is precisely the kind of life he hates. When his wife calls again, he can't help but tell her he is feeling lost. "Why don't you just stay there?" she asks sarcastically, knowing it is impossible. Bob concedes and asks about the kids, returning to his father persona. "Do I need to worry about you, Bob?" Lydia finally asks.

**All Is Lost**: Disillusioned, Bob returns to his old ways, smoking a cigar and drinking alone at the bar... and he ends up sleeping with the redheaded singer. The next morning, Charlotte catches him and becomes angry. Bob gets a call from his wife and tells her that he will soon be home. In a restaurant, Charlotte feels hurt and makes fun of his age, while Bob counter-attacks with her need for attention. All mutual understanding lost, they seem more apart than ever, the *whiff of death* surrounding this once-promising relationship.

**Dark Night of the Soul**: That night, the fire alarm goes off, and they find each other at the hotel's entrance, again alone and lost among many unknowns. They make amends and share a last night at the bar, taking each other's hands. "I don't want to leave," she says. "So don't. Stay here with me. We'll start a jazz band" is his answer. Sadly, they are obviously joking, as they still don't seem to believe that it is possible to change their lives and be together.

**Break into Three**: They share a peck in the elevator, the place they met, but nothing else happens. When will the tension break? The next morning, *A and B Stories cross* as Charlotte gets a fax from John. It seems almost inevitable that Bob and Charlotte will go on with their lives.

**Finale**:
1. Gathering the Team: In the morning, Bob calls Charlotte from the lobby to try to see her once more.

2. Executing the Plan: Bob, ignoring a blonde bimbo who is trying to hit on him, meets Charlotte and says goodbye. Although

she seems open to his suggesting something, he does not dare to say anything more. And off she goes, maybe forever...

3. High Tower Surprise: Just when he thought he had lost her, Bob spots Charlotte's blonde hair in a crowded street. It is his last chance, either now or never!

4. Dig, Deep Down: Bob "digs, deep down," jumps from the taxi and chases Charlotte, embracing her and releasing the tension between them. At last, they are being sincere with their feelings.

5. The Execution of the New Plan: Bob has a plan for both of them, which he whispers in her ear. There has been much debate about his actual words, which remain unheard. But what is important (show, don't tell) is that afterwards, he kisses her, at last showing his love for her and thus signaling his own change.

**Final Image:** Bob gets in the taxi, smiling at Charlotte. He is a changed man. In the beginning, he was out of touch with himself, but after acknowledging his feelings for Charlotte, he is starting a new phase in his life, having found "acceptance." We don't know what will become of Bob and Charlotte... but we do know they will never be the same.

## BLUE VALENTINE (2010)

Can you "love like crazy" your wife, your daughter and your family... and still be completely stuck in life? This small ($1m) independent film by one of my favorite directors, Derek Cianfrance, perfectly manages to photograph the beginning and the end of the love story of Dean and Cindy as if twice frozen in time.

In many ways, *Blue Valentine* tells the story of one of those "crazy loves" that happens in so many movies: the magical encounter, the mutual seduction, the drama and difficulties of being together... but interestingly, it is told from the point of view of who the lovers have become after five years, when decadence, drinking and lack of passion have taken their toll on the "perfect" love story, leading to an almost inevitable separation.

What is especially interesting is that this film's clever structure features not one, but two parallel storylines... and that, my friends, equates to two potential beat sheets. Can a film keep its general, logical overall structure while having two non-linear plots happening back and forth in time that also perfectly fit the Blake Snyder Beat Sheet?

The answer is yes — indeed, this fantastic movie is one example of the flexibility the Blake Snyder Beat Sheet offers. In the right hands, it can become a powerful creative tool with which to make miracles like this heart-breaking story of love and separation.

ROP Type: Separation Passage

ROP Cousins: *Silver Linings Playbook*, *Three Colors: White*, *Cashback*, *A Separation*, *The Squid and the Whale*

## BLUE VALENTINE
*Written and Directed by* Derek Cianfrance

**Opening Image**: A clear Opening Image if there ever was one: Dean (Ryan Gosling) starts off sleeping alone on the couch, a symbol of his current state in the "time-out chair of life"; by the end, he will have had quite a rude awakening from his dream of a family life. Yet we learn he is in a sense a family man, evidenced by his close relationship with his charming daughter Frankie (Faith Wladyka), the opposite of what we will see in the end.

**Set-Up**: As Blake advised in *Save the Cat!® Strikes Back*, we visit the "at home," "at work" and "at play" scenes of the main character — "at play" being the scene where father and daughter wake up mom Cindy (Michelle Williams) sleeping alone in bed, "at home" being the family breakfast where Dean behaves like a child and "at work," where Dean (who drinks and drives) has a job as a painter, while Cindy is a nurse at a clinic, where she is hit on by her boss, Dr. Feinberg... and does not seem to mind. Clearly, there are many *things that need fixing* in their lives.

**Theme Stated**: "Dean, I don't need to clean after two kids." This line, spoken by Cindy, pretty much summarizes their main problem: despite what she expects in a husband, Dean behaves as an immature child, something exciting when falling in love... but maybe a drag when you have a family. Or is it that Cindy has forgotten how to have fun?

**Catalyst**: Cindy finds Megan, their lost dog, dead in a ditch, which makes her late for Frankie's school show. But instead of supporting her, Dean can only blame her to disguise his own guilt, asking her, "How many times did I tell you to lock the f****** gate? Huh?"

**Debate**: How does a couple end up like this? Did they really love each other once? To answer these questions, we go back in time about five years earlier (although it seems much more), to learn about their love and relationship expectations. Here, Dean is a young man working for a moving company. He thinks "men are more romantic than women," and his philosophy is that girls "marry the guy that has a good job and who's gonna stick around." Is he right? Is that enough to keep a couple happy?

**Break into Two**: Dean buries the dog, breaks down in tears and watches old family films while Cindy stands strong and cleans the house. Immature Dean does not realize that she expects him to support and help her, so instead, he avoids his responsibility again and suggests to Cindy that the pair have a reckless romantic weekend: "Let's go get drunk and make love." She clearly does not feel like it, but as her own character flaw dictates, she ends up going along with the plan. Ironically, at the hotel Dean chooses the Future Room.

**B Story**: In the liquor store, Cindy finds Bobby Ontario, a former boyfriend who immediately hits on her and who looks like the complete opposite of Dean: young, well-groomed and fun. Also, although we won't find about it until later, Bobby is Frankie's true father and the proof that Cindy's life could have been very different. Can it still be?

**Fun and Games:** This section starts with another flashback where we see a young Cindy stuck in her previous relationship with Bobby, an abusive father and a grandma who tells her, "You gotta be careful that the person that you fall in love with is worth it to you." Back in the present, Dean and Cindy are about to start their "romantic" weekend in a cheesy love hotel. There, they hold on to their roles: he continues to be immature while she acts responsible. Little by little, they try to bring back the passion... but it doesn't seem to work. They are each attempting to solve this crisis the "wrong way."

**Midpoint:** In this case, the Midpoint refers to the *false victory* of their falling in love. In the past, Dean encounters her on the bus and *raises the stakes* with his childlike romantic wooing, and in a night to remember, they live their own *public coming out* as their relationship charmingly flourishes among bad jokes, street tap-dancing and ukulele-serenading.

**Bad Guys Close In:** But again in the present, the "internal" Bad Guys that have accumulated over the years slowly seep out as Cindy asks Dean why he doesn't do something else in life if he is so talented. A good ROP character, he defends his being stuck: "This is the dream." For Dean, there is nothing more to achieve in life than having a wife, a daughter and a job that lets him drink. Dean tries to have sex with Cindy, but she punishes him — their drunken romantic weekend is not working. Back in the past again, we learn that Cindy is pregnant. Dean forces her to confess: "Is it mine?" "Probably not."

**All Is Lost:** In accordance with our flashback/flash-forward storytelling, at minute 70, Cindy is about to get an abortion, but she stops the procedure at the last minute. Meanwhile, in the present, she is woken up by a call from work and decides to leave Dean behind. The romantic weekend has been a total failure and they are "worse off than when the movie started."

**Dark Night of the Soul**: Again, we have dual parallel beats. In the past, Dean consoles the shocked Cindy, giving her all his support and care. In the present, Dean wakes up alone in the Future Room, wondering why she has left.

**Break into Three**: These beats also overlap. During the flashback, Dean says, "Let's do it. Let's be a family," showing that he deeply loves Cindy even though he is not even sure he is the father. And in the present, once he finds out where Cindy is, he gets drunk and is about to trigger the third and final act of their relationship.

**Finale**:
1. Gathering the Team: In the present, a very drunk Dean arrives at the clinic to ask Cindy for an explanation of why she left. / In the past, Dean walks to Cindy's home, ready to "gather with her team," or family.

2. Executing the Plan: In the present, Dean's plan is to force Cindy to go home with him, which he expects to happen if he insists, embarrasses her and lays a guilt trip on her. / Dean dines with Cindy's family, telling them about his own parents. Cindy talks about school, revealing how little her parents are involved in her life.

3. High Tower Surprise: As Dean tries to force her to go home, he ends up trashing the room and assaulting Dr. Feinberg. And to Dean's astonishment, the High Tower Surprise arrives: Cindy asks for a divorce: "I am so out of love with you." / In the past, Dean and Cindy make love in her room, and he gives her a song: "You and Me" by Penny and the Quarters.

4. Dig, Deep Down: Dean tries to use all of his usual manipulative tricks to get Cindy to stay with him, but this time, it doesn't work. So he has to "dig, deep down," to try to keep her: "You said for better or worse. This is my worst. But I am gonna get better." / In the past, Cindy is looking at herself, pregnant, in a mirror. She is "digging, deep down" herself, gathering strength to be with a man who she probably does not love that much.

5. The Execution of the New Plan: Dean finally decides to leave, and to prove that his final decision is a proactive one and not merely a reactive one, he sends his beloved daughter Frankie back with mom. / In the past, Dean and Cindy get married, carrying out their New Plan, which is to love each other for the rest of their lives.

**Final Image**: Dean leaves the house and walks away amidst fireworks that light up the sky (and usually accompany a celebration). He started off with a family: he had a wife, a dog, a daughter... and now he is a broken man and on his own. Will he recover, or will he drown in pain? The only thing we know is that he is not stuck anymore: he has accepted going on with his life, even it if is far from his loved ones.

## THREE COLORS: BLUE (1993)

In the first of Kieslowski's famous *Three Colors* trilogy, a woman must overcome the death of her entire family. While being a "Death Passage" if there ever was one, this masterpiece goes far beyond the movie-of-the-week premise to give us a serious insight into the process of overcoming grief by using love and creativity as catalysts.

When Julie decides to start a new life from scratch, she does so by leaving behind all that reminds her of her family instead of properly grieving. We doubt that the choice will really help her to overcome the loss — but what if, in the process, she discovers that she had actually lost her true self *before* the tragedy? And, now alone, will she take the opportunity to rebuild herself?

As Blake said, "Only the counterintuitive move of embracing pain will help," and in this case, Julie must regain the sense of who she really was, is and wants to be. Only then will she be able to start a new life and love again.

Like all masterpieces demonstrate, there are no easy solutions on how to live life, but this gem of a film allows us to better understand that sometimes the answers are not written in black and white, nor even in shades of gray, but entirely in blue.

ROP Type: Death Passage

ROP Cousins: *The Descendants*, *The Station Agent*, *Amour*, *The Sweet Hereafter*, *Ponette*

## THREE COLORS: BLUE
*Written by* Krzysztof Kieslowski and Krzysztof Piesewicz
*Directed by* Krzysztof Kieslowski

**Opening Image:** A car accident. Julie (Juliette Binoche), the mother, is the only survivor. As we will see in the end, something else has been destroyed, for family was the place in which Julie had decided to drown her own personality, future and independence.

**Set-Up:** After waking up from the accident, Julie seems like she is about to flee from the hospital, but in reality, she wants to kill herself by swallowing pills. She is ultimately unable to do so, indicating that there is hope for her, but she still must overcome her *Stasis=Death*. Can she regain her will to live?

**Theme Stated:** A doctor asks her, "Do you feel able to talk?" This is our theme: will Julie be able to overcome grief and express herself again as a human being and as an artist?

**B Story**: We meet Olivier (Benoit Regent), a friend of the family and her B Story hopeful lover, who shows how he cares for her by bringing a small TV set so she can watch her family's funeral. "Is there anything I can do for you?" he asks, showing his character's warmth. We learn then that Julie's husband, Patrice, was a famous composer who left an important Concerto unfinished.

**Catalyst**: At minute 11:30, Julie gets the first of her "blue musical panic attacks": a powerful symphonic melody that will haunt her in her intense moments of synesthesia — as we will learn later, it is the music of the unfinished Concerto still dwelling in her mind. She was secretly composing it in Patrice's name, a fact that a nosy journalist threatens to reveal to the world.

**Debate**: Will she let the world know the truth about her husband? And how will Julie cope with the loss of her family? Will she let the painful symphony out? As a hurt ROP hero, Julie chooses to avoid the pain, emptying the manor of any object that might remind her of her family, hoping that oblivion will take away suffering. "Why are you crying?" Julie asks her maid at one point. "Because you're not," the maid replies. Meanwhile, Olivier is gathering Patrice's papers at his office when he discovers that his deceased friend was having an affair.

**Break into Two**: To further destroy anything that can bring back memories, Julie instructs a notary to sell the house and to keep "a secret," as she prepares to disappear. She even dumps the unfinished score of the Concerto in the trash, renouncing the will to express herself through music. There is no turning back... except for one little thing: Julie decides to keep a blue glass bead lamp. Maybe there is hope for her, after all.

**Fun and Games**: The *promise of the premise* here is seeing someone as they elude any kind of human relationship to prevent the potential pain that comes with it. At first, Julie has to finish cutting away from her past: she burns, destroys and even eats every personal object that brings back memories. She decides to sleep with Olivier, destroying the act of sex as a symbol of love, after which Julie scratches her fist on a stone wall to replace her inner pain with outer suffering. She then decides to disappear and get a new home. When the real estate agent asks what she is doing in life, she answers with a simple, "Nothing." Also, she has begun to suppress her own instincts of caring for people, such as when she decides not to help a man who gets beaten. And she seems to be getting good at it — the synesthetic "blue musical panic attacks" are less intense; Julie is getting close to her goal of emptying her life of all love and sensibility.

**Midpoint**: The past is never very far, so Julie meets Antoine, the young man who witnessed the accident. He tries to return a golden cross to her, a symbol of salvation. Even though she experiences a brief panic attack when memories return, she manages to reject the cross and laughs at his story. It is a *false victory* and her *public coming out* — Julie has almost succeeded at living a life devoid of any kind of pain. But does she realize all she could lose in the process?

**Bad Guys Close In**: As Julie's goal is to avoid any feeling of caring, the Bad Guys in this story are mostly encounters with other people — like Olivier, who has tracked her down, showing that he has not given up on her. Or a flutist who plays her own melody and says, using his flute case (symbolizing music) as a pillow, "You have always to hold onto something," reminding her that her own music could be her salvation. Or her mother, who, due to dementia, has lost all memories and ability to care for anyone. Does Julie want to end up like her? Meanwhile, pressure is building, the "panic attacks" get stronger and Julie literally tries to drown them in blue water. By not caring, Julie can become mean and cruel, as she realizes when she finds a little rat and its offspring in her home, and disposes of them using the neighbor's cat. Consumed by guilt, Julie confesses to Lucille, her prostitute neighbor. And maybe because Julie showed some openness and caring by reaching out, Lucille puts her to the test by asking for her help. Julie hastily complies — she can still be saved, but there is a long way to salvation... especially when Julie sees what is happening on a nearby TV set.

**All Is Lost:** On the air, Olivier is announcing that he has been asked to complete the Concerto. Also, some private photos are shown, in which Patrice can be seen with a mysterious red-haired woman, forcing Julie to realize that her husband had an affair. The *whiff of death* surrounds her — not just the literal death of her family, but also in the way she remembers her husband.

**Dark Night of the Soul:** Julie tracks down Patrice's assistant (Florence Vignon), who confesses that she kept a copy of the Concerto, which will allow Olivier to finish the score now that it is in his possession. When asked why she did it, the assistant answers, "That music is so beautiful. One can't destroy things like that." As in love or caring, some things are too precious to die.

**Break into Three:** In a powerful Break into Three moment, *A and B Stories cross* when Julie confronts Olivier, accusing him of wanting to finish the Concerto. And in pure B Story Character fashion, he replies that it is the only way to make her emotionally alive again. She also asks him about Patrice's lover, for now she must choose to either confront her past or live in denial. Her choice as she Breaks into Three is inspired and reinforced by Olivier's caring.

**Finale:**

1. Gathering the Team: Julie tracks down Sandrine, Patrice's lover, and follows her into a restaurant.

2. Executing the Plan: In a restroom, Julie confronts Sandrine, who seems sad, because "now you will hate the two."

3. High Tower Surprise: Sandrine reveals she is pregnant, and Patrice is the father! Julie only asks if he loved her, and she says yes, adding, "Will you hate us?"

4. Dig, Deep Down: Julie returns to the swimming pool in an apparent attempt to toy with death. But when she gets out of the water, she "digs, deep down" by visiting her mother

and deciding she does not want to end up like her, unable to show love.

5. The Execution of the New Plan: Julie restarts her life. She resumes working on the score with Olivier and learns that he bought the mattress on which they slept together, discovering how much he loves her. This prompts Julie to give Patrice's estate and name to Sandrine's baby, showing acceptance and forgiveness. And when Olivier tells Julie it's either him or her who will finish the Concerto, Julie takes her own score to his home. In doing so, she not only signals that she is going to accept him as a lover, but also is committing herself to claim authorship of the Concerto and, despite her dead husband's memory, to continue her own career as a musician.

**Final Image:** A beautiful moving frieze of all the characters in the film starts with Julie and Olivier making tender love, while Julie, finally at peace, cries. Over Julie's silent crying, the completed chorus of the Concerto plays, singing the words of 1 Corinthians 13: "If I have not love, I am nothing."

## TRAINSPOTTING (1996)

Irvine Welsh's maze-like multi-point-of-view novel was adapted by John Hodge with the intention of producing "a screenplay which would seem to have a beginning, a middle and an end," and ended up resulting in a film ranked #10 in the BFI 100 Top British Films of all time. So this indie jewel is our gateway into, or more accurately out of, a tale of drug addiction and all that surrounds it — in this case: Scotland.

As an "Addiction Passage," *Trainspotting* tells the story of Mark Renton, a young punk trying to quit heroin, one of the most addictive substances on earth... but maybe not as addictive as feeling safe among the wrong friends.

Mark starts by having consciously chosen his heroin addiction to avoid the responsibility of adulthood, and he knows he is spinning in the hamster wheel of drugs. He will soon figure out that his life might be dramatically shorter if he does not change his ways.

We like Mark from the beginning because he has resolved to quit, but as in any good ROP, he tries to do it "the wrong way." He thinks that heroin is all that he has to give up to change, but in reality, he will have to "quit" a place without a future, a job without expectations, a family without understanding and, especially, a group of friends without hope.

ROP Type: Addiction Passage

ROP Cousins: *Requiem for a Dream*, *Withnail and I*, *The Addiction*, *Shame*, *Drugstore Cowboy*

TRAINSPOTTING
*Written by* John Hodge
*Based on the novel by* Irvine Welsh
*Directed by* Danny Boyle

**Opening Image**: "Choose life. Choose a job. Choose a career... I chose not to choose life. Who needs reasons when you have heroin?" This unforgettable and oft-quoted beginning gives us a clear picture of who Mark Renton (Ewan McGregor) is and how he needs to change. His transformation will be complete when he starts choosing what he is avoiding now: a job, a career, a TV set... that is, *life*.

**Set-Up**: We visit Renton's world, a hopeless little Scottish town with seemingly nothing to offer youngsters like him... except for drugs. Renton spends his days in a filthy crack house with his James Bond-obsessed friend Sick Boy, dim-witted Spud or their dealer, "Mother Superior." We also meet two of their non-drug addict friends, sporty boy Tommy, and Franco, a tough psychopath, whose lifestyles and hopes for the future are not very different from Renton's. As a sign of their sordid rejection of life, a baby has been left alone in one of the rooms. One of them is probably the father, but no one seems to care.

**Theme Stated**: Just when Renton decides to quit heroin, he tells the person least likely to be supportive, their dealer Mother Superior, who asks, "You need one more hit?" As our theme, how many "last hits" does Renton need to quit heroin forever?

**Catalyst**: The Catalyst in this movie is Renton's celebrated underwater bad trip in "the worst toilet in Scotland." This nasty experience prompts him to make his first serious attempt to leave heroin cold turkey with the so-called "Sick Boy method," which involves resisting withdrawal with the help of isolation and a junk-food cocktail.

**Debate**: Will Renton be able to overcome his addiction? He starts off well by quitting the drugs, but at the same time, he knows "the downside of coming off junk was that I would need to mix with my friends in a state of full consciousness." Renton is starting to figure out that drugs might not be the only problem, that he must also deal with his environment, in which even his non-drug addict friends seem to be destroying their lives with booze and mindless sex. He must make a living too, but as he and his friend Spud discover, drugs do not help them take a job search seriously.

**Break into Two**: When Renton and Sick Boy watch Tommy's sex tape, he realizes, "Something important was missing from my life." So he decides to go further out of his comfort zone to try and avoid his negative surroundings, to make new friends and to meet women.

**B Story**: "Heroin had robbed Renton of his sex drive, but now it returned with a vengeance." As all of his friends score while he faces rejection, he finally hits it up with Diane, a hard-drinking girl who, after a long night of sex, reveals that she is underage. But she is also a resolute, clever person who — as B Story Characters must — will help him see himself in a new light.

**Fun and Games**: The *promise of the premise* centers on how an addict in recovery lives a normal life. We follow Renton through several adventures in which he starts confirming that simply leaving the drugs is not enough. During a trekking trip to the countryside, Renton explodes: "It's shit being Scottish!" He is drinking hard and seems to have lost hope, so he is soon on heroin again, stealing and getting high. Things reach a dramatic point when the fatherless baby dies because of their irresponsibility... and their only response is "to keep going on" with drugs and crime.

**Midpoint**: Things can't go "well" forever and they are arrested. In their *public coming out*, Spud is given a jail sentence and Renton gets a warning: he will avoid prison if he undergoes treatment. Stuck in the same environment as before, this second time quitting does not seem promising. He *raises the stakes* by abandoning treatment (now he can go to prison) and symbolically climbs a wall, barely standing in balance — no matter on which side he falls, it will be "bad" for him — the "drugs" side is lethal, the "life" side holds rejection by his friends. "Choose life," says Sick Boy, mocking him, pushing him towards the "wrong way of coping."

**Bad Guys Close In**: Renton visits Mother Superior and goes on a bad trip, ending up at the hospital, while "You're Gonna Reap Just What You Sow" blasts. When his parents lock him up, his Bad Guys appear in the form of regret and memories of the dead baby, Spud in jail and the once-healthy Tommy, who is now an AIDS-infected junkie. When Renton is assured he is disease-free, Diane inspires him to go somewhere else, and he makes a sincere attempt by moving to London and working as a real estate agent. While things seem to be improving, Bad Guys Franco and Sick Boy move in with him, recreating the negative environment. After he is fired because of them, the worst happens: he must go back to Scotland.

**All Is Lost**: If that was not bad enough, back home at minute 70, Renton learns that Tommy has died a horrible death, slowly perishing alone for three weeks from toxoplasmosis. Now Renton must face the *whiff of death*, the near-certainty that something similar will happen to him if he does not change his ways.

**Dark Night of the Soul**: In a tender and heartfelt moment, very similar in form but opposite in spirit to the celebration of Renton's freedom, all the friends mourn Tommy in the bar.

**Break into Three**: Back in the crack house, the "clean" Renton is left speechless when his friends agree to make a deal selling drugs to some dealers in London. Renton tries to reject the plan, but the environment is overwhelming, even to the point of making him relent to testing the drugs personally. Or maybe Renton has something more in store for them.

**Finale**:
1. Gathering the Team: The "team" is the group of friends preparing for the heroin exchange while on their trip to London. Renton takes another of his "last shots." Is this really the final one?

2. Executing the Plan: They meet with the gangsters in a hotel room and, despite last-minute tensions, successfully sell the heroin. Now they can celebrate! Everything went according to plan... didn't it?

3. High Tower Surprise: While celebrating, Franco loses control and cuts a man's face. Renton realizes that he has to break away from him or his psychopath friend's temper will get all of them arrested.

4. Dig, Deep Down: Renton "digs, deep down" when he resists Franco's taunting, which could get him killed. He is trying to find his chance to flee.

5. The Execution of the New Plan: That night, Renton wakes up, drinks water (a symbol of purity) and steals the money, leaving his former friends behind.

**Final Image**: Renton has changed — he wanted to quit heroin and has done so, and he has also left behind his toxic environment. At last, he has ended up becoming the opposite of who he was at the beginning by deciding to "choose life, choose a job, choose a career..." at least for the time being.

## THE 400 BLOWS (1959)

Can you put films like *Porky's*, *Sixteen Candles* and *American Pie* in the same category as French New Wave masterpiece *The 400 Blows*? Wow, critics gonna criticize! But no matter how many readers of *Cahiers du Cinema* are now waving their *foulards* in protest, the fact is that the "Adolescent Passage" story reflects one of the most universal themes and storylines: the coming-of-age.

In this groundbreaking film by François Truffaut, we follow the adventures of Antoine Doinel, a schoolboy who doesn't feel he has a place in a society that only has authority as an answer for his "life problem": growing up.

Ironically, family, school, police and the correctional system are institutions designed to make children fit in, so when Antoine begins to feel different and wants to look for his own path in life, he naturally starts by coping "the wrong way," which avoids the inevitable — he must be on his own to figure out his place in life.

Let's see, then, how a classic, rebellious and successful *auteur* film from 1959 fits the Blake Snyder Beat Sheet like a charm, proving that good narrative and a solid structure can make a film stand, almost 60 years later, as tall as Antoine Doinel's figure in the final famous frame of the film.

ROP Type: Adolescent Passage

ROP Cousins: *Heavenly Creatures, An Education, Fish Tank, Juno, The Virgin Suicides*

## THE 400 BLOWS
*Adapted by* François Truffaut and Marcel Moussy
*Dialogues by* Marcel Moussy
*Written and Directed by* François Truffaut

**Opening Image**: Credits show us the ever-*classique* Eiffel Tower, but Truffaut is telling us something more: all kinds of buildings (a symbol of society) prevent us from seeing the whole tower, a visual statement working as an Opening Image that advances one of the themes of the film — how must the individual struggle to set himself apart from an oppressive society that threatens to drown him?

**Set-Up**: We meet our young hero, Antoine Doinel (Jean-Pierre Léaud, who would play the character in five more films), in his "at work" moment, that is, in school. There he is caught, ridiculed and punished by the teacher, the first of the authority figures Antoine will have to escape from. Then "play" arrives, even if he is prevented from attending recess; instead, he voices his rebellion by writing a protest on the wall, only to be caught again. Finally, "at home" we are introduced to his family: a seemingly uncaring mother and a light-hearted father. As we will see, authority is not lacking here, either.

**Theme Stated**: "Recess isn't a right, it is a reward," says the teacher when punishing Antoine. Ironically, freedom has to be earned by submitting to society's strict rules — failing to do so results in the loss of freedom, and can even lead to imprisonment.

**Catalyst**: As a punishment for writing the protest, Antoine is ordered to conjugate this humiliating sentence: "I deface classroom walls and I mistreat French verses." This seemingly unimportant moment will trigger all of his future reactions and decisions, setting the plot in motion.

**Debate**: What is Antoine's life like, and why does he (and we) feel that he does not fit in? Talking to his best friend René, Antoine refuses to accept authority, fantasizes about stealing money from their parents and beating the teacher. Later at home, Antoine tries to fulfill his homework/punishment, but his ever-angry mother prevents him from doing so.

**B Story**: Antoine's best friend is René, the equally neglected son of a wealthy family, and also his companion when it comes to getting in trouble. But unlike Antoine, René knows how not to get caught and recognizes the limits of rebellion — something that, as we will see, he will not be able to teach Antoine.

**Break into Two**: The next day, Antoine remembers he didn't fulfill his penalty, so to avoid being punished again, he plays hooky with René, thus entering Act Two's *upside-down world* of freedom from responsibilities, where he can do as he pleases with no authority figures over him... as long as he and René don't get caught.

**Fun and Games**: Quite literally, Antoine and René have Fun and Games at the cinema, playing pinball and visiting an amusement park. Antoine discovers the *upside-down world* of family when he sees his mother kissing her boss! The next day, Antoine returns to school, but again is severely reprimanded and humiliated when he lies about his absence — he says his mother had died, a falsehood that is quickly discovered. Antoine tries for the second time to escape home and authority, testing the hardships of life in the streets and ultimately coming back to a temporary calm at home.

**Midpoint**: This *false victory* (a happy home) quickly ends when Antoine is suspended for breaking the school-world rules by plagiarizing Balzac. This is his *public coming out*, but before being taken to the principal, he escapes again. *A and B Stories cross* as René is punished but also escapes.

**Bad Guys Close In:** Time starts running out for Antoine, as the metaphorical *clock* of his options goes on *ticking*. He and René flirt with petty crime as they begin stealing — first a poster, and then an actual clock. Antoine and René pretend to be adults, playing backgammon, drinking wine and smoking cigars, but their adventure takes a dark twist as they set foot in the underground when they steal a typewriter and try to sell it on the black market.

**All Is Lost:** As he is about to return the typewriter, Antoine is caught and taken to the police station, where he is charged with vagrancy and theft. The police chief proposes to take Antoine to a correctional center, and his stepfather accepts. Antoine is "worse off than when he started" — no family, no school, no freedom, all responsibility.

**Dark Night of the Soul:** In a long Dark Night of the Soul beat, Antoine is put in a holding cell next to thieves and prostitutes as he contemplates the city lights, his former world of freedom. The police wagon then takes him to prison, where he spends the night alone.

**Break into Three:** Antoine's last hope vanishes when his mother visits the judge and actually persuades him to take Antoine to a center for juvenile delinquents. Antoine's fate seems sealed as he is about to enter the dark world of Act Three.

**Finale:**
1. Gathering the Team: Antoine does not have a "team" *per se*, as he cannot trust any other people and must rely only on himself. This scene gives us a good view of the singular fate that society designates to rebellious children: jail. The only other option is flight, but Antoine learns that one kid who had escaped has been caught.

2. Executing the Plan: In an impressive scene even by today's standards, Antoine demonstrates good behavior by answering

all of the psychologist's questions. Here, we also learn details of Antoine's past that explain his attitude.

3. High Tower Surprise: A double surprise awaits him: first, René comes to visit but is not allowed to see him, thus ending their friendship. Then, Antoine's upset mother arrives to tell him that because of a letter he sent his father (presumably talking about her lover), they do not care for him anymore, and he will be sent to a labor center. He has definitely lost his family.

4. Dig, Deep Down: Almost immediately, Antoine "digs, deep down" when he gathers the strength to escape from the labor center while playing a soccer match. After throwing the ball in-bounds, he leaves the field, crawls under a fence and runs away.

5. The Execution of the New Plan: Antoine keeps sprinting, faster than Forrest Gump ever ran! He goes on until he reaches a distant beach, fulfilling his dream of seeing the sea, and having a whole future for himself.

**Final Image**: At the beginning, Antoine had a family, a school and friends. Now, he is alone and far from responsibility and society's rules. Just as how the houses prevented us from seeing the Eiffel Tower in the Opening Image, Antoine's lonely figure stands as tall as the famous monument. Now, there is no society that can hide his powerful presence from us.

The "complication" for these lovers is the "ticking clock" looming over them in *Before Sunrise*.

# 6  BUDDY LOVE

If there is anything just as primal in our human instinct as survival, it's love. And as Blake taught us, primal-ness is the key ingredient of any good story. It's also elemental as a foundation for our hero's transformation, the primary goal we want to achieve when we work on a narrative.

Love stories are the bread and butter of many screenwriters and novelists throughout the world, and while at first the term "rom-com" may not seem to belong to the "deeper" indie world, you'll soon realize there are many kinds of love to write about.

That's why we put the "Buddy" before the "Love." We are not only referring to the romantic, we're talking about that special connection you may feel toward another being, one so strong that it could change your life — be it the love of friends, family, a significant other or, as we will see, the relationship with a special animal.

Our first subgenre, **Pet Love**, refers to that strong, primal connection between a man or an animal with a non-human species. Mainstream cinema has plenty of films to show for this (picture any boy + dog / horse / whale / dolphin / alien / etc., flick), but indie cinema also has its share, as in *My Dog Tulip*, *Best in Show* or our chosen film, *Kes* (boy + kestrel) from British auteur Ken Loach.

**Professional Love**, our second subgenre, centers on unlikely couples in the workplace or business environment who are usually forced into partnerships by the job they have to accomplish together. In Hollywood films, cop duos are the classic example, led by *Lethal Weapon*, but our independent realm is also full of these stories, although in a more realistic setting — from France's super-successful *The Intouchables* to Euro-period pieces like *A Dangerous Method* by David Cronenberg, to intimate works as charming as Kaurismaki's *Drifting Clouds*. Still want your share of cops? Watch *Hot Fuzz* and die laughing!

And there is, of course, **Rom-com Love**. As Blake put it, these are stories where two people "are just too blockheaded to realize they're perfect for each other." Hollywood specializes in these, but international writers and directors have also told many stories of romantic love in a fun, quirky, yet passionate way — so independent and European filmmakers, audiences and indeed lovers must be as blockheaded as Americans! Consider the unexpected indie hit *Once* or Richard Linklater's real-time trilogy starring and co-written with Ethan Hawke and Julie Delpy, from which we have chosen *Before Sunrise*.

We're not done yet! There's the **Epic Love** subgenre, in which two lovers, friends or acquaintances have to confront external sweeping events like wars, catastrophes, political changes or moral standards to be together, such as in *The Reader* (Nazism and German guilt), *The Unbearable Lightness of Being* (the Soviet invasion of Czechoslovakia), *The Boy in the Striped Pajamas* (the Holocaust), *Hiroshima Mon Amour* (WWII) and even friendships, as in *The Last King of Scotland*.

We'll conclude with **Forbidden Love** stories, in which our protagonist's own condition (be it racial, sexual, age difference, opposing families, etc.) separate our lovers, as in *Let the Right One In*, *The Graduate*, *My Beautiful Laundrette* or our chosen example, *Blue Is the Warmest Color*.

Keep in mind that, as in most films, there is a "love story" lurking in the background, many times in the shape of a B Story, which makes it easy to mis-categorize many films as Buddy Love stories. But a true Buddy Love will have these three critical components:

First, we need an **incomplete hero**, someone whose life is in a perpetual *Stasis=Death* moment. To be whole, they will need something else that another person will bring. So, many times, the "side A" of our buddy team is calm, steady and even boring, like cold serious scholar Carl Gustav Jung in *A Dangerous Method* or plain-as-vanilla teenage student Adèle in *Blue Is the Warmest Color*.

How can you "complete" them? Easy: create a **counterpart** who will fill those gaps. As a writer, you should not only develop your duo as different as possible, but as complementary too. The "side B" of our team is usually quirky, unique and often bizarre, especially when placed next to the hero. As in many a traditional "meet cute," we immediately think they couldn't be more unalike... but love will just take time to bloom. In many cases, the counterpart is the theme-propellant B Story Character and will know more about life and love than our protagonist. Compare our aforementioned examples with their respective counterparts Sabina (hysterical, masochistic, sex-obsessed patient) or Emma (blue-tinted hair, aspiring artist).

How can two people be meant for each other yet not realize it? The reason, and what we need next, is a **complication**, a situation that both "keeps them together and forces them apart." It can be their own condition (social, sexual, economical, etc.) or an outer menace or situation: a patient/doctor relationship (*A Dangerous Method*), a vampire/possible victim link (*Let the Right One In*), marital status (*Once*), sexuality (*Total Eclipse*) or poverty (*Montparnasse 19*). In each of these cases, the two are tied together by the event or situation that is keeping them apart! Whether they overcome the complication or not is what keeps us watching.

What about our classic love triangles? They are covered in what we call the **three-hander**, in which the hero or heroine "leaves the wrong guy for the right one." And what if both characters change their ways to be together? This dual arc is called a **two-hander** by *Cat!*-lovers. And you'll never believe it, but if the story deals with two couples, we call it... a **four-hander**! I bet you didn't see that one coming (I wouldn't have, for sure). And a last piece of (love) advice from Blake: most of the time, "it's usually the girl who knows it's true love and the guy who doesn't have a clue." In my case, that is absolutely true, too!

## LOVE YOUR BUDDY, WILL YA?

So you want to write about two people who are as different as can be, yet you think must end up together? Then this genre is for you! Here's your recipe for a great story:

1. First, take an "incomplete hero," someone who seems to be missing something from his or her life (spiritual, ethical, physical) but doesn't seem to realize it at first.

2. Mix him with a "counterpart" that dares to be all that the hero doesn't even think to be, and behold how well they complement each other... although they wouldn't admit to it.

3. Spice things up with a "complication," an inner or outer situation that both joins them together and keeps them apart.

Now relax, call your best buddy or buddette, and watch the following movies together! You may fall in love, even if he or she is into mainstream cinema — and we know that hurts!

## KES (1969)

Life in a mining village in 1969 England surely was tough, much more so for a kid who doesn't seem to properly fit in his environment. With an estranged father, a distracted mother, an abusive brother, bullies at school and an environment where not many people appreciate him... this is the kind of situation in which one needs a friend the most! Even if the friend is a hawk.

*Kes*, based on the 1968 novel *A Kestrel for a Knave* by Barry Hines, is an early example of the social realism that has defined the long career of British auteur Ken Loach, and it's stood the test of time. Barely 50 years have passed since kids were treated like Billy Casper was, and we are still left to wonder what has changed today for many underprivileged children.

This film is also a fine example of "Pet Love" stories, in which the primal bond (and the "complication" that joins and separates them) between man and animal bring each other to completion. After the film's tragic ending, we know that training Kes has changed our hero's life forever, which gives us hope for his future.

Faithful to its social intent, the film also becomes a denouncement of the situation in industrial British society during the '60s, focusing on an educational system that berates children for not fitting in, while Billy himself shows (and learns) that with care, dedication and respect, one can educate and befriend even the wildest bird in the sky without taking away any of its freedom.

BL Type: Pet Love

BL Cousins: *My Dog Tulip*, *Wiener-Dog*, *Truman*, *A Boy and His Dog*, *Beginners*

KES
*Based on the novel by* Barry Hines
*Adaptation by* Barry Hines and Ken Loach and Tony Garnett
*Directed by* Ken Loach

**Opening Image**: Our "incomplete hero," Billy Casper (David Bradley), is woken up in the early morning by his cruel half-brother Jud. Billy does not even try to confront Jud, but just takes his verbal abuse and demeaning treatment.

**Theme Stated**: "Another few weeks, you'll be up with me [in the mines… Now] they wouldn't have a weedy tw*t like thee," says Jud in his hard Yorkshire accent. Right now, no one thinks much of Billy, but he will show everyone how talented he can be.

**Set-Up**: We see Billy in his everyday life. He gets up early in the morning to work as a paperboy, and we soon notice some of his *things that need fixing*. For example, he claims he doesn't steal anymore, but he shoplifts a bottle of milk for breakfast. He is also constantly reprimanded, such as when he cuts corners at work or trespasses on someone's property. Billy is never praised or given positive re-inforcement, not even in class, where he seems to have problems focusing. Instead of being helped, he is scolded. We know that if his life stays the way it is, Billy's opportunities will evaporate, a *Stasis=Death* situation for a youngster.

**Catalyst**: At minute 12, his friends invite him to go "nesting" the next day, that is, looking for birds' nests. He's the only one who shows up, and while wandering through the woods, he spots a magnificent bird: a kestrel.

**Debate**: Billy tries to get nearer, but he's stopped by the landowner. However, they talk about the bird and Debate if it can be trained, as the breed is especially difficult to deal with. This is our "complication," and it sounds, thematically, like Billy himself. Can a boy with no knowledge of birds train a kestral? Billy tries to get a falconry book from the library, but even in this place of free culture, it is difficult for him to access the book... so he has to steal it, showing that he still needs to change. To make matters worse, his brother laughs at him when he returns home. No one supports Billy. Will he succeed?

**Break into Two**: We meet Billy's mother, who has no problem with her older son betting at the races and with whom she discusses their latest flirtations. Billy isn't really listening to them, as he is immersed in reading, entering a world of knowledge which will take him into Act Two.

**Fun and Games**: Billy finds his own Fun and Games while reading, but as director Ken Loach is famous for his portrayal of the middle class and their environment, we also get a glimpse of the Fun and Games of a typical Saturday night. It is soon made clear that the adults do not exactly behave like grownups. Billy's mother is right when she says maybe he could have a chance with another kind of education, but she doesn't seem too keen to provide it. That night, Jud arrives home drunk and while he sleeps, Billy insults and pretends to hit him, not daring to actually do it... yet. He flees from home, steals the kestrel (aptly named Kes) from the nest and starts raising him, fulfilling the *promise of the premise* about "a boy and his hawk." We begin to see a different Billy — focused, in control and calm. Indeed, the bird "complements" him! At school, he attends PE, where another grownup (their teacher) behaves like a bully and even cheats at soccer to win the match.

**Midpoint**: Billy suffers a "Midpoint defeat" when the teacher sees him trying to go home without taking a shower. Billy is forced to get naked and shower with cold water, suffering further humiliation in public. Soon after, during another collective assembly, *A and B Stories* (represented by teachers, as we will see) *cross* as a girl reads Matthew 18, 10-14: "Never despise one of these little ones, I tell you," and tells the parable of the stray sheep. *Stakes have been raised* about the children's future, but no teacher seems to grasp that there are many stray sheep among them, like Billy.

**Bad Guys Close In**: Things start looking even worse for our protagonist when he is caught daydreaming about Kes and forced to visit the Headmaster's office, setting the tone for this beat. It is announced that the youth employment officer will visit them soon, a symbol of the sad future these boys face. None of the teachers seem to care for them, as they will soon be out of school and working in manual labor, yet the Headmaster physically punishes him and some other innocent pupils, ironically saying, "You are the generation that never listens."

**B Story**: Our B Story, similar to *The Black Stallion*, the "Pet Love" example provided in *Save the Cat!® Goes to the Movies*, comes late. In this case, it pertains to another teacher, Mr. Farthing, who not only lets Billy speak about his hawk in front of the whole class (allowing him to show his passion), but also defends our protagonist from a bully and, soon after, goes to watch him training Kes. "Hawks can't be tamed," Billy tells him, maybe talking about himself, "they're manned. It's wild and it's fierce and it's not bothered about anyone." Aren't young kids the same?

**All Is Lost**: Billy's stealing tendencies return, and he spends the money Jud had given him for betting on food. Billy sees Jud coming to school and knows he will get a beating if he is caught.

**Dark Night of the Soul**: Billy tries to find some place to hide, but even as he sneaks into a warehouse, he knows that soon he will be caught.

**Break into Three:** *A and B Stories cross* as no teacher seems to care for him, and when the ruthless headmaster finds Billy, he makes him go to the employment officer, the symbol of his impending "adult" life outside of school.

**Finale:**
1. Gathering the Team: Looking distracted and alone, Billy summons his strength as he goes to see the employment officer.

2. Executing the Plan: Billy attends the meeting and pays no attention whatsoever to the officer, since he appears to be worried about something else. In this important life moment, it seems that it is the officer who is deciding Billy's future, although Billy succeeds at resisting working in the mine, like his brother.

3. High Tower Surprise: Billy runs to check Kes's barn. The bird is not there, so he starts looking for him everywhere. Billy realizes he is in even deeper trouble when he discovers that his brother would have made a small fortune if he had used the money Jud gave him to properly place the bet.

4. Dig, Deep Down: He "digs, deep down," returning home to confront his family. Jud confirms that he killed Kes in retribution, and Billy finds the kestrel's body in a trash bin.

5. The Execution of the New Plan: Enraged, Billy fights with his brother, something he did not dare to do at the beginning. We understand that things will never be the same for either of them, and that Billy has started to mature.

**Final Image:** Billy respectfully buries Kes, the bird that "completed" him and reciprocally taught him courage, self-esteem and talents no one seemed to believe he had. A quite open-ended film, we are left to wonder about Billy's future, but we know with certainty that his relationship with the hawk has transformed and completed him.

## A DANGEROUS METHOD (2011)

Christopher Hampton is one of my personal writing heroes and main influences. It is always a pleasure to study how masterfully he adapts historical themes dealing with complicated, multi-layered characters and real, dark, passionate stories.

The challenge is especially difficult because that source material often seems too intellectual for big audiences or too quiet to spawn a proper thrilling pace, but Hampton always manages to boost the possibilities of his narrative by placing his characters in situations that are the most extreme and primal of human instincts: sex and death.

Such is the case with this wonderful film, which deals with the development of psychoanalysis at the beginning of the 20th century, featuring three key psychologists of the time — Sigmund Freud, Carl Gustav Jung and Sabina Spielrein — who walk into the vast, uncharted territory of the mind, where one could only return cured... or irreversibly harmed.

Just mentioning those three names suggests a love triangle, and we would be correct to anticipate such, but unexpectedly, it is not exactly "the girl" that the two men are after. In a nice twist, it is the respect of the patriarchal figure which Spielrein and Jung desire at the same time they love and analyze each other — which makes their "Professional Love" story flourish among dreams, masochistic relationships, deceit and despair.

BL Type: Professional Love

BL Cousins: *Hot Fuzz, Drifting Clouds, In Bruges, The Intouchables, Broadcast News*

A DANGEROUS METHOD
Based on the play *The Talking Cure* by Christopher Hampton and the book *A Most Dangerous Method* by John Kerr
*Screenplay by* Christopher Hampton
*Directed by* David Cronenberg

**Opening Image:** Sabina Spielrein (Keira Knightley), suffering from a severe case of hysteria, is admitted to the Burghölzli Clinic in Zürich, in a distressed state — quite different from what we will see at the Final Image. We meet her doctor, Carl Gustav Jung (Michael Fassbender), a man full of lively energy and positive passion for his job... quite the opposite of his persona at the end.

**Theme Stated:** "I'm not mad, you know?" says Sabina. And since this movie deals with the beginnings of psychoanalysis and defining "sanity," it is also a warning that doctors and patients were walking through uncharted territories... which could cure them or make their conditions worse.

**Set-Up:** We explore more deeply our main character, as Dr. Jung is a man of opposites. He has a scientific mind yet is open to believe that supernatural coincidences happen for a reason. He has a lovely, wealthy, pregnant wife, yet among the *things that need fixing*, he does not really pay much attention to her, instead being obsessed with work. He is obviously the "incomplete hero" whose life needs a jolt. He'd like to meet a certain Dr. Freud and is not bewildered at all when Sabina tells him that an angel speaks to her in German — she is the obvious quirky "counterpart." But when he leaves for military service (entering a *Stasis = Death* moment), she relapses into hysteria, showing how much she needs "the talking cure."

**Catalyst:** An opportunity arises for Jung to have Sabina, who wants to be a psychologist, as his aide. They will work together. It is also the "complication" that starts off our "Professional Love" process that will keep them together and, at the same time, pull them apart.

**Debate**: Is Jung right in giving her such responsibility? Will she be up to the task? And most importantly: what can happen between them? A chance to set up tension and Debate is laid out during a psychological test, which results in doubts whether Jung's marriage is strong enough to withstand the temptation. And then, Sabina Debates with Jung about a dream she had, revealing that much of her neurosis derive from a masochistic relationship of a sexual nature.

**Break into Two**: Probably inspired by this revelation, Jung decides to meet Freud at his home in Vienna. Jung is about to enter the *upside-down world* of psychoanalysis, and the B Story Character is around the corner — an influence from which there will be "no turning back."

**B Story**: Another mirror "Professional Love" story starts when mentor-mentee, father-son figures meet at last! Jung and Freud (Viggo Mortensen) have their first, historic 13-hour conversation.

**Fun and Games**: An exploration of love, admiration and human relationships starts with mild (for now) disagreements between Jung and Freud over questions of method, race and social status, while Sabina seems to improve enormously. She develops her own theories about the destructive / creative nature of sex, which makes her further fascinated with Jung. Temptation seems to grow when another psychologist shows up for treatment but ends up treating Jung. Otto Gross (Vincent Cassel) rejects all kinds of self-repression and wants patients to be really free, even if they destroy themselves. "Do not pass by the oasis without stopping to drink," Gross says to Jung, encouraging him to have a relationship with Sabina.

**Midpoint**: *Stakes are raised* when Sabina insinuates herself to Jung, and they can no longer resist each other — they have sex, which feels to him like a "Midpoint defeat." He tries to terminate the relationship, but she convinces him to go on, turning their encounters into masochistic sessions. *A and B Stories cross* when Freud announces to Jung that among his disciples, he is the "crown prince."

**Bad Guys Close In**: Bigger disagreements start building between them. Jung wants to explore such subjects as telepathy or parapsychology, while Freud wants him to remain in the field of the apparently more scientific sexual theory. Meanwhile, Jung and Sabina continue their relationship, which threatens to "make the team disintegrate" as word is spreading that Jung is sleeping with one of his patients. Terrified, Jung leaves Sabina, enraging her so much that she seeks Freud's help and mentorship, which Jung successfully blocks — for now. Sabina counterattacks and blackmails Jung forcing him to confess to Freud that he lied, making her successfully his new pupil and distancing herself from Jung even more. The "team further disintegrates" when Jung takes Freud to the US and while on the trip, the mentor refuses to be psychoanalyzed by the mentee, afraid of losing his authority. Back at home, Sabina asks Jung to work together again, while they fool themselves into thinking they can avoid their "Professional Love" story. Of course, they start having sex again and this time, she is the one to leave him, hurting him deeply. Sabina realizes how much the old master and pupil have grown apart from each other.

**All Is Lost**: After an editorial meeting, Jung and Freud have a deeply symbolic and subtext-drenched conversation about the erasing of the father figure, and possibly affected by the talk, Freud suffers a stroke and almost dies in Jung's hands.

**Dark Night of the Soul**: In a series of deeply bitter letters, the two former friends and mutual admirers sadly certify the death of their relationship.

**Break into Three**: As they quote Hamlet saying "the rest is silence," Jung symbolically crushes his mentor's last letter and at the same time Freud puts the photograph of his rejected pupil away in a box. Both men are devastated, but too proud to change. With the *A and B Stories crossing* for the last time, their mirror "Professional Love" is finished. Now, what about Sabina?

**Finale:**

1. Gathering the Team: Sabina "gathers" with Jung's wife, who tells her that his husband is deeply depressed and only she can analyze and perhaps cure him. However, Sabina's plans are very different — she is pregnant (by a doctor she has married) and has come to say goodbye.

2. Executing the Plan: Sabina sits with a saddened Jung and tries to make him see how lucky he is for everything he has. But he seems distressed, and tells her about a prophetic dream he has had about a coming tide of blood washing over Europe (World War I).

3. High Tower Surprise: They both realize that they keep looking for each other in their new relationships, Sabrina's new husband and Jung's new mistress. They (and us too!) realize that their love was deeper than they thought.

4. Dig, Deep Down: Sabina tells him to cure people, trying not to hurt himself more in the process, but Jung answers that "only the wounded physician can hope to heal," revealing how much walking in the perilous path of this "dangerous method" has changed him.

5. The Execution of the New Plan: They separate to never see each other again.

**Final Image:** Sabina started off as a very distressed, mentally ill patient, but her character arc has made her a balanced, talented psychologist ready to help others. Meanwhile, the optimistic and passionate Jung has turned into a bitter, depressed individual. They have been changed forever, in so different ways, by their "Professional Love" story.

## BEFORE SUNRISE (1995)

One night, one city, and just two characters — director Richard Linklater took a huge creative challenge when he decided to have just these ingredients, resulting in a film in which its main characters do little more than walk and talk! Of course, there *is* more: the incredible, charming chemistry between Ethan Hawke as Jesse and Julie Delpy as Céline that — for now — has lasted three wonderful films.

Structure-wise, *Before Sunrise* is a seamless film, with no apparent act breaks, no major plot occurrences, no spectacular twists, no great revelations, no big arguments... seemingly un-beat-able too? It's just that everything happens underneath the surface, and our Beat Sheet does as well.

Look twice: under all that apparently light dialogue, there is a large amount of subtext, and behind those naturalistic, improv-like performances, there are dozens of hours of rehearsing. Most importantly, the story contains all of our BL components: an "incomplete hero" who doesn't seem to believe in romantic love, a "counterpart" who can help him learn otherwise, and "a complication that ties them together and sets them apart," that is, the little time they have to spend with each other.

Meet then, our "Rom-com Love" story, in which, like the classic Hollywood counterpart, the smiles, laughs and feel-good mood is present, but there is also the fear that our lovers will not end up together. Will they re-unite in six months as planned? Well, back in the day, audiences had to wait for almost a decade for the sequel to learn the answer! And thankfully, 30 years later and *another* sequel, Jesse and Céline's love story is still being told.

BL Type: Rom-com Love

BL Cousins: *Once, Four Weddings and a Funeral, (500) Days of Summer, Punch Drunk Love, Me and You and Everyone We Know*

BEFORE SUNRISE
*Written by* Richard Linklater and Kim Krizan
*Directed by* Richard Linklater

**Opening Image**: A seemingly straight railway track momentarily crosses another. What if the two tracks joined, making one way where before there were two? Our film starts with undeniably symbolic trains and the people who populate them, like young Jesse (Ethan Hawke) and Céline (Julie Delpy) who, for the time being, are headed in the same direction.

**Set-Up**: Upon hearing an Austrian couple's discussion on the train, Céline gets up and sits down, not very far from Jesse, who rises to the occasion and tries his best lousy pick-up lines on her. Soon, we learn that he is a backpacking American on his way home, and she is a French student returning to Paris. He plays the literary lone traveler while she plays the misunderstood young daughter. He is so full of himself and she is afraid of everything. And while they try to play it cool, we are already smiling — it is so evident that they are into each other!

**Theme Stated**: Although in this clever, thematically subtext-drenched film, many of the things they say could be considered "stated themes," let's choose the title of the book Jesse is reading: Klaus Kinski's autobiography: *All I Need Is Love*. And isn't that what they both need? But wait — do they need the same *kind* of love? They will have just one night to figure that out!

**B Story**: Quite an easy beat in a film with basically two characters, so look no further: Jesse and Céline are our "Rom-com Love" buddies, and the film will basically deal with how meeting each other for less than 24 hours will change them forever and, more specifically, how their philosophy about love itself will change, too.

**Catalyst**: At minute 13, the train stops and Jesse boldly invites Céline to spend the day with him in Vienna.

**Debate**: In pre-"but we're not even Facebook friends" times, wasn't it crazy to spend the day in a foreign city with someone you just randomly met? Jesse "helps" Céline Debate why she should leave the train with him, and he convinces her to imagine it's a time-travel adventure. After they get off, they seem a little awkward, still Debating if what they did was okay before discussing what they should do for the day... like maybe attending a theater piece later (we don't think so — insert your mental wink emoticon here).

**Break into Two**: Their wanderings through Vienna begin, along with this: "We're stuck together, so we'll ask each other a few direct questions." Time to start their 24-hour (*clock ticking*) dating challenge! There is "no turning back" for the two of them!

**Fun and Games**: They both have evident Fun and Games, first on the tram when they ask each other silly questions about their (sex) lives — they are exploring the *upside-down version* of conventional dating, where you have anything from months to a lifetime to figure out if that person is the right one. They barely have a day, and thus the *promise of the premise* is delivered. We soon learn that they apparently have quite different views about love: Céline seems the hopeless romantic and Jesse the rugged nonbeliever. As they spend the day together, however, the distinctions become blurred, especially when they share a kiss and continue having a fun time at an amusement park with a Ferris wheel (one you cinephiles should recognize).

**Midpoint**: They seem to be moving toward true sincerity when Céline says, "I am having a great time," a *false victory* and a *public coming out* in her own way, being frank when speaking about how she, as a woman, should be devising a strategy to "get" Jesse. Also, the *stakes are raised* when they talk about what they don't like about each other. "Were we having our first fight back there?" *A Story* (the possibility of their being together) and *B Story* (their differences about how love should be) *cross* when a street poet says, "I carry you, you carry me, that's how it could be." But will they dare to think that their love can really happen? Also acknowledging that *clocks are ticking*: "What good is saved time if nobody uses it?" Well, they'd better make the most of this situation!

**Bad Guys Close In**: There are no extraneous characters, but the writers have provided internal Bad Guys: insecurity, fear, differences — anything that could separate the duo. They start confessing the truth about their past relationships and discuss what isolates men and women in regards to love — things such as "men justifying their fooling around" and "women destroying men." Their chat becomes more personal when they finally talk about what they want to find in a relationship: "Loving someone and being loved means much to me," says Céline, while soon after, Jesse implies that personal fulfillment is more important for him than love. They seem to be falling further apart, the "team disintegrating," until they decide not to solve their differences then and there; after all, they will only be together for a short time.

**All Is Lost**: They finally acknowledge that their night is about to end and they will become separated forever: "After tomorrow morning, we'll probably never see each other again, right?"

**Dark Night of the Soul**: They contemplate the "death" of their short love and Céline says, "It's depressing, no?" Also, two tramways (a recurrent visual thematic symbol in the movie) move apparently in the same direction — but this time on different tracks.

**Break into Three**: The couple get some wine and go to the park, the sexual tension sizzling by now! Although they aren't certain that "doing it" could hurt them, Jesse makes *A and B Stories cross* when he says, "If somebody gave me the choice right now of to never see you again or to marry you, I would marry you." A romantic *Moment of Clarity* if there ever was one!

**Finale:**

1. Gathering the Team: In the morning, they enjoy their last moments together, gathering the strength to soon separate. They dance in the street and afterwards, Jesse says, "You cannot conquer time," quoting W. H. Auden.

2. Executing the Plan: Their "plan," as devised during the night, is simply to go back to the train station and split. "I guess this is it, no?" They try to say goodbye, but it is hard.

3. High Tower Surprise: The Surprise comes when they kiss and all rational thoughts aside, they reckon that they love each other too much, that it is a once-in-a-lifetime opportunity, so they agree to see each other again in six months.

4. Dig, Deep Down: Now that it is clear that they love each other, both have to "dig, deep down" to say goodbye for real and to trust the other's love.

5. The Execution of the New Plan: Their new plan is to separate and then see each other again in six months.

**Final Image:** At the beginning, they didn't know each other, but they were going in the same direction. Now, they are in love and heartbroken, traveling in opposite directions. Jesse has found out that he is a romantic at heart, and Céline has discovered that she is more rational that she once thought, certifying the "two-hander" nature of the film: meeting another has indeed changed them forever. You may be wondering... did they finally see each other as planned? Well, to find out, you'll need to watch the rest of the trilogy... and fall in love, if only briefly, with Jesse and Céline again.

## THE READER (2008)

"Epic Love" stories, as defined by Blake, are those in which "sweeping events bring our lovers together"... and also set them apart. We are clearly talking about the necessary "complication" for our film's couple of buddies, which usually implies such dramatic settings as wars, difficult times and complicated environments.

These epics may span for many years, horizons or situations — in this case, almost four decades. In it, we have an "incomplete hero" in teenager Michael Berg, who falls in love with tram conductor Hanna Schmitz, bringing many complications into their lives: age, environment, and especially... secrecy.

Kate Winslet won a great number of awards for her fantastic, restrained performance in playing the crude yet sensitive lover of stories, who has a very complicated past. Both Colin Firth and young David Kross do justice to their roles as well, infusing their characters with sadness, melancholy and tension.

Holocaust, German guilt, shame and forgiveness are some of the ingredients of this German/US co-production featuring the talented English director Stephen Daldry (*The Hours*, *Billy Elliot*), and playwright and screenwriter Sir David Hare, adapting the novel by Bernhard Schlink — an undeniable mixture of talents and awards! So what are you waiting for? Start reading this Beat Sheet... or have someone special read it to you.

BL Type: Epic Love

BL Cousins: *The Unbearable Lightness of Being*, *Paradise Now*, *Wuthering Heights*, *Hiroshima Mon Amour*, *The Boy in the Striped Pajamas*

THE READER
*Based on the book by* Bernhard Schlink
*Screenplay by* David Hare
*Directed by* Stephen Daldry

**Opening Image**: Berlin, 1995. A man carefully sets down breakfast for a much younger woman, with whom he has spent the night. As we will see in our Theme Stated, she complains about her inability to know what he is thinking. And that is the main change our character will undergo: from being closed-off toward others to opening up... a change that will take him almost 40 years.

**Theme Stated**: "Does any woman ever stay long enough to find out what the hell goes on in your head?" asks Michael Berg's (Colin Firth) apparent one-night stand. In this film, we will focus on two things about Michael: his inability to settle down with a woman (because, as we will find out, he has not forgotten a certain "counterpart") and the inability to open up and reveal his deepest secret — because secrets, and the consequences of keeping them, are the theme of this movie.

**Set-Up**: Back in 1958, we meet young Michael (David Kross), a "kid" living in postwar reconstruction Germany. He feels sick during a tram trip and is helped in a classic "Save the Cat!" moment by tough Hanna Schmitz (Kate Winslet), who embraces him and takes him to his home. After spending some months there while recovering from scarlet fever, Michael visits Hanna to thank her. Although she seems distant, Hannah lets him see her changing clothes and Michael, ashamed, flees.

**B Story**: Our B Story involves, obviously, Michael and Hanna, an unlikely couple "set apart" by many circumstances, the most obvious one being their age. For this and other reasons, their relationship will be built upon secrecy, a further "complication" that will also keep them together.

**Catalyst**: Michael returns to Hanna's home but gets dirty with charcoal. She tells him to clean himself in her bathtub, but then she appears naked and embraces him. They make love for the first time.

**Debate**: Is it possible that two people of different age, social class and upbringing can love each other? For now, it all seems to be about sex for them, and Michael returns there after school so that he can see her more. The secret builds: Michael does not tell anything to anyone, neither family nor friends, starting to isolate himself with Hanna. Also, when he asks to know her name, she suddenly becomes serious. "You look so suspicious," he says. He still doesn't know how many secrets Hannah hides. And if there were any kind of thematic doubt, Michael's teacher says, "The notion of secrecy is central to Western Literature." Someone said secrecy *and* literature? Michael starts reading a book to Hanna, and she seems delighted. They still don't know how important reading will be for their lives.

**Break into Two**: They argue bitterly over a misunderstanding, and Hanna says, "You don't matter enough to upset me." Michael cries and tells her that they have been together for a month and that he loves her. He asks her if she feels the same way, and she concedes. Their true "Epic Love" story has officially begun!

**Fun and Games**: What is it like for a teenager's first love to be with an older woman? And can it be sustained with sex, laughs and reading aloud? The *promise of the premise* (and the film's title) are delivered when she decides to have him read aloud to her before each sex session. And Fun they have! It is laughter, tears and enjoyment for them while exploring the world of books. More classic Fun and Games moments come when they go for a cycling holiday, when Hanna cries upon hearing children singing in church and when he writes a poem about her. Also, Michael has interactions with his classmates at school, but he leaves them, including a girl who has a crush on him, to be with Hanna every day.

**Midpoint**: A particularly long Midpoint starts when Hanna gets a promotion at work but seems distressed by it. Soon, she and Michael have a nasty argument but they seem to make amends by having sex. Soon after, he suffers a *false defeat* when Hanna moves away without telling him. He finds himself alone and with no friends, and in a flash forward to 1995, a mature Michael performs his *public coming out* during a "Midpoint celebration" at a restaurant with his daughter: "I am not open with anyone." Back again in time, now in 1966, Michael is shown studying at law school, still seemingly alone. Has he forgotten Hanna?

**Bad Guys Close In**: The Bad Guys come in many shapes and sizes for Michael when he learns that Hanna is being put on trial — she used to be a SS guard at Auschwitz and during the infamous Death Marches! And what's worse, at the trial he discovers that the rest of the defendants have decided to accuse Hanna of plotting it all. When a key piece of evidence involves Hanna's signature and Hanna accepts blame, Michael realizes she liked to be read to because she is illiterate. But Hannah decides to keep her inability to read and write a secret, even if it means a life sentence. Meanwhile, Michael knows he could help her if he told the judge that Hanna is illiterate, but he struggles with "internal" Bad Guys. He is determined to keep their relationship secret because of the shame it would mean to disclose that he was with someone who had such a terrible past. Meanwhile, 1970s Michael has divorced and has been unable to forget Hanna, so even though he will not talk to her, he starts sending her tapes of him reading the books they loved. Hanna uses the books to teach herself to read and write, and she sends letters to Michael, but he never answers. In the 1980s, Hanna is about to be released from prison, and they finally reunite, but Michael hides his feelings for her, his shame about her past too great. "That's over now, isn't it?" she asks.

**All Is Lost**: Unable to bear the fact that nothing will ever be the same with Michael, Hanna hangs herself in her cell, symbolically stepping on some books to achieve that sad demise.

**Dark Night of the Soul**: Michael receives the news of her death and realizes how much they loved each other. He breaks down, starting to show his feelings for the first time.

**Break into Three**: In her last letter, Hanna only wrote "Hello" to Michael, but she also gave him a mission to complete.

**Finale**:

1. Gathering the Team: Michael travels to New York to meet Ilana Mather (Lena Olin), one of the few survivors of the group that Hanna guarded when she was an SS to give Ilana the money that Hanna saved during her imprisonment.

2. Executing the Plan: Michael tells Ilana about the trial and tries to convince her that Hannah was illiterate during the war, attempting to clear her name, at least in that regard.

3. High Tower Surprise: On the defensive, Ilana asks Michael, "Why don't you start by being honest with me? What was the nature of your friendship?" Michael is asked to be sincere and disclose the truth.

4. Dig, Deep Down: He "digs, deep down" to open up to someone about their secret love for the first time: "When I was young, I had an affair with Hanna... I've never told anyone."

5. The Execution of the New Plan: Acting on a suggestion by Ilana, his "new plan" is to put the money Hanna left in an organization to encourage literacy, as a means of poetic justice.

**Final Image**: Michael meets with his daughter again and takes her to the old church where Hanna cried upon hearing the choir. He starts telling his daughter about the affair with Hanna. Doing so, he ends a 37-year silence, overcoming his shame and acknowledging that he had always loved Hanna... and he always will.

## BLUE IS THE WARMEST COLOR (2013)

It's not every day that a French indie film receives words of praise from Hollywood king Steven Spielberg, who, as part of the 2013 Cannes Festival judging panel, publicly lauded this film "of deep love and deep heartbreak." It not only went on to win the Palme d'Or, but it was given to the director AND to its two lead actresses, a first in the festival's history.

It is also a story of "Forbidden Love," which has natural ties with doomed love films like *Brokeback Mountain* or the various versions of *Romeo and Juliet*. It is "forbidden" because in both romance dramas and real life, many passionate loves are simply not meant to happen.

The film is also particularly long, just a minute short of three hours, but as you can guess, this doesn't affect its strict adherence to our Blake Snyder Beat Sheet. It only serves to demonstrate that you can have the freedom to play around with the beats and their impact, for example, like having a particularly long Break into Three.

All the rest of the elements are also present: an "incomplete hero" who must figure out her life and sexuality, a bizarre "counterpart" who has everything already figured out and possesses qualities that the hero needs, and a "complication" (Adèle's youth and lack of experience) that brings them together and — at the same time — sets them apart. So let's enjoy this terrific film and... fade to blue!

BL Type: Forbidden Love

BL Cousins: *Harold and Maude*, *The Graduate*, *Let the Right One In*, *Benny & Joon*, *My Beautiful Laundrette*

## BLUE IS THE WARMEST COLOR

*Based on the graphic novel by* Julie Maroh
*Screenplay, adaptation and dialogue by* Abdellatif Kechiche and Ghalia Lacroix
*Directed by* Abdellatif Kechiche

**Opening Image**: Adèle (Exarchopoulos) leaves home early in the morning and walks to the bus stop in the distance. This is our first "bookend," or Opening Image, since our ending will be a very similar one, with the distinction that Adèle will be a very different woman — her life will have "changed for having known another."

**Theme Stated**: In class, the teacher asks, "When you cross paths and you both exchange glances spontaneously, like with love at first sight, is there something less or more in your heart?" This is the theme of our story, and as we will see, relationships are complicated and involve both gaining and losing.

**Set-Up**: We get a better glimpse of Adèle's life. She seems like a good student; she is pretty and popular and causes no trouble to her parents. She has some *things that need fixing*, like how easily influenced she is by her nosy girlfriends, who place so much peer pressure on her that she hooks up with a boy named Thomas whom she doesn't really like.

**Catalyst**: Adèle's world is shaken. Just like her teacher set up for us, she crosses a stranger — a girl with blue hair, a lesbian who seems so different from her — and they exchange an intense glance. Enter the "unique and bizarre" counterpart for our hero.

**Debate**: The inner Debate becomes an intense one for Adèle, since she apparently has always been heterosexual. She decides to date Thomas, but that night she masturbates thinking about the blue-haired girl. At school her friends push her even more, so that she ends up having sex with the boy. However, she feels "messed up and crazy," so she sorts out her thoughts with her gay friend Valentin. Further doubts arise when a female friend kisses Adèle and afterwards claims it was not to be taken seriously. Adèle feels depressed, so Valentin takes her to a gay bar.

**Break into Two**: Fascinated to see so many gay people living openly, Adèle is later surprised to glimpse the blue-haired girl in the street. Curious, she follows her and makes the proactive decision to enter a lesbian bar, thus also entering the *upside-down world* of Act Two.

**B Story**: At the bar, she finds the blue-haired girl, Emma (Léa Seydoux). She is a Fine Arts student from a better upbringing, is well-cultured and ambitious, but also older than Adèle. They seem too different, don't they? But it is clear that there is an electrifying connection between them. Emma leaves with a girl who appears to be her current girlfriend but asks what school Adèle attends.

**Fun and Games**: As is typical in "Buddy Love" stories, the Fun and Games section of the script becomes the opportunity to explore the world of the friend, lover or colleague who is about to change the hero's life. In Adèle's case, this happens merrily (as when they exchange conversations linking Sartre to Bob Marley), but also unhappily — when her nosy friends see Adèle with Emma, they confront her and she has to defend herself. Also, Emma won't kiss Adèle on the lips, implying she is still dating another person, an important set-up for later. Adèle starts spending more time with Emma, who takes her to museums and opens a new world of culture and sensibility to her.

**Midpoint**: After a picnic in which they finally kiss, *Sex at 60* occurs, shown in the controversial but naturalistic way the movie became famous for. There is a *public coming out* (pun intended) when Adèle and Emma attend the Gay Pride Parade. It is also a *false victory*, since their relationship is flourishing and Adèle is at ease as a lesbian — further supported when they have a "Midpoint party" at the home of Emma's parents, who are nice, well-cultured, open-minded, and accept the girls and their lifestyle.

**Bad Guys Close In**: What are the obvious Bad Guys in a relationship? Doubt, jealousy and temptation. First, the couple has dinner at Adele's parents' house, where Emma deduces that Adèle has not talked to her parents about their relationship, forcing Emma to pretend that they are only friends and that she has a boyfriend. Not only that, Adèle's parents frown upon Emma's choice of painting as a profession. Adèle is now a practicing teacher and temptation courts her in the form of one of her colleagues, whose advances she has to dodge but is obviously flattered by. And when they have a party with Emma's artist friends, Adèle can't help but feel out of place, also being hit on by Samir, an actor. Jealousy crawls in the distance when Adèle sees Emma flirting with Lise, an old friend, who is pregnant. That night, Emma tells Adèle that she should become a writer, further showing their differences and how she does not really appreciate Adèle's teaching career. Soon after, when Emma is working at Lise's, Adèle gives in to temptation and ends up kissing (and probably more than that) her male colleague.

**All Is Lost**: *Oh la la!* Adèle arrives home some time later and discovers that Emma knows about her infidelities. Emma calls her a liar and kicks her out of her home and her life.

**Dark Night of the Soul**: In a classic Dark Night of the Soul moment, Adèle cries alone at night. When the semester ends, she enrolls in summer school, seemingly to avoid being alone. Has she forgotten Emma?

**Break into Three**: It is implied that around three years have passed when Adèle and Emma reunite at a bar. In this very long (almost 15 minutes!) and intense Break into Three, *A and B Stories cross* as they acknowledge their feelings — Adèle still loves her, and Emma has strong feelings, but she is in a fulfilling relationship with Lise. She tells Adèle that she will always have a place in her heart, then she leaves as Adèle breaks down in tears.

**Finale:**

1. Gathering the Team: Some time has passed, and Adèle has become a full-time teacher, as she wanted. She puts on make-up and a bright blue dress, "gathering her (seduction) tools."

2. Executing the Plan: Adèle's plan consists of attending Emma's opening exhibition to see if she can win her back.

3. High Tower Surprise: Their past passion and closeness seem lost, as Emma does not really pay attention to her; in fact, Emma (symbolically not having blue hair anymore) seems bothered by her presence and dedicated to Lise.

4. Dig, Deep Down: Adèle "digs, deep down" to leave the place when she bumps into Samir, who had flirted with her at the party earlier. Even if she seems interested, now that she is left alone again...

5. The Execution of the New Plan: ... Adèle realizes it is time to move on. Samir tries to find her, but takes the wrong way.

**Final Image:** As in the beginning, Adèle is a woman walking alone toward the horizon, but this time against a symbolic sunset. We know that she is a very different person, and we realize that she is finally able to leave behind the one who completed her. She may be alone, but she is ready to face the future.

 The "High Tower Surprise" is a thrilling surprise for the bad guys — and the audience — in the Finale of *The French Connection*.

# 7 WHYDUNIT

The world of tough private detectives, men in trench coats, blonde *femme fatales*, expressionist lighting, sax music at night, dark motivations, gun shots and endless double whiskies are not really the first things that come to mind when we talk of indie film, are they?

But when you think of independent masterpieces like *Brick* by Rian Johnson (which Blake covered in *Save the Cat!® Goes to the Movies*), you'll realize that the human obsession to find the answer to every deep mystery, and our willingness to step toward the darkest corners of morality to unveil the enigma, is as current in non-mainstream film as in Hollywood — it is after all, a dark reflection of ourselves.

Thus we present you the "Whydunit," a most classic of genres, present in our culture since the mythical times of Osiris, Cain and Oedipus — who did it, and more importantly, why? We crave the revelation and will do anything in our power to discover it, even if darkness must swallow us to do so.

The Whydunit genre corresponds with the type of story in which a **detective** must discover a **secret** that is at the core of the case, but most importantly, he or she will have to perform a **dark turn** to crack the mystery that will show us "what evil lurks in the hearts of men."

So let's get to know the components of this genre better. To start, we need a **detective**, a character who may work as such or not, so that it's quite possible our POV character is an amateur sleuth. What's important is that our detective usually "thinks he has seen it all, but is unprepared for what he'll find," meaning that not even the toughest, most jaded private dick could anticipate the grimness he or she will unveil. Perhaps unsurprisingly, this revelation usually does not change our main characters, as their cynical view of the world is just confirmed. Yet even if *they* do not change — look in vain for any trace of change at the end in the faces of Michael Caine as Jack Carter in *Get Carter* or Gene Hackman as "Popeye" Doyle in *The French Connection* — *we* change watching them. That is the power of the Whydunit.

The detective usually "unveils the clues," sharing each one with us as we accompany him on his trip into the "ever smaller chambers of a Nautilus shell," as he strives to find the answer to a **secret**. This is an enigma, a question that must be uncovered — something life-threatening, as who planted the bomb in *Michael Clayton*'s car, who murdered the hero's wife in *The Constant Gardener*, who kidnapped the main character for 15 years and why in *Old Boy,* or something, well, simpler like who "micturated" upon the Dude's rug in *The Big Lebowski*. No matter what, the secret's lure is so strong that the detective will do anything to know the answer... including breaking the rules.

The third element of this genre, the detective's **dark turn**, is the particular moment where the pursuit of the secret makes the hero choose a "wrong way"— breaking the rules of trust (as in *Michael Clayton*), the rules of the underworld class (*Get Carter*) or keeping with the investigation even though you know it can destroy you (*Pi*). In any of these cases, going against the rules means that he is setting himself up as "part of the crime," or will make us realize he has been "guilty of a similar crime all along." Thus, the Whydunit detectives become part of the darkness they are investigating.

Of course, mysteries and evil await in many shapes and sizes so as always, we have five types of Whydunits to investigate. The first one is the **Political Whydunit**. As its name suggests, politics are our chosen realm, but not only governmental — any kind of corporate, industrial or law-related world will serve our purpose. That's the case in Costa-Gavras's '70s masterpiece *Missing*, big pharma under-world-set *The Constant Gardener*, properly political *Tinker Tailor Soldier Spy*, the power games dealt inside a medieval abbey in *The Name of the Rose*, or our chosen one, *Michael Clayton*, in which lawyers are not always on the correct side of the law.

Our setting could even be a nonexistent, surreal or made-up world, including dreams, hallucinations or the trippy fantastic environments in which some protagonists (*and* directors) live. As mainstream examples of the **Fantasy Whydunit**, Blake cited *Blade Runner*, *Who Framed Roger Rabbit* or *The Sixth Sense*; as our indie, auteur and cult examples, we will reference David Lynch's *Mulholland Drive*, Alejandro Amenábar's *Abre los Ojos* (remade in the commercial film realm as *Vanilla Sky*) and the so visually powerful debut of Darren Aronofski, *Pi*.

Cop Whydunits speak for themselves. In this subgenre, it is a lawman who will have to unveil the "secret" as part of his everyday job, but this case will be the most important and shocking of his or her career. The Coen's *Fargo* is one of the best examples, along with Friedkin's *The French Connection*, the Korean masterpiece *Memories of Murder* and the French series *Crimson Rivers*.

On the other hand, the **Personal Whydunit** is solved by an individual who is *not* a cop, but an amateur sleuth or someone who might even be from the other side of the law. What matters is their drive and their "dark turn," as we see in Argentina's *The Secret in Her Eyes*, Austria's (and Haneke's) *Caché*, Spain's *Thesis*, France's controversial *Irreversible* and our groovy British classic *Get Carter*.

Finally, the classic noir detective aesthetics or narrative devices will have a genre of its own, if only in our European, auteur or indie realm. It's called **Film Noir Whydunit**, and the well-known look, characters and plots of the dark classics of Hollywood's Golden Age, along with the hardboiled worlds of Hammett, Cain and Chandler will be a mirror for these productions. Just watch all-time French classic *Le Samourai* or more modern proposals like the *Millenium* trilogy (preferably the Swedish version), *Blood Simple*, the blue-period films of Takeshi Kitano and, even though it may not seem like it in the first place, *The Big Lebowski*.

Keep in mind that our plot is usually concerned with "turning over the cards," that is, showing us the clues as the detectives unveil them, and you will find that in many instances, the sleuth will start investigating one mystery to find another one that encompasses the first. We call this a **case within a case** that lets us — and the detective — discover what has been the story (and often the theme) all along.

Finally, a piece of advice from Blake if you're writing a Whydunit: figure out who, what, when, where and why your bad guy did it... and make your gumshoe follow those steps in reverse.

## WHY DID THEY DUNIT?

Do you have what it takes to solve the mystery, both in your script and in your case? You'll need:

1. A "detective," an amateur or a pro who thinks he has seen it all but is "unprepared for what he'll find."

2. A "secret" to uncover, one that our sleuth is so obsessed with that when "turning over the cards" he cannot help but go on... and we cannot help but watch.

3. A "dark turn" in which he will break his own rules, his group's or society's, showing that his drive is an obsessive one and thus making him "part of the crime."

Beware of who you find in that last dark chamber! What if you find... yourself?

## MICHAEL CLAYTON (2007)

It is always good news when an experienced screenwriter takes the director's seat, even if it's his first feature, as in the case of Tony Gilroy and *Michael Clayton*. Add to the mix Sydney Pollack, Anthony Minghella and Steven Soderbergh as producers and a cast that includes George Clooney, Tilda Swinton and Tom Wilkinson... and its success was not a surprise.

The resulting film was nominated for seven Academy Awards® (including Best Picture, Best Director and Best Original Screenplay). And there's no doubt about it, it's a wonderful movie whose narrative, universe and visual style made it an instant classic.

It's also a great example of our "Political Whydunit" subgenre, taking place in the realm of "governmental or corporate power," in this case, law firms, organizations, multinationals — you get it! So we're talking about "thriller" in its most traditional sense.

Of course, *Michael Clayton* includes all our elements: a "detective" in the form of a lawyer who has seen it all, because his work deals with complex schemes, who finds himself making a "dark turn" to solve a "case within a case," that is, to reveal a "secret" that very powerful and wealthy people want to keep hidden. But Michael, just like us, needs to know the secret. Will he be changed by the revelation?

W Type: Political Whydunit

W Cousins: *Z*, *Good Night and Good Luck*, *The Quiet American*, *The Constant Gardener*, *The Name of the Rose*

MICHAEL CLAYTON
*Written and Directed by* Tony Gilroy

**Opening Image:** The "reborn lawyer" monologue of Arthur Edens (Tom Wilkinson), a very disturbed man, opens the film, quite the opposite of what we will see at the end. We also find an anxious woman, Karen Crowder (Tilda Swinton), hiding in a bathroom. And finally, in the middle of the night, we see the busy offices of a law firm knee-deep in a crisis, full of nervous people who have sold their souls to their jobs. In this world, can you remain sane... let alone be decent?

**Theme Stated**: "Who else could be trusted?" says Arthur, referring to Michael Clayton (George Clooney). Trust is the theme of this film, but would you rely on the words of such a distressed man as Arthur? To do so would surely take the kind of loyalty and faith one can only put in friends and family. Yet can your own work disturb you so much that you become the opposite — untrustworthy?

**Set-Up**: Enter lawyer and "fixer" Michael Clayton, a man who deals with the dirty work at the law firm. Soon we realize that Michael, drinking and playing high-stakes poker, must ironically have personal *things that need fixing*: he has gambling debts and he invested in his recovering, drug-addict brother Timmy's restaurant, but Timmy relapsed, the restaurant closed, and Michael owes Timmy's loan sharks $75,000. So why does everybody trust Michael? Soon, we understand as we witness his charm, seeming serenity, fast decision-making skills and clarity of mind when dealing with a difficult client. Yet he still seems to be in a *Stasis=Death* situation when he says he only considers himself a "janitor." Meet our cynical "detective" who thinks he has seen it all, and get ready to discover how unprepared he is for what is about to happen.

**Catalyst**: While driving at dawn, Michael stops and leaves his car, impressed by the magnificent view of some horses in a field. Suddenly, his car explodes! And Michael has to run.

**Debate**: What a way to start our Debate section! What has happened? Why has someone tried to kill Michael? The film cuts to a flashback four days earlier, helping us to consider possible answers. More characters are introduced, like his young son, who is obsessed with an adventure novel in which no one can be trusted. "Sounds familiar," Michael tells him. At work, he expertly fixes other people's problems, though he seems weary of it. There is much stress and pressure involved, which in the past drove him to a gambling addiction. At the same time, we meet Karen, General Counselor for U-North (an agricultural products conglomerate), a woman not unlike Michael, also under a lot of pressure.

**Break into Two**: Arthur, legendary senior litigating partner of the firm, and the man of the distressed opening monologue, has apparently stripped naked while giving a deposition. Michael "gets the case" and has to go to Milwaukee to "fix" it. The "case within a case" has begun, and there is "no turning back," as Arthur holds the "secret" Michael will have to uncover.

**B Story**: The B Story pertains to both men and the trust they have in each other. Michael finds Arthur, who claims that he has been working about 12% of his life on a case defending the reputation of U-North, who he believes to be responsible for the death of hundreds of farmers... at the same time while crazily proclaiming he is "Shiva, the God of Death." Can Michael trust a man like him?

**Fun and Games**: The exploration of how work, pressure and stress can affect people and even turn them crazy is the *promise of the premise* that this beat delivers — not only because we see a video of Arthur getting naked, but also because this section deals with the defense of the U-North case he was working on. Karen, who must "fix" it, meets Michael and decides that neither he nor Arthur are trustworthy. Karen's suspicions are confirmed when she illegally gets Arthur's briefcase and finds a memo about a product made by U-North that turns out to be carcinogenic — this is the "secret" she will have to hide. Michael soon learns that Arthur has escaped his careful watch, and Karen seeks Mr. Verne, a kind of "fixer" like Michael, but with seemingly less scruples. Verne starts monitoring Arthur's house and calls, and their suspicions become very real: Arthur is building a case against U-North.

**Midpoint**: Michael suffers a *false defeat* when he can only get $12,000 to pay off his brother's debt and is given a *ticking clock* warning: he has seven days to get the rest of the money. He *goes public* when he tells his boss Marty that he is "45 years old and broke" and fears losing his job in a soon-to-happen merger. Michael asks for a loan, but all he gets is a week to find Arthur to secure his own job. Talk about *raising the stakes*!

**Bad Guys Close In**: Michael has to find his mentor Arthur no matter what, but when he finally does, the latter uses his vast legal knowledge to keep Michael at a distance: their friendship is "disintegrating." Michael tells Arthur, "I'm not the enemy." And Arthur's response, "Then who are you?" strikes at the core of Michael's internal struggle.

The Bad Guys Close In when Arthur leaves a message at the firm's answering machine telling about the carcinogen, prompting Karen to nervously ask Mr. Verne to kill him in order to cleap-up the mess once and for all. Soon, Arthur is dead, and of course, it has been staged to look like suicide. Michael blames himself for the death of his friend and visits a key witness against U-North, noting that it made no sense for Arthur to commit suicide at that stage in the case. So our "detective" performs his "dark turn" against both his personal and his family's beliefs when he asks his policeman brother to give him a seal to trespass into Arthur's apartment. There, he discovers a seemingly unrelated clue inside a copy of the same book his son was reading: a receipt from a copy shop... and something we may find familiar (remember our Catalyst) — an illustration of horses on a hill. Just as Michael is taking this in, a voice yells, "Freeze!"

**All Is Lost**: Michael is arrested, so he will not be able to carry on with his investigation of Arthur's documents. The *whiff of death* surrounds the case as he realizes he may never find answers to the "secret."

**Dark Night of the Soul**: Michael contemplates the extent of his options when his angry brother bails him out, disappointed for having trusted him, recalling the theme.

**Break into Three**: Michael presses on and follows his last clue: the copy shop receipt. And *A and B stories cross* when he discovers Arthur's legacy: a memo explaining U-North's plans to keep the carcinogen secret. This sounds like Break into Three material because now Michael has a way to prove that his mentor was not (totally) crazy! But at the office, Marty offers Michael the $80,000 he requested earlier, which comes with a three-year contract. Michael decides not to give Marty the memo, knowing he would lose everything. Meanwhile, Karen has gotten the memo, too.

**Finale**:

1. Gathering the Team: Michael has a plan: he gathers the money and pays the loan shark, afterwards going to the poker room we saw at the beginning. The Bad Guys have gathered too, to kill Michael.

2. Executing the Plan: Michael leaves the game early, demonstrating that maybe he won't relapse after all. He gets a call from work, thus executing his plan of continuing to work for the company. Meanwhile, Mr. Verne sets a bomb in his car.

3. High Tower Surprise: Back in the present at our "horses on the hill" location, the car explodes. The baddies think that he has been killed, and Michael supports this notion by throwing his belongings into the burning car.

4. Dig, Deep Down: Michael "digs, deep down" when he trusts his drug-addicted brother (the one most likely to fail him) to help him at the most dangerous time. But after having paid the loan sharks, it is his brother who thanks him.

5. The Execution of the New Plan: Michael's new plan involves confronting Karen and making her believe that it's easier to buy him than to kill him. When she complies and trusts him, attempting to buy him off, he reveals that he was recording the conversation and his policeman brother arrests her. Michael has shown what kind of a person he's chosen to be.

**Final Image:** Michael gets in a taxi and tells the driver to give him $50 worth of a drive. We began with a very distressed man, and we are ending with an apparently calm one. As in most "Whydunits," our "detective" has not changed, but rather we have — thanks to the revelation. Is he more cynical than before? We must wonder, as in the unforgettable last shot, for only a second... Michael Clayton smiles.

## Pi (1998)

Darren Aronofsky is, no doubt, one of the most interesting filmmakers and auteurs that emerged in the late '90s. He's the living example of how you can start in the independent realm with a self-financed first film, and with a budget of about $68,000, produce a film that is multi-awarded and launches a mainstream career.

This film is also a good example of our "Fantasy Whydunit" subgenre, one in which the "secret" is investigated in a magical, supernatural or hallucinated world, like the surrealistic Chinatown that our main character inhabits along with his constant feelings of paranoia, social anxiety disorder and hallucinations.

Maximillian Cohen is our "detective," one who thinks he has "seen it all" about the real world and is only interested in mathematics. Well, he is truly unprepared for what he will find, which goes beyond math. And while you can tick the "cynical" box too, in this case he will change at the end — if only at a great loss.

With a "secret" that must be uncovered — apparently a long string of random numbers — and a classic "case within a case" scenario, what Max is looking for turns out to be much more than he expects. And to discover it, of course, he will have to make that dreaded "dark turn" that causes him to become part of the darkness that falls... when you stare too hard at the sun.

W Type: Fantasy Whydunit

W Cousins: *The Naked Lunch*, *Open Your Eyes* (*Abre los ojos*), *Mulholland Drive*, *eXistenZ*, *Alphaville*

Pi
*Story by* Darren Aronofsky and Sean Gullette and Eric Watson
*Written and directed by* Darren Aronofsky

**Opening Image:** Our "detective" to be, Max Cohen (Sean Gullette) is waking up, nose bleeding, an image that we will see repeatedly. But has he really woken up? Max suffers massive headaches that make him pass out, but he is also paranoid and hallucinates — this makes up the Fantasy of the Whydunit. At the end of the film, we will see if he has really "woken up"... to life.

**Theme Stated:** "When I was a little kid, my mother told me not to stare into the sun," Max narrates. Looking into the sun almost blinded him, but he doesn't realize that learning about certain "secrets" is similar to staring at a star — we can end up blind or worse. Max will have to learn this lesson, and this time, for real.

**Set-Up:** We get to know Max better and the many *things that need fixing* in his life. He lives alone, is reclusive, unemployed, dirty, and does not take care of himself; his entire room is filled with wires and circuits, a symbol of his ignoring all that is not mathematics in life. However, he has a "Save the Cat!" moment by playing math games with a little girl while awkwardly ignoring his sweet neighbor Devi's (Samia Shohaib) kindness. Max tells us that he thinks "mathematics are the language of nature," so he is determined to find a pattern behind everything, for example, the stock market. He does not want to get rich, but only wants to crack the code. He looks at the trees, but doesn't seem to see beauty, only numbers. Max, who is Jewish, has a chance encounter with a Hasidic Jew, Lenny (Benk Shenkman), and after having another panic attack, notices he is being followed by a strange woman from Wall Street. But is it all real or just paranoia?

**Catalyst:** "Stop thinking. Just feel. Use your intuition." This is what mentor Sol ("sun" in Spanish) tells Max when they meet to play the Japanese game *go*. But as we will see, ceasing to think and to just feel is precisely what Max finds difficult. Will he achieve this goal by the end?

**B Story**: Our B Story or "mentor love story" pertains to Sol. As we can deduce, he used to be a great mathematician who hastily worked to find patterns in the number Pi, but never found them. Retired after suffering a stroke, he seems to live a nice life among his books and tropical fish.

**Debate**: Can Max follow Sol's healthy advice? Or is he really more interested in surpassing him? Who is the strange woman that Max avoids? He Debates with himself why Sol quit his research when "he was so close to seeing Pi for what it really is." Why did Sol apparently stop believing when he almost had the answer? Further questions arise when Lenny tells Max that he works with numbers too; he is trying to crack a code that the Qabalah may contain.

**Break into Two**: Max has a revelation and decides to apply a new theory to his work, apparently basing it on the Golden Ratio. But before hitting the "enter" key on his computer to execute the calculations, he hesitates when he hears Devi making love in the next room. Those are the real-world feelings he is missing! Even so, he pushes the key and enters Act Two.

**Fun and Games**: His powerful computer, aptly named Euclid, melts down when trying to make the new calculations and spits out a printed paper with a seemingly random string of numbers. Max deems it an error and throws it away, noting a strange secretion on the computer. Meanwhile, Sol keeps advising him to relax to get perspective or he will become blocked, but Max realizes that part of Euclid's results were true. Now the "secret" that he has to unveil is clear, as the "case within a case." What was the string of numbers? Can he use it to predict the stock market's patterns? He keeps having hallucinations and has to dodge the woman again. To avoid her, he ends up going with Lenny to the synagogue, where he finds a new lead: the pattern they are looking for in the Torah is 216 digits long, just as the one Euclid found. However, Sol disapproves and thinks that Max can end up as a numerologist if he loses scientific rigor. The Wall Street woman, Marcy, tempts him with a new chip that could make his computer work again.

**Midpoint**: Agitated from this "Attention Attraction," Max gets one of his attacks, this time *in public*. He tries to find out if a hallucination is real and ends up waking up near Coney Island. For a moment, he feels at peace, far from his seclusion and the city — at last connecting with nature. He seems to be getting the "knowledge that he has to change," but before he can embrace the notion, a nautilus shell gives him a new idea. At home, he studies the strange secretion under the microscope and achieves a *false victory*; he finds spirals and the secretion seems to be organic! He may be onto something big.

**Bad Guys Close In**: Obsession further pushes the "disintegration of the world" for Max. He ignores Devi (he is "losing an ally") and performs a double "dark turn": first he calls Lenny to help with the Torah code (thus being anti-scientific), then he accepts Marcy's chip in exchange for information. When Max is about to press "enter" again, he hesitates, as if knowing the consequences. The computer fails again, he hears Devi having sex again, and Max finds a strange bulging vein on the side of his head. Still, he gets the code again and learns it by heart.

**All Is Lost**: After memorizing the code, all goes white — he still does not know it, but getting the number into his head was dangerous. All Is further Lost when he wakes up and finds Devi in his apartment, but he kicks her out. No one will care about him now.

**Dark Night of the Soul**: Max contemplates himself in the mirror. He is "beaten and he knows it." He has shaved his head and is studying an anatomy book, and even though we don't understand why, we are sure it is bad news.

**Break into Three**: Max continues studying the stock market and realizes that he is able to predict stocks' futures: the number did something to his mind! *A and B stories cross* as he visits Sol, and has a *Moment of Clarity*. Before showing him the numbers, the computer had become self-conscious. Max insists on investigating, and Sol warns that it could destroy him.

**Finale:**

1. Gathering the Team: Max returns home, but on the way he has to flee from Marcy and her thugs — the stock market is crashing because they are using Max's incomplete number. Lenny appears to save Max, but in fact kidnaps him.

2. Executing the Plan: At the synagogue, the rabbi reveals to Max that the number may be the name of God, but he "executes his plan" of refusing to reveal it.

3. High Tower Surprise: Max returns to tell Sol about his discovery, but finds that Sol has died! It turns out that Sol had returned to the investigation about the number, and it killed him.

4. Dig, Deep Down: Now Max knows what can happen to him, and at home, he is about to have another attack. But this time, he "digs, deep down," avoids taking meds and destroys the computer. He has a vision and, upon waking up, burns the number. Even so, it is still in his mind. So he "digs, further down" and...

5. The Execution of the New Plan: ..."executes his new plan," performing a trephination on himself with a power drill.

**Final Image:** Max is sitting in the park, again looking at the leaves. He does not see patterns and numbers. As he plays the math game with his little neighbor, he is unable to perform the mental calculations of his past. Blissfully ignorant, now he can smile, relax and enjoy life.

## THE FRENCH CONNECTION (1971)

Legend says that director William Friedkin once argued with Howard Hawks, who defied him to film a chase unlike anything that had been done before. Today, *The French Connection* is famous for its gritty realism, wonderful performances, cold documentary style and, of course, its foot and car chases — Friedkin won!

It's also a good example of our police procedural subgenre, which we call "Cop Whydunit." In these films, a lawman decides to solve a case but progressively finds himself sucked into the "secret" he is trying to uncover, at some point performing a "dark turn," which involves breaking society's or his own rules, setting himself up to be part of the crime.

The "secret" in this case involves a Lincoln Continental car and the drugs that could be hidden inside, but our policemen will only find them after they realize they have a "case within a case." To crack it, they will have to go on a "trip into the ever-smaller chambers of a nautilus shell," which involves putting their sanity at stake.

The investigation will not leave us, however, with a changed man: our "detectives" are a kind of narrator, an avatar for that dark trip we will experience via their discoveries. And cynical as they are, no matter how dark the last revelation in the last chamber, they will probably not change — we will do that for them.

W Type: Cop Whydunit

W Cousins: *Insomnia*, *Violent Cop*, *The Offence*, *Fargo*, *Memories of Murder*

THE FRENCH CONNECTION
*Based on the book by* Robin Moore
*Screenplay by* Ernest Tidyman
*Directed by* William Friedkin

**Opening Image:** The film begins and ends with the killing of a policeman, the first being the one who was tailing French drug dealer Alain Charnier (Fernando Rey). Also, pay attention to the magnificent Lincoln Continental so out of place in 1971 Marseille. Seldom have cars had so much prominence in a film as in this one, and this particular automobile holds our "secret."

**Theme Stated:** "Never trust anyone," says Jimmy "Popeye" Doyle (Gene Hackman) to his partner Buddy "Cloudy" Russo (Roy Scheider), based on real-life cops Eddie Egan and Sonny Grosso, respectively. Yes, it is true that in the world of criminals, no one should be trusted, but does the theme also apply to Popeye himself? As we will see, no matter how a good detective Popeye is, the "case" and the "dark chambers" he will visit can make him untrustworthy.

**Set-Up:** Our "detectives," Popeye and Cloudy, are a couple of street cops "who have seen it all," and are used to busting small-time crooks and dealers using imaginative methods like a Santa Claus disguise. But they are also violent and abusive, and we soon realize that Popeye has a work addiction problem. It seems hard for him to leave the precinct — instead of going home, he wants to go for a drink, merely an excuse to keep working overtime. At the same time, in Marseille, Charnier is making a deal with a famous French actor to smuggle drugs into the USA. How will they do it? This is the "mystery" that our detectives will have to solve.

**B Story:** The secondary story in this film surrounds the relationship between Popeye and his partner Cloudy, two cops who must trust and support each other in tough, early '70s New York City. Is Cloudy aware that the obsessive, violent and aggressive behavior of Popeye could not only endanger their friendship but his life?

**Catalyst:** As usual, the "case" starts with "something small or unrelated," such as going to the aforementioned bar and finding a suspicious group of people apparently just having fun. This is already a glimpse of our "dark turn," the work obsession that will deprive Popeye of whatever humanity he has left.

**Debate**: Is Popeye's hunch right? Can these people just be having fun? Is it worth spending a night working overtime in a stakeout just because he has a hunch? At last, they follow the suspect, Salvatore Boca (Tony Lo Bianco), to a small bar and find his attitude suspicious. They probably have a case after all.

**Break into Two**: Not coincidentally, in Marseille, Charnier makes a deal with French celebrity Henri Deveraux, who will be key in the scheme. Popeye and Cloudy start to spy on Boca — their fates will ultimately meet when the "secret" is revealed.

**Fun and Games**: The *promise of the premise* in police procedurals is "digging for clues," so these films usually have very clear Fun and Games beats, often our protagonists carrying on their everyday work while "showing us the clues as they discover them." In this story, they work undercover, investigating the suspect's family, getting court orders, performing bar raids and finding that chief mobster Joel Weinstock may be involved. The case progresses, and their boss decides to further authorize them to carry on with the investigation, involving some feds who do not particularly like Popeye. It seems his behavior in the past led to the death of a police officer. Again, is he trustworthy? The cops start following Boca to learn more about his meeting, and we witness some of the best foot chases ever shot in the history of cinema, still fascinating today for their flawless narrative and clever montage.

**Midpoint**: After a full day of tailing the people connected to the case, Popeye, Cloudy and Agent Mulderig (Bill Hickman) reconvene. Popeye gets territorial over the case, telling Mulderig, "My partner and I made this case and we don't need any Fed screwing it up!" Mulderig responds, "You haven't shown me anything yet." And so the *stakes are raised*; after this *false defeat*, Popeye and Cloudy need to prove that they're really onto something, or they're going to be off the case — a blow to their reputations and egos.

**Bad Guys Close In**: The next day, Popeye spots Charnier, but the drug dealer is clever enough to mockingly evade the detective. Bad Guys Close In for Popeye as he is taken off the case by his superiors and then Charnier's bodyguard attempts to kill him. Popeye commandeers a citizen's car and gives chase. The legendary (and still spectacular!) car chase beneath the elevated train follows.

**All Is Lost**: Popeye finally finds the bodyguard and, as he begins to flee, shoots him in the back. With Charnier missing and the bodyguard dead, Popeye's prospects aren't looking good. They can only follow Boca, who leaves the Lincoln in the street — the key to unlock the mystery. After a long stakeout at night, their cover is blown when some crooks attempt to steal the car's tires. Afterwards, the cops look in the car, but it seems clean. All Is Lost as the case faces the *whiff of death*.

**Dark Night of the Soul**: After towing the car to a police garage, Popeye and Cloudy spend a long "dark night" tearing the car apart to find the drugs, but uncover nothing. They consider the car as the symbol of their failure, until...

**Break into Three**: ... *A and B stories cross* when Cloudy realizes the car weighs more than it should, and they deduce that the drugs must be hidden in it somewhere. They push further and finally find heroin in the rocker panels. Now, they have the evidence and can proceed with their final plan.

**Finale**:
1. Gathering the Team: Very cleverly and in an unexpected way, the film doesn't show the cops' plan and preparations, but only those of the baddies: Charnier meets Deveraux to ask him for one last favor, which as we imagine, deals with his reacquiring the car.

2. Executing the Plan: Charnier meets Boca, Weinstein and the drug mobsters, and they execute their deal. The French dealer gets his money and hides it in another car.

3. High Tower Surprise: Just when the mobsters are about to leave, they find the police waiting for them! Popeye salutes Charnier and a new chase begins.

4. Dig, Deep Down: Boca is gunned down by the cops as Popeye "digs, deep down" to find Charnier in an abandoned factory, and when he sees him shoots — only for Cloudy to discover that Popeye has inadvertently killed a fellow cop. In his obsession, Popeye has ended up becoming "part of the crime."

5. The Execution of the New Plan: Apparently indifferent to what he just did, Popeye continues to chase Charnier, showing no remorse but only the ongoing obsession to catch his nemesis, much to Cloudy's surprise. Popeye is "not changed, only more cynical."

**Final Image**: A last, loud shot is heard, and we discover the fates of the characters in the final credits. Several of the small-time dealers received very short sentences and Weinstock went free. Popeye and Cloudy were suspended from narcotics duty and reassigned. Charnier was never found.

## GET CARTER (1971)

"Personal Whydunits" don't necessarily pertain to cops, but rather to an "amateur sleuth" who will investigate a mystery, only to discover things about himself that he'd really wished he didn't know. Such is the case of Jack Carter, a hitman who sets himself on a mission of knowing who killed his brother Frank up in Newcastle, and more importantly, the "why" of our Whydunit.

This great and now respected British film (made with MGM's help) was famously forgotten until a new generation of filmmakers like Tarantino and Ritchie found in its harshness, crude violence, industrial landscapes and amoral characters, the inspiration for their own work. It's the kind of quiet, tense, elegant film that is seldom made today.

In any case, *Get Carter* contains all the elements of the genre, with Carter as a sarcastic, jaded "detective" unveiling clue after clue, pursuing his investigation through the "ever-smaller chambers of a nautilus shell," in whose deepest darkness he ultimately finds... himself.

Carter will need to solve the "case within a case," if he is to uncover the "secret," enabling him to discover what the story has been about all along. And even for such a violent and immoral character, there is still room for that indispensable "dark turn" in which he will break his own and his culture's rules in pursuit of the crime, realizing how guilty he has been all along.

W Type: Personal Whydunit

W Cousins: *Blow-Up*, *The Secret in Their Eyes* (*El Secreto de sus Ojos*), *The Conversation*, *Memento*, *Oldboy*

GET CARTER
*Based on the novel by* Ted Lewis
*Written and Directed by* Mike Hodges

**Opening Image:** Jack Carter (Michael Caine) looks out of the window of his bosses' home, his mind somewhere else because he has just been told his brother has been killed. He is a henchman of the London mafia, and he seems uninterested while the others watch pornographic images (already here, we are setting up something!). At this point, Jack literally does not have a clue about who killed his brother. We can bet that the discovery will not change him much... but we will be changed instead.

**Theme Stated:** "Remember: they are killers, just like you," says Jack's boss, meaning that whatever he is going to find about his brother Frank's death will be bad news, and he may also die while trying to get answers.

**Set-Up**: Regardless, Jack travels north to Newcastle. We get to know him a little better: he is cold, focused, sardonic and a drug addict. Upon arriving at Newcastle, he asks a woman named Margaret about Doreen, Frank's daughter, but he doesn't learn anything yet. While he is apparently being watched, Jack visits his brother's home, finding a double-barrel shotgun, which will become a symbol of his brother-hood... and of revenge.

**Catalyst**: Jack visits Frank's body in an open casket, ready for the wake, but none of Frank's friends — not even his daughter — show up.

**Debate**: Artfully written as the entire duration of the funeral, our Debate beat introduces us to Doreen, whom Jack offers to take out of the city with him — he has plans to move to South America when all ends. He tries to get more clues about Frank's death, but the only thing he gets straight is that Frank was drunk when he died. Carter does not believe the police report, even when Margaret finally shows up at the funeral and confirms it.

**B Story**: At a bar after the funeral, Doreen erupts in a fit of rage, stating that no one really knew what Frank was like. Although Jack has no way of knowing at this time, Doreen is the B Story Character whose personal and spiritual story he will learn through, ultimately linking him to the deepest "secret" of the mystery.

**Break into Two**: Jack starts his investigation in earnest, visiting the race track to find an old buddy who might have some information, a man named Albert Swift. But Albert sneaks out as soon as he sees Carter.

**Fun and Games**: In any good Whydunit, the Fun and Games section focuses on the detective's investigation: the interrogation, clues, red herrings. Typically, the detective will have to visit many different strata of society, from the richest mansions to the poorest industrial slums. So Jack finds chauffeur Eric Paice, who claims to know nothing about Frank. Following him, Jack sneaks into the house of crime boss (and porn tycoon) Cyril Kinnear (played by playwright John Osborne). A great *pope in the pool* scene takes place when a poker game entertains the audience while exposition is being delivered. Jack is warned by a man named Thorpe to leave town, but Jack turns the tables and Thorpe gives him a name to investigate: Brumby.

**Midpoint**: Carter has a brief *false victory* as he goes to Brumby's home thinking he's got his man, but he realizes he has made a mistake, not seeing, as we do, that *A and B stories* have just *crossed*. When he goes back to the motel, he has *Sex at 60* with the landlady; *stakes are raised* and *clocks start ticking* when his colleagues from London visit to force him to abandon his quest. Naked and threatening them with a shotgun, he *publicly comes out* and performs his "dark turn" when he locks them up and destroys their car, breaking his own group's rules.

**Bad Guys Close In**: Carter flees from his Bad Guy mates and feels no remorse when a kid has been badly hurt because of him. We also learn an important clue: because Carter slept with his brother's wife, it is possible that Doreen is actually his daughter! As his lack of morals becomes more apparent, he is rescued by Kinnear's girlfriend Glenda who takes him to Brumby. Brumby tries to bribe Carter by giving him the ultimate clue for the case, revealing Kinnear killed Frank. Now he asks Carter to kill Kinnear, but he rejects his money and instead beds Glenda, finding she is also an amateur porn actress for Brumby.

**All Is Lost**: While Glenda is taking a bath, Carter switches on a projector and is appalled to see Doreen "acting" in the porn film.

**Dark Night of the Soul**: Carter can't help but silently cry as the last of the clues have been revealed. He has discovered that the very same underworld in which he dwells has ruthlessly swallowed up the sweet girl that is probably his daughter. He literally cannot stop looking, suffering this penance for getting involved. He has discovered the "secret," and now realizes he was part of the crime all along.

**Break into Three:** *A and B stories cross* as Carter discovers the "case within a case." He forces Glenda to divulge who else was involved, implicating Eric and Kinnear. He puts Glenda in the car trunk, finds Albert, and kills him after making him confess — they killed Frank because he had found out about the film. Now it seems there is only room for revenge!

**Finale:**

1. Gathering the Team: Eric and Carter's mates "gather" to kill him, but he manages to defend himself, doing nothing when they throw his car (and Glenda) into the sea.

2. Executing the Plan: Carter's plan consists of actually executing all those involved, one by one. He kills Brumby, overdoses Margaret and convinces Kinnear to set up Eric, before turning the latter in to the police.

3. High Tower Surprise: Kinnear hires a mysterious man wearing a ring, who will turn out to be another killer.

4. Dig, Deep Down: Jack "digs, deep down" as he chases Eric by foot, crossing railways, wastelands and beaches, and finally forces him to die the same way Frank did: full of whiskey.

5. The Execution of the New Plan: Once matters are solved, Carter is about to throw his brother's shotgun into the sea, maybe signaling that he will start anew, but...

**Final Image:** ...a single shot from the killer hired by Kinnear strikes him cold and leaves him dead on the beach with no one left to avenge him. We can only assume, as in any good Whydunit, that the truth probably didn't change Carter... but we surely have changed for him.

## THE BIG LEBOWSKI (1998)

If one thing defines cult movies, it's the lack of appreciation that critics, press or audiences (sometimes one, sometimes all) show when they are first released. But time and an ever-growing fandom put such films in their place, making them not only ultimately successful, but — in this case — inducting them into the National Film Registry, inspiring themed festivals… and even a religion!

*The Big Lebowski* is perhaps the quintessential Coen brothers film along with another Whydunit, *Fargo* (beat out by by Blake in *Save the Cat!® Goes to the Movies*). In this case, and despite its luminous colors, upbeat music, bathrobes and bowling uniforms, we are talking "Film Noir Whydunit."

How so? Start with the fact that the Coen brothers reportedly took inspiration from the work of Raymond Chandler (*The Big Sleep*, anyone?), including the complicated plot, double-crossing characters and the many secrets that need to be solved by our detective. Add to this the take-off tropes like the alcoholic detective, the *femme fatale* redhead, the powerful tycoon, the stray dangerous blonde…

Translate this to our *Cat!* vocabulary, and you'll have our "detective" who in his dudeness is quite unprepared for what he will find, a "secret" seemingly unimportant (who micturated upon a rug that clearly "tied the room together") — and don't forget the "dark turn" that will get him more involved than he ever wanted, setting himself up as part of the crime. Join us as we enter into a "world of pain," and let's go for this beat sheet!

W Type: Film Noir Whydunit

W Cousins: *The Girl with the Dragon Tattoo*, *Brick*, *The Samurai* (*Le Samouraï*), *The American Friend*, *Blue Velvet*

## THE BIG LEBOWSKI
*Written by* Ethan Coen & Joel Coen
*Directed by* Joel Coen

**Opening Image:** Let us follow a tumbleweed through the city of Los Angeles and meet Jeffrey Lebowski, AKA the Dude (Jeff Bridges): slacker, deadbeat and lover of White Russians. What will have changed in him by the end?

**Set-Up:** After paying with a post-dated 69-cent check for a carton of milk for his cocktails, the Dude returns home, only to be assaulted by a couple of thugs claiming that he owes money to a certain Jackie Treehorn. As a warning, one of them urinates on his rug, but after all, it seems like a misunderstanding. However, the Dude is desolated for having lost such a rug and visits another Lebowski, the "Big" one himself (David Huddleston) to seek compensation, for he is the millionaire achiever whose young wife Bunny is the one who indeed owes money to Treehorn. Lebowski demeans the Dude for his lifestyle (a running theme, as we'll see), and dismisses him.

**Theme Stated:** "Ever thus to deadbeats, Lebowski," says one of the thugs who assault and berate him in his home. A variation of the classic Latin quote, "Ever thus to tyrants," this is our ironic theme, as most of the characters in the movie act similarly to the Dude. From the false millionaire, to the scheming Germans or to Maude (who wants a son without commitment), all are like the Dude — they want to achieve something… for nothing in return.

**Catalyst:** Before exiting the Big Lebowski's mansion, the Dude sets the theme and the movie in motion by stealing a rug and meeting Bunny (Tara Reid), the Big's nymphomaniac wife.

**Debate:** Will there be consequences for the theft of the rug? Will Lebowski suffer any consequences? He seems to be very much at ease. In the meantime, we get to know his buddies better, gun-toting violent defender of all things Jewish, Walter Sobchak (John Goodman), and silent Donny (Steve Buscemi). There is a *double bump* when the Big Lebowski calls to meet the Dude, furthering our Debate section when he offers the Dude what appears to be an easy job: Bunny has been kidnapped and the Dude must deliver $1 million. Who has kidnapped her? This is the "secret" that will have to be unveiled.

**Break into Two**: Lying at home on his new rug, the Dude is assaulted again, this time by different people, including a *femme fatale* redhead, Maude (Julianne Moore). Lebowski is way more involved than he thought, and there is no turning back now. The film's first dream sequence signals the act change.

**B Story**: The love story pertains to Maude and the Dude. It's not a traditional love story by any means, but fits well in the noir tradition, as we will see that she is using him in various ways.

**Fun and Games**: After the dream sequence, the Dude has to fulfill the *promise of the premise* by carrying out the delivery of the money. Unfortunately, he asks Walter, who has a plan of his own to keep the million for themselves, to come along — and he leaves the kidnappers a "ringer" full of dirty underwear instead. Upon returning to the bowling alley, the Dude thinks that Bunny will be killed, but Walter believes that she has, in fact, "kidnapped herself" to keep the money. Then there's a new problem: the money is stolen along with the Dude's car. He gets a call — the woman who stole his rug wants to see him.

**Midpoint**: *A and B Stories cross* when his Dudeness officially meets Maude, daughter of the Big Lebowski and an avant-garde artist and feminist who also wants the money back, since her father took it from the family foundation. In a spoken *Sex at 60*-brimmed scene, they discuss the enjoyment of coitus, and Maude reveals that Bunny is actually a porn actress who probably wants to scam her father. Maude *raises the stakes* by offering the Dude 10% of the money when he recovers it, then gives him a doctor's number. El Duderino celebrates a *false victory* in the limo, stating that he "can't be worried about that sh\*t."

**Bad Guys Close In:** Seconds later, he notices the Bad Guys Close In when he sees a VW Beetle following him. He is taken to another limo, where the Big Lebowski shows him a severed toe and threatens him should he not recover the money; we witness the "dark turn" of the Dude as he lies to the Big that they dropped the money. Other Bad Guys, a bunch of vinyl-dressed Germans, assault the Dude at home and request the money or they will cut his "chonson." The Dude "abides" and finds his car, along with a lead that takes him to the 15-year old who supposedly stole the car and the money. Things don't end well, and the Dude is assaulted at home again, this time taken to see Jackie Treehorn himself, the one who wants to find Bunny to collect a debt. "All the Dude wanted was his rug back," the Dude says before passing out, drugged by something Jackie put in his "Caucasian."

**All Is Lost:** "Darkness washed over the Dude" as he dreams again, a seemingly pleasant bowling-themed dream that turns into a johnson-cutting nightmare. He wakes up and is hit again, now by policemen. No leads, no money, no help... *No nada!* What can he do now?

**Dark Night of the Soul:** A weary Dude sadly returns home, but he is so angry that he says he hates the Eagles and is kicked out of the cab. But wait: wasn't that Bunny passing by in a convertible, with all her toes intact?

**Break into Three:** The Dude gets back home to find it has been trashed. Luckily, *A and B stories cross* and he finds Maude there, so at least he can have sex with her! But he soon finds that she only intends to get pregnant. Before almost collapsing, the Dude has a revelation: Maude explains that her father has no money (it was all her mom's), so the kidnapping may have been a way for him to steal from his own foundation.

**Finale:**

1. Gathering the Team: The Dude "gathers his team," basically consisting solely of Walter, who complains it is Shabbos and he shouldn't be driving.

2. Executing the Plan: They both confront the Big Lebowski and confirm their theories. He demands his money, and the Dude and Walter finally leave the house penniless. At last, the "secret" has been unveiled!

3. High Tower Surprise: Unexpectedly, at the bowling alley, the Germans, who don't know that the plan has been uncovered, ask for the money, and a confrontation takes place. In the aftermath, Donnie dies of a heart attack.

4. Dig, Deep Down: The Dude and Walter "dig, deep down" to say goodbye to their dear friend, while the Dude has to "dig" a little more to remain friends with Walter when he inadvertently dusts him with Donnie's ashes.

5. The Execution of the New Plan: Their "new plan" is to go on like nothing happened and to live a tranquil life of bowling and drinking — that is, "abiding."

**Final Image:** The Stranger bookends the film by finishing his monologue. Has the Dude or Los Angeles changed by the revelation of this adventure? Most likely not, but there is something comforting in that nothing will change in his Dudeness's realm.

 *The Artist*, our "Fool," is finally "Triumphant" as he dances his way through the Finale with his loving B Story Character, Peppy.

# 8  FOOL TRIUMPHANT

We all know one: a particular person with an incredibly bright aura surrounding them, whose "foolishness" consists of not noticing reality as you and I do. Their innocence makes us think that they will not get very far, but despite it all, they surprise everyone with survival, success and fulfilled dreams. They are the stars of our "Fool Triumphant" genre.

It's a classic story: the "village idiot" who doesn't seem to "get it" but who ends up becoming king because of his talents, even if the fierce and unbelieving opposition do all that they can to stop our "fool." Yet all their efforts will be in vain, because our main character is strangely blessed: good karma, destiny or the divine seem to be on his side!

It's quite normal that many of our FT tales are comedies, and in the mainstream film world, there seem to be actors who have made their specialty playing them — ask Ben Stiller, Will Ferrell or Owen Wilson. But it's nothing new; all these actors have almost a century of precedents, following in the footsteps of Charlie Chaplin, Buster Keaton or Harold Lloyd, all known for playing clown-like characters whose candor and innocence usually enabled them to triumph in the end. So don't be surprised that even in our own independent world, many of these films will be comedies, too.

In a nutshell, to build a "Fool Triumphant" tale we will need, of course, a **fool**, someone who must confront an **establishment**, which is represented by a business, organization or group that appears too powerful for him to either defeat or fit in. Lastly, we need a **transmutation** for our fool, as he or she will become something new, albeit usually leaving their innocence untouched.

Just like in every other chapter, we have five subgenres, in this case differentiated by the environment our fool will find himself knee-deep in. The first of them is the **Political Fool**, and as its name suggests, our realm will be that of power in all its forms. Is there anything more classic than a naive newcomer in the reins of government, stalked by powerful wolves? Such is the example of films like *The Great Dictator*, *Quai d'Orsai*, *Bob Roberts* or our chosen example, *The King's Speech*.

How about the **Undercover Fool**? As its name suggests, our protagonist will take the identity or position of someone else, having to swim perilous waters to keep his innocence or goodness. Such is the case in *Life Is Beautiful*, *Un Prophete*, *Eastern Promises* or *Cruising*. Don't confuse this type of story with the **Fool Out of the Water**, in which our main character will find himself in a world he does not belong, but where his powers and skills will ultimately have a new impact, like in *The Artist*, *The Counterfeiters* or *The Big Blue*.

And then there's the **Society Fool**, in which the "establishment" is particularly closed-off and which will require our hero's hardest efforts to penetrate, becoming probably the most somber of our FTs — films such as *My Left Foot*, *Billy Elliot*, *I Am Sam* or *Match Point*. In contrast, the **Sex Fool** delves into the world of love through sexuality, with our "court jester" having his or her (inner) purity at stake — such is the case of *Boogie Nights*, *Jeune et Jolie*, *Melissa P.* or *The Dreamers*.

Now, how do we identify (or create!) our "fool"? As Blake said, this character's most important feature is that he must be disregarded at first, and of course, he is unaware of what he is missing, something which others will realize and try to take advantage of. And while having his talents and powers overlooked can be seen as a disadvantage, it is also his greatest power — no one thinks he can succeed!

Fools often look like they don't have a clue, and are usually calm, gentle, quirky, well-mannered or simply childlike in their behavior. Other characters, more jaded ones, will think that the fool is easy to take advantage of... and while this is so most of the time, we have to consider the "dark fool," the one who will use his demeanor and apparent weakness to profit from others, to thrive or simply to survive. Such is the case of Malik in *Un Prophete*, Chris in *Match Point*, or Lea (Isabelle) in *Young & Beautiful (Jeune & Jolie)*.

The fool thus finds and naturally opposes an "establishment" in which he stands out as different and unique. The world he inhabits is usually powerful, dangerous and potentially lethal for his innocence, so we fear for our hero. Establishments are heavy, formless and menacing, such as prison (*Cell 211*), governments (*Bob Roberts*), Hollywood (*Sunset Boulevard*, *The Artist*), concentration camps (*Life Is Beautiful*, *The Counterfeiters*), or the mafia (*Eastern Promises*), just to name a few.

Sometimes establishments are so big and powerful that we need a character to represent them, which we call the **Insider**. He is "the jealous brother that gets it," as Blake said, someone who acknowledges the fool's powers and sees him for what he is: a menace to their own ambition. The Insider will try to destroy the hero, either by straight opposition or by trying to corrupt the hero's innocence.

The **transmutation** is the last of our fundamental components for any FT, and this takes the form of a beat in which our hero gets a new persona, even **getting a new name**. In regard to their character arc, our hero will not usually lose their trademark innocence, so their change usually requires them to acquire a new status, name, job or personality. In *Boogie Nights*, doesn't Eddie Addams transform into Dirk Diggler (and afterwards into darker Brock Landers)? And in *The King's Speech*, doesn't the Duke of York become "Bertie" to become, in the end, King George VI?

The transmutation may also imply a **change of mission** — our hero was in the adventure to obtain a particular goal, but halfway into the story, they feel forced to readjust their priorities to continue being who they are. It's no coincidence that in our two movies about actors, *Boogie Nights* and *The Artist*, both Georges Valentin and Dirk Diggler decide to take their own careers into their own hands.

A final thought: as we will further explain in Chapter 10, the "Fool Triumphant" and the "Superhero" genres and stories have many things in common, but there is a particular difference — with the exception of the "dark fool," our innocents do not realize or know about their own specialness. In our Superhero genre, on the contrary, the hero's pains come from knowing how special he is.

## FOOL-ING AROUND WITH YOUR FILM!

An audience's favorite in both the mainstream and indie realms, the old story of the "village idiot" can still be told a million times. To find your court jester and confront the system from within, you will need:

1. A "fool" who is clueless about his own powers, innocent in character, gentle in his manners and seemingly an easy target for the "Insider" who underestimates his powers.

2. An "establishment" or group that our foolish hero stumbles into that seems too strong to defeat, and where he obviously does not fit.

3. A "transmutation" the fool will have to undergo, which usually implies a new persona born in the process and, many times, a "name change."

Are you an indie filmmaker? Just picture yourself trying to produce a Hollywood film. Who knows? Be enough of a "fool," and you may make it!

## THE KING'S SPEECH (2010)

Tradition and storytelling tell us that in every king's court there is a fool. But what if he was appointed king? While this may be an infrequent occurrence (Roman emperor Claudius comes to mind in more than one sense, especially when Derek Jacobi plays the role), "Political Fools" are easily found in both literature and cinema, especially when history meets the elements of dramatic structure.

Such is the case of David Seidler's screenplay about King George VI, formerly the Duke of York, whose stammer had to be overcome before becoming king. In Seidler's tale, he found a good friend in the process: his speech therapist Lionel Logue.

As for the rest of our FT requirements, the British monarchy sounds like a real tough "establishment" for a "fool" to challenge, doesn't it? Traditions, obligations, a one-track mindset... and also the place where, by definition, a king isn't exactly free, making it the perfect environment for a "transmutation" to occur.

Of course, we have an *Insider* in the form of a jealous brother, and a "change of mission," too. It's a film that became a major box-office success, won dozens of awards, and with a budget of about $15 million, earned more than $400 million. And of course, it's also a film that perfectly fits the Blake Snyder Beat Sheet and our "Fool Triumphant" rules.

FT Type: Political Fool

FT Cousins: *The Great Dictator*, *Bob Roberts*, *In the Loop*, *The Madness of King George*, *Goodbye Lenin!*

THE KING'S SPEECH
*Screenplay by* David Seidler
*Directed by* Tom Hooper

**Opening Image**: Can a microphone be something frightening? It certainly is for an individual who stutters yet must address an audience at a packed stadium! Meet our "fool," Prince Albert, Duke of York (Colin Firth), who finds it very difficult to speak in public and is therefore unable to inspire his subjects or gain their respect. Wait until our Final Image, when he must speak to a much larger audience, as a changed man in a changed world.

**Theme Stated I**: "Let the microphone do the work," Albert's assistant tells him. The king-to-be will get this sort of advice continually from people all around him, but what is easy for the majority may not be that simple for him. This is the introduction to the theme, which is expanded after the Debate.

**Set-Up**: We get to know Albert a little better, and we come to admire his perseverance. He patiently (well, sometimes not that patiently) subjects himself to the most embarrassing and ridiculous methods to cure his stammer, but to no avail. As a good "fool," he is overlooked and disregarded by his Royal Family and is himself particularly naive about his own "powers." This determination that he is demonstrating in the Set-Up will ultimately lead to his cure. But for now, tired of not getting any results, Albert is ready to give up. Doesn't it sound like *Stasis=Death*?

**Catalyst**: His supportive wife Elizabeth (Helena Bonham Carter) searches for a final chance at her husband's "transmutation" by finding a peculiar Australian speech therapist named Lionel Logue (Geoffrey Rush), who only demands "trust and total equality" to treat this notable patient.

**Debate**: Will Albert accept? Can someone like Lionel really help him? And can a nobleman really give the kind of "total equality" that

Lionel demands? For starters, another of the usual FT beats happens when Albert gets a "name change" from Lionel — from now on, he will be "Bertie." Lionel is making a clever move here, side-stepping the "establishment" that burdens Albert. To prove his worth, Lionel bets a shilling with Bertie, that he will be able to speak without stammering. Under Lionel's tutelage, Bertie reads a piece without hearing himself, but considers the matter hopeless and leaves.

**Theme Stated II**: The Duke meets his father King George, a notable orator and symbol of the "establishment" who warns him that with the scandalous behavior of his brother the heir, Bertie will have to talk a lot more in public. "We have become actors," he says. "We're expected to have charisma. And we're expected to instill trust and faith in the people through our speech."

**Break into Two**: Later at home, Bertie is restless and nervous, and decides to listen to the recording of his voice that Lionel made. Astounded, he hears himself speak without stammering... and is left appropriately speechless.

**B Story**: Bertie and Lionel are two men who couldn't be more different but will develop an unlikely relationship — from being unable to trust each other, to becoming mentor and mentee, confidants and friends. But much must happen for that to become a reality!

**Fun and Games**: How does a king behave when not in public? And how does he work on his speech impediment? Can our "fool" really be triumphant? There is a long road ahead for Bertie, who has a temper and orders Lionel to treat him as royalty, which Lionel refuses to do. Soon they are having quite un-kingly literal Fun and Games, jumping, relaxing and doing bizarre exercises that help Bertie slowly improve at speaking in public. Meanwhile, the "establishment" plot slowly evolves — we meet our *Insider*, jealous brother David (Guy Pearce). Soon after, their father dies and, luckily for Bertie, it is David who will become King Edward, although we suspect he is not truly ready for the task.

**Midpoint**: *A and B Stories cross* when Bertie visits Lionel and they drink together. The Duke *comes out* (showing us a glimpse of his inner pride) when he reveals that his father's last words were for him: "Bertie has more guts than the rest of his brothers put together," a moral *false victory* if there ever was one. Relieved at not having to be king, Bertie talks more intimately to Lionel, even joking, "Lionel, you are the first ordinary Englishman I've really spoken to." Quite another *coming out*! But Bertie still has room for change, for when Lionel asks, "What are friends for?" he answers, "I wouldn't know." He has one in front of him and still cannot see it.

**Bad Guys Close In**: Bad Guys come in all shapes and sizes for Bertie. He meets Wallis Simpson, the divorced American woman who is the lover of King Edward... and realizes that Edward intends to marry her, something that could cause a national crisis. The *Insider* accuses Bertie of wanting the throne (isn't he a bit right?), so our "fool" seeks Lionel's advice. But he feels his speech counselor is overstepping and decides to stop seeing him, "disintegrating the team." Also, Bad Guys Hitler and Stalin are creating tension in Europe, and Churchill is sure there will be a war. Edward abdicates to marry Wallis, and Bertie has a "change of mission" when he is made king, his greatest fear.

**All Is Lost**: Bertie, now King George VI, tries to speak before the Archbishop (Derek Jacobi!) and the noblemen of his country. Burdened by the looks of those before him, he is unable to utter a word.

**Dark Night of the Soul**: Bertie cries in his wife's arms when he realizes the magnitude and complexity of the task that lies ahead, especially the coronation ceremony. It is clear that he needs help... and a friend.

**Break into Three**: Bertie swallows his royal pride and visits Lionel at his home, and they both apologize to each other, as *A and B Stories cross* and he finds the courage to go on. Bertie pays the shilling he owed Lionel for fulfilling his promise, and they make the proactive decision to go on together.

**Finale:**

1. Gathering the Team: Together as a "team," Bertie and Lionel "make plans for the attack" on how to deal with the ceremony at Westminster Abbey, and they "amend hurts" when Lionel's enemies try to break the king's trust in him. "I have a voice," says Bertie.

2. Executing the Plan: The coronation is successfully held, and the King is crowned for all the world to see. Everything seems right, until...

3. High Tower Surprise: ...the situation in Europe gets worse when the British declare a state of war against Hitler's Germany. Bertie has a new, much more frightening task: to deliver a radio address to all of his empire, to inspire his people to stand united.

4. Dig, Deep Down: Forty minutes before the broadcast, Lionel coaches Bertie for his ultimate challenge, making him "dig, deep down," using many not quite kingly words that start with a loud "F." But Bertie also "digs, deep down" in another way — he is humble enough to thank Lionel, who instructs him: "Say it to me as a friend."

5. The Execution of the New Plan: With the entire world listening, the King's speech is delivered and he inspires all. He is now a real king and, for the first time, Lionel calls him "Majesty," a title he has earned. As a great "fool" character, he has not revolutionized the "establishment," but he will make a big difference.

**Final Image:** All hail the King! We started with a mere duke who made people feel embarrassed, and we finish with a wise king who is acclaimed by his subjects, ready to lead the country into its toughest challenge. Most importantly, we started with a man with no friends, and we close with two companions for life.

## LIFE IS BEAUTIFUL (1997)

Another film that caught the world by surprise, this $20 million budget Italian motion picture became a worldwide success and enjoyed a long, triumphant run when it won not only the Grand Prix at Cannes, but also the Academy Awards® for Best Foreign Language film, Best Actor and more. *Piu bello!*

As its name suggests, *Life Is Beautiful* is an inspiring movie about keeping faith and high spirits in the toughest situations, a challenge made unforgettable by the performance of Roberto Benigni as Guido, our "undercover fool," who will pretend that his family's imprisonment in a concentration camp is a mere game — all to protect his son from its horrors.

Guido is the ultimate "fool," with his joy of living, naiveté and wonderful way of using reality to pretend that he is inhabiting some sort of fairytale in which he is a prince and his beloved Dora is a *principessa* in their storybook world. His gentle manners, innocence and "village idiot" demeanor will enable him and his family to sustain their morale in a time of need.

Finally, the "establishment" is meant for us to be terrifying, and nothing is more frightening than a Nazi concentration camp! For Guido, the only way of challenging its strict rules is by pretending that the camp is something entirely different. Thus, our fool will use his "transmutation" into a prisoner to actually preserve his family's lives and hopes.

FT Type: Undercover Fool

FT Cousins: *Eastern Promises*, *The Drop*, *The Danish Girl*, *A Prophet* (*Un Prophete*), *Cruising*

## LIFE IS BEAUTIFUL
*Story and Screenplay by* Vincenzo Cerami & Roberto Benigni
*Directed by* Roberto Benigni

**Opening Image:** After an unknown narrator tells us about the nature of this "fable" (a bookend with the Final Image), we meet Guido Orefice (Roberto Benigni), a young Jewish man who is traveling to Arezzo in 1939 to meet his uncle and open a bookstore. Guido has a full life ahead of him, with great passion and joy.

**Theme Stated:** "Buon giorno, principessa!" Good day, princess! This thematic cry of joy will be repeated throughout the movie, signifying not only Guido's will to remain in his fantasy world, but the declaration of optimism that he will use to bring happiness, even in the toughest of times.

**Set-Up:** Let's get to know Guido a little better. Not only he is good at using reality's accidents to his advantage (even being mistaken for the king of Italy), but as soon as he finds someone he likes, he pretends to live in a fantasy world, calling himself a prince. Aptly, he soon meets "princess" Dora, with whom he is smitten. Upon arriving at his Uncle Eliseo's, something wrong is in the air — Eliseo has just been attacked by what appear to be fascists. It is too early for Guido to worry about them; instead, he notices some fun occurrences he will later use as part of his fantasies, showing his prowess at spotting them (and showing the talent of the writers for funny Set-Ups).

**Catalyst:** At minute 11, Guido literally runs over Dora with his bicycle, which means that she lives in the same city, and he hopes for them to find each other sometime "in a standing position."

**B Story:** Dora is the "love story" of our film, and from the very beginning, Guido shows an intense admiration and infatuation with her, which slowly becomes mutual. This love will inspire him to take the greatest risks and make the ultimate sacrifice.

**Debate**: Can the couple really be together? Can a humble Jewish waiter and the daughter of a conservative Catholic family find true love in the midst of fascism's rise? While the Debate begins, Guido gets a job as a waiter from his uncle and learns to use Schopenhauer's will-powers. We also meet an important character, our *Insider*: German doctor Lessing, who shares a love for riddles with Guido.

**Break into Two**: Guido decides to seduce Dora by pretending to be (again, showing his "undercover" talents) a school inspector, and after he openly mocks the fascist discourse on racial superiority, he asks Dora out.

**Fun and Games**: This section aptly starts at the theater, during a performance of Offenbach's "Barcarolle." We realize (although Guido hasn't yet) that Dora is dating another man, but out of cheekiness, he "steals" her and uses all the previously set-up moments to have Fun and Games with her. Later, Guido has to wait tables at a party, not knowing that it's Dora's engagement celebration! He says goodbye to Dr. Lessing, who gives him a last riddle and a great set-up for later, while Guido sends Dora a big cake, so that she expects him to appear at any moment. However, when he hears that she and her boyfriend will be married soon, he gets nervous. How can he fight against that?

**Midpoint**: When jittery Guido drops a tray full of candy, Dora hides under the table to kiss him and ask him to take her away. In the best prince-like fashion, he takes his uncle's green-painted horse and steals her from the party, as *A and B Stories cross*, having his own *public coming out* as a prince, his *false victory*, and a little bit later, their out-of-sight *Sex at 60*, which serves as a transition to our next beat.

**Bad Guys Close In**: Some years later, Guido and Dora have had a son, Giosué, who feels totally at ease in his dad's fantasy world — so much so that he doesn't realize (as we and Guido do) that Bad Guys are Closing In. In the streets, there are German patrols, and Jewish people are forbidden to enter many businesses. A couple of policemen go to Guido's bookstore to look for him, and soon, on Giosué's birthday, Guido and Giosué are put on a train with all the Jewish people of the city. Bravely, Dora demands to go with them.

After arriving at the camp, Guido decides to use all his imagination and resources to make Giosué believe that they are really playing a game, and the prize is a real battle tank! No matter how bad things get (they do not have food, Uncle Eliseo is killed in the gas chamber, and soon Giosué is the only living child in the camp), Guido finds a way to make him feel safe, and to communicate to Dora that they are still alive. *But for how long?* we ask ourselves. One day, a stroke of luck leads Guido to believe that they will get out of the camp — Dr. Lessing is there and recognizes him.

**All Is Lost**: The doctor does not want to help them out of the camp. He just wants Guido to solve a riddle for him.

**Dark Night of the Soul**: As Guido continues talking to the doctor, we realize that no matter how hard a fighter he is, this time he knows it may be too late.

**Break into Three**: How do you *cross A and B Stories* for our Break into Three if our B Story Character Dora is away from Guido, so they cannot see each other? Cleverly, Guido uses Hoffmann's music to send a message of hope to her — he will continue fighting for his family. He tries to escape, but when he finds a mountain of dead bodies in the mist, he realizes that he will have to look for another way.

**Finale:**

    1. Gathering the Team: Guido and the other prisoners "gather" to see the Nazis burning all evidence and killing as many prisoners as they can. Guido knows it is now or never! So he takes little Giosué...

    2. Executing the Plan: ...and tells him the plan: to remain hidden until no one is in sight. With Giosué safe, Guido enacts his own plan: looking for Dora while dressed as a woman and taking the "undercover" game to the very end.

    3. High Tower Surprise: And the end seems near, indeed, when he is spotted by some Nazis and taken prisoner, presumably to be executed.

    4. Dig, Deep Down: When they walk in front of Giosué, Guido "digs, deep down" to remain "in character" and to pretend that it is all still a game.

    5. The Execution of the New Plan: Guido is shot dead by the guard, but his plan succeeded. Giosué remains hidden until the next day, and he gets the promised battle tank — the American army is here to liberate the prisoners.

**Final Image:** Although Guido is dead, he managed to save his family, so now his narrator son, reunited with Dora, have their full life ahead of them. We feel sad for Guido, but we remain inspired by how he — as many others — sacrificed all for family and gave them and us the gift of a beautiful life.

## MATCH POINT (2005)

A book like this wouldn't be complete if we didn't have a film by one of the American symbols of auteurship and independent film-making, to the point of being labeled a legend: Woody Allen. Fool Triumphant stories are common in Allen's films, and he himself has played the part several times (even in real-life Hollywood, one could say), but can he give the genre a twist? You bet!

"Society Fools" refer to those individuals who don't belong to a certain social environment because of class, money or upbringing, a fitting situation for a broke tennis player trying to fit in with a rich British family.

This is how protagonist Chris Wilton tries to engage the traditional, one-track mindset "establishment" of wealth and power, which he is welcome to join as long as he respects its rules. As a good "fool," Chris will try to challenge the establishment, but as in many a tale, he will be defeated, performing a negative "transmutation" that will give him what he wanted, only to realize that maybe it was not what he really *needed*.

The rest of the elements of our genre are present, including the *Insider* Nola who knows the "fool's magic powers" and who will ultimately threaten him. There is a "change of mission," too. So let us follow the steps of Chris on his rise to the highest echelons of British society to discover if luck is all you need to be happy.

FT Type: Society Fool

FT Cousins: *My Left Foot, Zelig, Shine, Billy Elliot, Sling Blade*

MATCH POINT
*Written and directed by* Woody Allen

**Opening Image:** The fascinating slow-motion image of a ball moving back and forth over a tennis net sets the thematic tone of our movie — which deals with luck — and also sets the film's mood and style. We meet unemployed, penniless Chris Wilton (Jonathan Rhys Meyers), a promising yet early-retired tennis player, our "fool," whose situation at the end will be very different.

**Theme Stated:** In a very Allen-esque way, the theme is set at the very beginning of the film, with Chris's words: "The man who said, 'I'd rather be lucky than good,' saw deeply into life." Is it really better to have good luck than to have the skill or ability to create the life you want?

**Set-Up:** Let's get to know our "dark fool" a little better: Chris does not want to "do the tennis tour thing anymore," so he gets a job at an exclusive club where he will have access to wealthy pupils. He is clever and sensitive, delving into such high culture as opera, and Dostoyevski's *Crime and Punishment* (did someone scream "Theme!"?). But this humble, limited world seems like *Stasis=Death* to him, so he jumps at the opportunity to befriend Tom Hewitt (Matthew Goode), a well-to-do young man with an opera-loving family. Very soon, Tom's sister Chloe (Emily Mortimer) will be smitten with Chris, giving him real entree into the "establishment." Will he be able to fit in, or as a "fool," will he challenge its rules?

**Catalyst:** It was not all going to be that easy, of course! At minute 12, Chris meets the *Insider*: Tom's fiancée, struggling American actress Nola (Scarlett Johansson), presented playing a game of table tennis (did someone scream "Theme!" even louder?). They feel a mutual attraction, both "dark fools", trying to get into the establishment and become *Insiders*.

**Debate**: What will be the consequences? How will they affect each other's plans? Will Chris be able to become Chloe's fiancé, as Nola has with Tom? He is on his way developing his gentle "fool" manners and finally bedding Chloe. He even goes under the radar of Eleanor's (Tom's mother) Insider-spotting abilities. The family doesn't only love him, they get him a good job in the business world. Things seems to be going great for Chris, but we know his attraction for Nola is dangerous.

**Break into Two**: Chris bumps into Nola on the street. She is nervous before an audition, and he decides to accompany her for moral support. While he waits, a wonderful silent, almost-still shot of Chris simply thinking seems to tell us that he is making a decision. And when Nola returns, we know their love story is about to begin.

**B Story**: Nola is drinking too much and talks about her past, and we realize they are very similar indeed — both come from modest upbringings and have let their rich lovers groom them with luxury and affection. Life could be great for both. Nola says, "You're gonna do very well for yourself, unless you blow it... by making a pass at me." We see Chris's "change of mission": from just wanting to have a rich girlfriend, to also wanting to keep Nola for himself.

**Fun and Games**: The *promise of the premise* consists of Chris's further entering into the "establishment" of wealth, tradition and family values of the English upper class, including activities like skeet shooting, which is a nice way to set up our main character's access to a gun. Here also, Chris finally sleeps with Nola. Though he wants to pursue an affair, she keeps him at a distance — she doesn't want to ruin her relationship with Tom. Finally Chris marries Chloe and they start living together in a luxurious flat with a view. Chris soon learns that Nola and Tom have split up, as Tom has started dating a woman that his mother approves of. Chris tries to find Nola, unsuccessfully. It seems that he has lost her, so his initial plan of staying with Chloe is the only choice. We learn that Chloe is having trouble getting pregnant, causing some stress in their relationship.

**Midpoint:** Chris finds Nola by chance at the Tate Modern and he *publicly comes out* when he risks asking her for her new phone number even though his wife is nearby. Soon he experiences a *false victory*, starting an illicit relationship with Nola, who is much less wealthy now.

**Bad Guys Close In:** Preoccupied with his affair, Chris begins to neglect his work and even loses some money in the stock market. Meanwhile, Chloe is still desperately trying to "get lucky" so they can start a family. On top of that, Nola becomes pushy and needy, wanting to see him more and more. Chris almost freaks out when he realizes the reason: she is pregnant! Chris's response? "What unbelievable bad luck!" Nola refuses to get an abortion, asking Chris to leave Chloe and raise the child with her. And elsewhere, Chris has a close call when a friend accidentally catches Chris in a lie in front of Chloe. Is Chris running out of luck? Nola continues to put the pressure on and finally Chris lies to her about having to leave London for a few weeks. In a conversation with a confidant, Chris reveals that he doesn't believe he's capable of creating his own success in life — if he doesn't hang onto his good luck, he'll have nothing.

**All Is Lost:** Nola discovers that Chris is really in London, so she ambushes him at his home, calling him a liar. She delivers an ultimatum: either he leaves Chloe, or Nola will call her and reveal all.

**Dark Night of the Soul:** Chris lies awake during his textbook Dark Night of the Soul. He contemplates his fate, and is about to make a desperate decision.

**Break into Three:** Chris takes a gun from the locker of Chloe's father and *A and B Stories cross* when Chris tells Nola he's leaving Chloe, and arranges to meet Nola after work the next day. Chris is ready to put his plan into action.

**Finale:**

1. Gathering the Team: Chris "gathers" Nola by lying to her and summoning her home.

2. Executing the Plan: Chris's plan consists of killing Nola's neighbor to make the police believe that there was a robbery. He waits for Nola there and, with no second thoughts, he shoots her, too! After that, he meets Chloe and acts as if nothing had happened.

3. High Tower Surprise: Even though his plan seemed successful, the police contact him. He gets rid of the last pieces of evidence, but in a clever mirror of the film's Opening Image, one of the "stolen" items he's disposing of — a ring — bounces and falls back to *his side of the net*. Will Chris be out of luck?

4. Dig, Deep Down: He "digs, deep down" in his lying and feelings to convince the police that he was not the killer, and they seem to buy it.

5. The Execution of the New Plan: Chris's "new plan" is to conceal his feelings of guilt and trust his luck to not be caught. The policeman in charge of the case brushes with the truth, but Chris's luck diverts his attention — the officer does not seem to have a case after all.

**Final Image:** Chris and Chloe finally have a son. Everyone seems happy about it except Chris. Even though he has achieved all he wanted, he seems weary and tired, trapped in the life he desired with people he does not love, a closing image drenched in irony. In the final lines, someone remarks about the baby: "I don't care if he's great. I just hope he's lucky."

## THE ARTIST (2011)

Because France is one of the historic powers in cinema, it is certainly not a small thing to say that *The Artist* became the most-awarded French film in history at that time. César awards, Golden Globes, BAFTAs and of course Academy Awards® were swept by this sweet movie, an homage to the old age of cinema and its silent stars, and also a $15 million film that earned back more than $130 million!

The film portrays a "Fool Out of Water," defined by Blake as a story where the protagonist "will end up finding his unlikely place (there), and where his skills suddenly have new impact." That is almost by definition the storyline of our movie.

The rest of the FT prerequisites are here: George Valentin is a silent movie star, gentle and innocent, who will find himself "out of water" in the new world of talkies, and whose talents will be disregarded by the "establishment." This, of course, is the new Hollywood of speaking actors, and as expected, our hero will not lead a revolution *per se*, but his presence and talents will ultimately make a difference.

The "transmutation" will not only involve George becoming a director, but also a new kind of actor, one that can dance and finally talk. We have an *Insider* too, but this time with a twist: instead of being the "jealous brother that 'gets it,'" Peppy Miller is the only one who seems to understand the fool's talents and will try to help him, despite his opposition. As writers know, change is difficult, and more so if it implies *literally* finding your voice!

FT Type: Fool Out of Water

FT Cousins: *The Big Blue, District 9, Midnight Cowboy, After Hours, The Counterfeiters*

THE ARTIST
*Written and directed by* Michel Hazanavicius

**Opening Image**: The year is 1927. George Valentin (Jean Dujardin) is a silent movie star in the heyday of his career, lauded by the audience and his producer Al Zimmer (John Goodman). But gentle as he is, he also seems to be a touch vain and too proud. Will he be more humble at the end?

**Theme Stated**: "I won't say anything. I won't talk," says George's subtitles in a scene from his latest silent movie. Ironically, this works as our Theme Stated, as his silence is also a symbol of his inability to adapt to the new times, in which he will definitely have to talk.

**Set-Up**: At the premier, George is cheered by the audience. He enjoys that all eyes are upon him, but at the same time, disregards the value of his co-star, not wanting to share the attention. Sure, George is nice and everybody likes him, but he is a little too self-centered. Some *things will need to be fixed*! Outside the theater, he meets one of his fans, and the press implies that there is something between them, which George's bored wife clearly dislikes. That girl is named Peppy Miller (Bérénice Bejo), fascinated by movie stars, trying to become one herself.

**Catalyst**: When chance causes them to meet again at the studio the next day, it is dancing which helps them realize how good they both can be together (and the Finale is cleverly set up). Nonetheless, Al decides to fire Peppy on the spot because of the bad publicity. George immediately "Saves the Cat," securing her role as an extra in the film.

**Debate**: They start recording a scene in which they just bump into each other and dance for a second. But in each take, George seems to be more and more distracted, until he stops the filming. Later, they meet again in his dressing room and he sees her caressing his suit. He gives her "something that others will not have," painting a little black mole on her face. But George is married, so it is impossible for them to be together. Or can they be... somehow?

**B Story**: Obviously, the "love story" of our film is the relationship between the aging star and the rising new talent — not just because they feel attracted to each other, but also because she will be the one who will finally change him for the best and will give him a new life as an actor.

**Break into Two**: George seems comfortable as a silent movie star, but one day, Al shows him a new technological invention: sound in movies. George just laughs at it: "If that's the future, you can have it." George has still not realized that there is "no turning back." Unless he changes, he will be literally out of the picture(s).

**Fun and Games**: This beat starts with one of the only two scenes in the film with actual sound. In a nightmare, George begins living in the *upside-down world* of sound, where everything can be heard except his voice. It is just a dream, but a premonitory one. The next day, he discovers that the studio will only make talkies, which means he is out of work. Another era has dawned, along with the need for fresh faces (among them, Peppy's). George "changes his mission" and begins his "transmutation" when he spends time, effort — and lots of money — to make his own silent film.

**Midpoint**: George gets his *false victory* when he manages to finish the film, but he notices Peppy's film premiere is the same day, so the *stakes have been raised*. Later, *A and B Stories cross* as George dines with his chauffeur Clifton and hears Peppy demeaning old actors and their "grimaces" in an interview. Full of pride, George *publicly comes out* to reject her and leaves the restaurant.

**Bad Guys Close In**: Although silent, Bad Guys Close In for George in many shapes and sizes. First, the 1929 Wall Street crash threatens to bankrupt him, but he still trusts in his movie. Sadly, almost no one attends; Peppy does, but George does not see her. What he *does* see is the big billboard with her name on it, making him even more resentful. After this, his wife abandons him, and although Peppy tries to make amends, George rejects her again.

A year passes and George is not only drinking too much, he is pawning his best clothes. Ashamed at not having paid the faithful Clifton in a year, George fires him, further "disintegrating the team" and remaining alone. To survive, George auctions all of his beloved belongings, souvenirs and furniture, painfully seeing how two elderly people buy everything. What he does not know is that they work for Peppy: she has bought everything and is still protecting him from a distance. George wanders alone through the streets (did you notice the "lonely star" billboard behind him?). George decides to see one of Peppy's films, and boy, is she a star! George laughs in earnest, showing that he is a good man inside and appreciates her, but is still too proud to "talk" to her.

**All Is Lost**: George watches his old films, his former glory, at home. In a vision, even his shadow abandons him, and he realizes that he has lost everything because of his pride. Drunk and angry, he trashes the room, burning his films — and his apartment. The *whiff of death* could not be stronger.

**Dark Night of the Soul**: George clings to a particular can of film while he "contemplates his death" and passes out in the smoke.

**Break into Three**: Luckily for him, his dog alerts a policeman, and he is saved in time. When Peppy learns about this, *A and B Stories cross* as she visits him at the hospital, discovering the film he saved is the only one in which they appeared together. George wakes up in Peppy's home and although happy to be alive, he is still a little uncomfortable with her helping him. But Peppy has a plan.

**Finale:**

1. Gathering the Team: Peppy "gathers the team," in this case, all the film crew, and cunningly blackmails Al: either George is back in the movies, or she will not work for him anymore. Reluctantly, Al accepts.

2. Executing the Plan: Clifton brings George the script for the film, telling him that he now works for Peppy. George rejects the script, demonstrating that he has not changed enough, and Clifton says, "Beware of your pride."

3. High Tower Surprise: Wandering inside Peppy's house, George finds all his belongings and recognizes the elderly couple from the auction — instead of feeling thankful, he leaves, still unwilling to swallow his pride. But the outside world now is a talking one, and he does not find a place in it.

4. Dig, Deep Down: Depressed, George returns to his burnt home and picks up a gun. Before he harms himself, Peppy arrives. "If only you would let me help you," she says. "No one wants to see me speak," he answers. But then he realizes what he almost did and "digs deep down" to "talk," asking for help.

5. The Execution of the New Plan: Peppy has an idea to bring George back to the movies with her through what united them in the beginning: dancing! In a fantastic number performed for Al, the two stars show what an extraordinary team they are.

**Final Image:** In the *synthesis world*, George and Peppy are together with a bright future ahead of them, both in the movies and in real life. George has finally accepted Peppy's help, demonstrating his newfound humility. At last, as if to confirm his relevance in this new world... we finally hear him talk!

## BOOGIE NIGHTS (1997)

Written, produced and directed by Paul Thomas Anderson, *Boogie Nights* is a truly special film about movies, dreams, love and how to remain innocent even in an "establishment," the porn industry, which "decent people" consider dehumanizing and lacking in moral fiber.

Meet the innocent, gentle-mannered "Sex Fool," one who will end up finding his own powers while making a difference bringing innocence to this world and finding success in it — thanks to his formerly-disregarded skills. But can he remain an innocent in this seedy establishment?

The "transmutation" here is one of the clearest you will find, since it includes a necessary "name change" and a new persona as Eddie Addams gets to be "Dirk Diggler" (his better self), but whose goodness becomes endangered when his darker, "Brock Landers" side takes over.

This Fool Triumphant film is further enriched by a large cast of great actors, giving the film a much-mentioned Altman-esque feel that makes it dynamic, easy and fast-paced, and also allows the writer/director to further explore similar "fool" themes shared by many of the characters. So let's go back to the '70s and... roll!

FT Type: Sex Fool

FT Cousins: *The Dreamers*, *The Piano Teacher* (*La Pianiste*), *Crash*, *Intimacy*, *Belle de Jour*

## BOOGIE NIGHTS
*Written and directed by* Paul Thomas Anderson

**Opening Image:** 1977, San Fernando Valley (California): a masterful continuous shot immerses us in a world of neon lights, disco music and celluloid in which several characters are introduced. We will soon know that they all belong to the porn industry (our "establishment") directed by suave, easy-going film director Jack Horner (Burt Reynolds). By the end, not only the world, but the era, environment, film industry and characters will be very different.

**Set-Up:** Meet our "fool," Eddie Addams (Mark Wahlberg), waiter and school dropout with a "gift": apparently, he is marvelously endowed and a great lover, too. Eddie is gentle, nice and lovable (in a non-sexual way), but suffers at home under an obsessive mother. "I plan on being a star. A big shining star," he says. As we will see, many of his future companions are a little bit of a "fool," living in their own self-made worlds of illusion.

**Theme Stated:** "I've got a feeling, beneath those jeans there's something wonderful just waiting to get out," Jack tells Eddie. This is our theme, not only referring to his maleness, but also to his big heart, which will change them all.

**Catalyst:** One night, Jack and his crew ask Eddie to come home with them. Although reluctant, he joins them and learns about Jack's ambition to make a "film that is true, and right and dramatic." Eddie has sex with Rollergirl (Heather Graham) and he is "in." In the industry, we mean.

**Debate:** Can innocence survive in this tough establishment? Can a sweet soul really be a "star"? Several new characters show us the darker side of the business: cocaine, underage actors, absent families, competition, lack of true love and commitment, self-esteem issues... and the list goes on. Eddie seems to be developing a relationship with

Jack's wife Amber (Julianne Moore). She is the *Insider*, the one who seems to "get" that everything around them is not as bright as it seems and who will not see Eddie as an actor, but as a substitute son.

**Break into Two:** As in every good Fool Triumphant story, our hero gets a *change of name*, this time solemnly announced: a new persona is born as Eddie Adams turns into magnificent-sounding Dirk Diggler. As Blake said, the "transmutation" is offered by circumstances that seem divine, and as if to confirm it, Jack says, "I think heaven has sent you here, Dirk Diggler."

**B Story:** In this case, the film's love story takes the shape of a mentor-mentee relationship between Eddie (sorry, Dirk) and Jack. His respect and faith in Dirk as an actor will give Dirk the self-esteem he needs, and in dark times, Jack will be the one to put Eddie back on the right path.

**Fun and Games:** At last, the '70s world of porn films is finally explored, surely the *promise of the premise*. Script, lighting and camera roll record the *upside-down world* of love and human relationships, bad acting and extraordinary, well, performances. Parties, leisure, debauchery and sleaze are the world in which Dirk finds himself at home. New clothes, shoes and bad haircuts mark the passing of time and the fulfillment of Dirk's ambitions — critics and audiences love him, and he is on his way to becoming a star.

**Midpoint:** Dirk gets many industry prizes in his *false victory* and *publicly comes out* at the ceremony, still showing that he is a "fool" at heart with his gentleness: "These movies we do... they can help." But the *stakes are raised* and new times are ahead as Dirk gets a new persona: Brock Landers, a darker, more violent character that mirrors his own slow, dark turn. *A and B Stories cross* when Jack realizes that he has fulfilled his own dream: "It's a real film, Jack." The *clock starts ticking* as an era ends: "Goodbye '70s, hello '80s."

**Bad Guys Close In:** The advent of video and the modernization of "the business" is a Bad Guy, though Jack refuses to change. Much worse Bad Guys are cocaine and shady new characters like Todd Parker. The "team starts disintegrating" when Dirk rejects Scotty (Philip Seymour Hoffman) and Little Bill (William H. Macy) shoots himself. Dirk, in Brock-character, justifies violence and grows apart from Jack over creative differences, and their producer gets imprisoned for owning child pornography. Bad Guys further close in when a young actor is hired, a possible new star rising.

Drugs, partying and stress also cause Dirk to have trouble getting erections, and he even fights Jack in front of his crew, getting fired. Dirk tries to start a side career (getting his "change of mission") in music. Hearing him sing a verse, we know he will fail, while the rest of his team find it difficult to make new lives for themselves because of their past in porn.

**All Is Lost:** Dirk has to work as a hustler in the outside world and gets severely beaten. Other characters reach their lowest, darkest moments of violence, aggression and morality when confronting real life.

**Dark Night of the Soul:** Injured and bleeding, Dirk lies almost dead on the ground in a parking lot.

**Break into Three:** *A and B Stories cross* by means of a parallel montage in which the characters' fates are shown, with a special focus on Jack's video adventure with Rollergirl and Dirk's beating.

**Finale:**

1. Gathering the Team: Dirk and his friends (among them, Todd) "gather" to begin a poorly-planned drug-related deal with fake powder.

2. Executing the Plan: They "execute the plan" by showing up at the dealer's house and performing the transaction. It seems to work, despite their clumsiness.

3. High Tower Surprise: The surprise is that Todd's actual goal was using the robbery as a means to get inside the dealer's house to rip him off. A shooting ensues, and Dirk escapes by the skin of his teeth.

4. Dig, Deep Down: Knowing that he has reached rock-bottom, Dirk "digs, deep down" to return to his mentor and friend, Jack. They embrace and Dirk asks him and Amber for forgiveness.

5. The Execution of the New Plan: "We all need to start again," says Amber. And indeed, that is their new "plan": to be together and work together again, and to help and support each other — opening a stereo store, going back to school, re-opening a bar with the family's help, becoming a magician, having a son...

**Final Image:** ...and of course, shooting films again. We see our "fool" Dirk Diggler rehearsing his lines, his confidence and self-esteem regained, but most importantly, his innocence untouched: "I am a star."

 The "Set-Up" introduces "Naif" Toto, whose love of film blossoms in the *Cinema Paradiso*.

# 9 INSTITUTIONALIZED

Life is made up of choices! And in our necessarily social lives, one of the most common decisions we make is whether or not to belong to a particular group, which usually means conforming to *their* rules. Deciding to belong has both advantages and disadvantages, and if it is already difficult to choose, when you realize there is something to lose no matter what you opt for, the decision becomes even harder.

The dilemma is made more difficult when — once we are inside the group — we find out that leaving it may be as hard as joining, and not only do we have to conform to its inner rules, but we also cannot defy them in the slightest without dire consequences. So the situation becomes more difficult.

There are several "institutions" to which we can belong, and they make up our five subgenres. First, we have the **Military Institution**, a world of orders, uniforms, ranks and obedience in which our individual self must be suppressed (and its mouth kept shut) for the common goal. Such are the stories present in *Platoon*, *The Experiment*, *Z*, *Land and Freedom*, *The Battle of Algiers* or our chosen film, *Paths of Glory*.

The **Family Institution** contains another realm of inner rules, regulations and customs, and we aren't just talking about Aunt Dora's Thanksgiving dinner etiquette! We're talking about any social group that can be considered a "family" (among the mafia, gangs, neighbors, roommates and friends — which is most dangerous?). Many films serve this subgenre, such as in *Boyz n da Hood*, *L'Auberge Espagnole*, *Brother*, *Gomorrah* or *The Fighter*.

There's also our **Business Institution**, the dreaded world of collective goals, water-cooler conversations, cubicles, casual days and after-work meetings — missing just one can make you an outsider! This is the world seen in films like *Margin Call*, *Smoking Room*, *Inside Job* or masterpiece *Glengarry Glen Ross*, our choice to examine.

Teachers and masters make up our **Mentor Institution** sub-genre, where our indoctrination and successful submission to the rules of the group (even if it is a gang of two) is symbolized by a mentor. This mentor figure may want the best or the worst for us, but their teachings are our "choice," as in *The Last King of Scotland*, *Apt Pupil* or *Cinema Paradiso*.

Finally, there is the very important and creatively challenging **Issue Institution**, in which multiple intersecting storylines, an ensemble cast and a powerful theme force several characters to make a choice and face the consequences. These issues and the choices they prompt are present in films like *Crash* (which Blake dissected in *Save the Cat!® Goes to the Movies*), *Short Cuts*, *Four Rooms*, *Cidade de Deus*, *Amores Perros* or our choice, pop masterpiece *Pulp Fiction*.

As always, we have three main components. Blake defined this Institutionalized genre as one in which an individual has to make a **choice** to belong to a particular **group**, which always involves a final **sacrifice**. This decision is never easy, because it may actually involve survival! And most of the time it is very difficult to predict which kind of life would be more difficult or dangerous for us when we must choose either "us" or "them."

As for the "group," any gathering of people, "work situations or closed societies with their own rules, ethics and bonds of loyalty" will serve. This is why unique jobs, seldom-seen societies or exotic social communities of whose customs we know little are great settings for these films.

The "choice" usually involves whether or not to belong to the group or leave it. This is not as easy as it seems, because peer pressure and self-sabotage make deciding more difficult, and the inner rules affect our decision. It is common, in the beginning of the story, for the hero to weigh the "pros and cons" of being one of the guys, which often involves ceremonies, rites of acceptance and exploring the power hierarchy that rules the group. The longer we belong to the group, the "choice becomes harder" because of the graver consequences that entail either staying or leaving.

This all leads us to the "sacrifice," which always boils down to "them" or "me"? Will we ultimately surrender our individuality to the group to belong, or will we rebel against it and suffer the consequences? There are three possible endings in this situation: a willing submission to the group's rules to the detriment of our unique self; uprising against the system to destroy it, thereby losing something on the way; or "suicide," which leaves us with expressionless characters who have lost their individuality. The moral, remember, is, "Look before you join!"

This genre has a set of characters that often appear, either as main or secondary personages. The first is the **Brando**, named after the famous revolutionary actor — he will proactively defy any system you throw at him, as his true nature is that of a rebel. He is Colonel Dax in *Paths of Glory* or Butch in *Pulp Fiction*.

You may also have a **Naïf**, the kind of character who, like "us," does not have a clue about the system's workings, so he will serve as our avatar into the "group," perhaps being a little (or a lot) more vulnerable to its dangers, as Grace in *Dogville*, Chris in *Platoon* or Ted the bellhop in *Four Rooms*.

Third, you have the self-explanatory **Company Man**, the type of character that proudly and blindly defends the system and will use its powers against any kind of rebellion. Expect his help in becoming one with the machine, but greatly dread him if he smells your dissent! Blake defined them as often insane and, at times, sexually frustrated. Look at the roles of Kevin Spacey in *Glengarry Glen Ross*, Adolphe Menjou in *Paths of Glory* or Harvey Keitel in *Pulp Fiction* and you will know what we mean.

Let's keep Blake's words at the forefront: all "Institutionalized" stories are a cautionary tale about "not paying attention to the voice inside." Whenever we are in a group, its dynamics may make us lose sight of our priorities, morals and personal boundaries, but "we who listen to our inner spirit are propelled by a power that can overcome all."

## TO BE(LONG) OR NOT TO BE(LONG)

Any time in life you are tempted to abandon your personal beliefs in favor of those of the group, you have an "Institutionalized" story at hand! You will recognize them because:

1. There is a "group," a closed environment of people with their own peculiar "rules, regulations and consequences for not following them."

2. At some point, you will be given a "choice" to belong, and you will feel like a "Brando" or a "Naïf," so beware (and don't turn into) the "Company Man."

3. However hard you try, you will not be able to avoid making a "sacrifice" when the time comes to decide if you want to stay in the group, and the ways to do this are by "joining, burning it down or committing suicide."

Be good and find your own perfect ending... on your own terms!

## PATHS OF GLORY (1957)

The military is probably the most absorbing of the many "groups" in which the individual may feel detached from his own self while belonging to a collective. Rank and file, orders, decorations and uniforms make any instance of going solo an almost impossible task. There is a clear behavior imposed: obey!

Stanley Kubrick's *Paths of Glory* is our choice for the "Military Institution" subgenre. In it, the military as a "group" will be challenged by an individual seeking justice for the common man while trying to force the upper ranks to treat a bunch of soldiers for what they really are — human beings — instead of as simply statistics among the millions to die in the fields of Europe during WWI.

That individual is Colonel Dax, our particular *Brando*, an idealist who still believes in his fellow man. He must face the "choice" of defending his men against all odds (and risking his career) while facing a final "sacrifice": to decide if it was worth putting "them" before himself ("me").

The result is truly a masterpiece, a film that 60 years after its release feels as current as the eternal tragedy that is war. Let's be thankful that once in a while, in such a violent and dehumanizing world, a human being like Dax will challenge any "group" to fight for human dignity.

I Type: Military Institution

I Cousins: *Captain Conan* (*Capitaine Conan*), *The Wind That Shakes the Barley*, *Elite Squad* (*Tropa de Elite*), *Gallipoli*, *The Hurt Locker*

## PATHS OF GLORY
*Based on the novel by* Humphrey Cobb
*Screenplay by* Stanley Kubrick & Calder Willingham and Jim Thompson
*Directed by* Stanley Kubrick

**Opening Image**: After the chords of the "Marsellaise" (France's national anthem), we witness a group of soldiers marching in perfect formation. We cannot see their faces or their individual features, we only observe them from a distance. Quite a different sight and visual approach from the one that Kubrick will use at the end of the film! Now they are only troops, an indistinct group. Afterwards, they will be recognizable individuals.

**Theme Stated**: "My men come first of all, George, and those men know it, too." Although it seems like an honorable statement, it is ironic: *Company Man* General Paul Mireau (George McReady) is lying and about to dispose of his soldiers' lives for his own benefit. He has already chosen between "them" and "me."

**Set-Up**: Mireau is visited by General Broulard (Adolphe Menjou), who assigns him a seemingly impossible task: to conquer a German position dubbed "The Anthill," a suicide attack that would kill a great deal of men. Mireau first refuses, but upon learning that a promotion is at the stake, he promises Broulard that the position will be secured. Of course, general that he is, he we will not do it by himself, so we move from the luxury of the officers' palace to the grimness of the trenches. There we meet our *Brando*, Colonel Dax (Kirk Douglas), who used to be the foremost criminal lawyer in all of France, and now "Saves the Cat" by defending his men's behavior during a battle.

**Catalyst**: Unfortunately for Dax, at minute 12 he gets a request: to take the Anthill. As we would expect, Dax refuses because he knows that more than half of his regiment would die in the attack.

**Debate**: Mireau's request turns into an order: Dax will take the hill or be put on furlough. Dax Debates with him about the impossibility of success, because it is basically crazy to even try — they will suffer heavy losses. He further Debates with himself whether he wants to be a part of such madness. He still doesn't want to personally command his men to their deaths.

**Break into Two**: Dax accepts the mission, clearly stating, "We'll take the Anthill." In doing so, he makes the proactive decision to stay with his men no matter the consequences. There will be "no turning back"!

**B Story**: This is the time to meet our B Story plot and characters, in this case, the ill-fated men who will unknowingly become the object of Dax's defense. For now, they are just soldiers in their own everyday conflicts, like Corporal Paris (Ralph Meeker), who witnesses a lieutenant panic and kill a fellow warrior (developing a grudge because of it), Private Ferol (Timothy Carey), deemed a "social undesirable," or death-obsessed but decorated Private Arnaud (Joe Turkel) — each of them having a personal conflict with the military "group."

**Fun and Games**: The *promise of the premise* is to show us life and death in the trenches of France in WWI. At first we move away from Dax's plot line to focus on our B Story narrative, including a night reconnaissance patrol. Soon, the day, hour, minute and second of the dreaded attack on the Anthill arrives. Dax bravely leads his troops, and witnesses his men die by the dozens. More problems arise when one of the companies is unable to get out of the trenches due to heavy fire, no matter how hard Dax tries to help. *Company Man* Mireau, who is supervising the attack, decides to have them bombarded by their own troops! When a commanding officer refuses to join the obviously doomed attack, the bloodthirsty general calls for the court martials of three men, one from each of the three companies involved in the battle.

**Midpoint**: As often happens at this beat, a "Midpoint meeting" is held between the main characters. In this case, Mireau *raises the stakes* by demanding many men be executed to inspire fear and discipline within others ("They are scum"), while Dax defends them, *publicly coming out* ("They are not cowards") as *A and B Stories cross*. Dax is unable to stop the court martials of the three soldiers — Paris, Ferol and Arnaud, but he still gains his *false victory* when he is appointed their counsel. *Clocks start ticking*, as he must prepare their defense for the trial that afternoon!

**Bad Guys Close In**: After the meeting, Bad Guys Close In on Dax when he refuses to obey Mireau's suggestion to drop representing the men, despite Mireau's threat to ruin Dax once everything is over. *A and B Stories cross* as the B Story soldiers we know all too well by now are accused of cowardice. Dax's "choice becomes harder" when the court martial begins and Dax realizes it is basically a travesty — no indictment is read, and no records will be kept of the trial. Dax tries to save the men, but the court "tightens the grip," and he states that he feels "ashamed to be a member of the human race." The military "group" is immune to his plea for humanity. Later, the soldiers sense death nearing as the "old values" of bravery and valor don't work anymore. Alone in their cells, their "world disintegrates," but they still hold on to hope.

**All Is Lost**: Hope is lost when a priest visits the prisoners and tells them that, despite Dax's efforts, all of them will be executed at first light.

**Dark Night of the Soul**: Thus starts the darkest night for these soldiers, one in which they will contemplate their death by various means: prayer, reason or drunkenness. They even fight, and one of them is so badly hurt, he may die before the new day arrives.

**Break into Three**: Dax continues confronting the military "group" to hold justice to the highest standard he can, such as when he designates as leader of the firing squad the man who held a grudge against Corporal Paris. Yet along with a revelation there comes some hope: Dax obtains information about Mireau's orders to bomb his own ranks and visits General Broulard, pressuring him about the scandal that could result... seemingly to no avail.

**Finale**:

1. Gathering the Team: Dawn arrives and the three soldiers are "gathered" to be shot. Paris tries to beg for his life, but he has only one decision left: to die bravely.

2. Executing the Plan: The "execution" of the plan consists of actually executing the soldiers, which is carried out and filmed in its ruthless, clockwork, military-precision cold-ness. Our innocent soldiers are unjustly shot to death.

3. High Tower Surprise: "Your men died very well," says spite-ful Mireau to Dax. But a High Tower Surprise awaits him: Brouleau announces there will be an official enquiry that will surely smear Mireau's name. Such a small victory, it seems... but then Brouleau suggests that Dax only defended his men to assume Mireau's position as general!

4. Dig, Deep Down: Outraged at Brouleau's accusation, Dax "digs, deep down" to decide if he must say what he wants to,

even if it will cause more problems: his time for a "choice" has arrived.

5. The Execution of the New Plan: Dax calls Brouleau a "degenerate, sadistic old man" and claims that he will never apologize. We don't know what consequences this accusation will have on his career, but he has made a choice... and a sacrifice.

**Final Image:** At a nearby tavern, Dax hears wild cheering and catcalling and sees his own men behaving like animals and terrorizing a young German singer, the first woman and "enemy" (Christiane Kubrick) we've seen in the film. Dax seems to reflect on their brutality: did he risk himself for men like these? When the frightened girl starts singing and all the soldiers sing along and cry with her, we see their tears in unforgettable close-ups, very different from the distance the director kept at the beginning. Dax seems to regain faith and gives them a few minutes more of joy... but soon his face turns serious again, which shows his "sacrifice" and the surrender of his individuality to the "group." He cannot allow himself to be human anymore, since the war is not over yet. Is it ever?

## DOGVILLE (2003)

The "family" in "Family Institution" can refer to a group affiliated by friendship or blood, but also, in our *Save the Cat!® Goes to the Indies* context, to any film in which that "group" accepts a stranger seeking protection, apprenticeship or survival by means of belonging. That is why, for example, crime "families" and the like can also be considered for this subgenre.

*Dogville* tells the story of a runaway woman, Grace, who seeks the acceptance of the inhabitants of the small town of the title. For that, she will have to conform to their rules and customs, and ultimately abandon her own free will to belong — the "choice" she must make in our story. And as we know, a final "sacrifice" will have to be made.

This is a wonderful film by controversial Danish director Lars von Trier, who takes a bravely different approach, abandoning naturalistic filmmaking for a theater-like set with invisible walls, probably inspired by German playwright Bertolt Brecht and even quoting him (check the lyrics of one of my favorite songs, "Pirate Jenny" for that).

Considering this uniqueness, plus the film's long duration (almost 3 hours), and we might think that there is no way it would fit our Beat Sheet. Well, we'd be wrong! Because no matter its formal peculiarities and apparent avant-garde-ness, *Dogville* perfectly follows all of our beats and, of course, in the right order. So, for once, let us... Save the Dog!

I Type: Family Institution

I Cousins: *Moonrise Kingdom*, *The Queen*, *Celebration*, *Brother*, *Boyz n the Hood*

DOGVILLE
*Screenplay by* Lars Von Trier
*Directed by* Lars Von Trier

**Opening Image:** "This is the sad tale of the township of Dogville." From above, we witness our "group," a small town in the Rocky Mountains. Sure, there are no walls, and the shacks are only made by chalk lines on the ground... but no one seems to notice. The town is full of lively people, quite a big difference to what we will behold at the end.

**Set-Up:** We get to know Dogville's inhabitants a little better, all seemingly happy people who mind their own business. True, everyone has individual quirks, but don't we all? Like gloomy Chuck (Stellan Skarsgård) the apple gardener, his obsessive wife Vera (Patricia Clarkson), their naughty children, the nosy store clerk or the church's caretaker, they all seem to live pleasantly, considering times are tough. At least there seems to be a balance.

**Theme Stated**: Tom (Paul Bettany), the town's ever-aspiring writer and philosopher, is worried about its people and their ability for tolerance: "What they really need is something for them to accept. Something tangible, like a gift."

**Catalyst**: After a gunshot is heard in the distance, Tom sees Grace (Nicole Kidman), a beautiful and fancily-dressed woman arriving in town, apparently fleeing from somebody. That "somebody" seems to be gangsters, and when they appear, Tom fools them into believing he has not seen any girl. They leave him with a number to call in case he sees her.

**B Story**: The B Story, or love story, deals with the nature of the love between Tom and Grace. While the rest of the townspeople will ultimately be shown to be selfish, Grace expects her relationship with Tom to be purer. Will she be right?

**Debate**: Tom asks Grace about herself, but she only reveals that she had a father until some "gangsters took him away" from her. She is doubtful about staying in Dogville, because she has nothing to offer in return to its inhabitants. However, Tom gathers the townspeople in church and they all Debate about the convenience of her stay. Isn't it crazy to hide a runaway with them? Couldn't it bring them trouble? Is she fit to live with them?

**Break into Two**: The people in the village decide to let Grace stay for two weeks, and after that, they will let her know if she can join the "group." There is no turning back, as she is on trial now. But what does this "choice" entail for her?

**Fun and Games**: Grace soon reveals herself to be a *Naïf* because she knows nothing about the rules, so she is a "virgin" to the citizens of Dogville. She offers to help, and after a lot of snubs, she starts being accepted. Thus she experiences the "pros and cons" of the group, finding happiness in helping, but also having to work hard. She discovers that many of the town's happy dwellers are not actually happy; indeed, they hate Dogville! She meets *Company Man* Chuck, who also comes from the city and seems to be in a perpetual bad mood. However difficult their lives may be, Grace tries to make them better, and ultimately she gets subjected to the town's verdict: 15 bells ring, which means everybody wants her to stay.

**Midpoint:** All the village celebrates with her, which allows Grace to have her *false victory*, as she is considered at one in the village. There is a "public coming out" and a whiff of *Sex at 60* when Tom confesses his love and she reciprocates, holding hands with him in front of everybody. "Stay with us as you damn please," they tell her. All seems great... until *stakes are raised* as the police come to town and nail a poster with Grace's photo on the wall. There is even a reward for her, as she is wanted in connection with a series of bank robberies.

**Bad Guys Close In:** This information triggers some changes in the dynamics of the village. The citizens feel that they are further endangered by Grace's presence, so she must make up for it by working more hours and taking reduced pay. "The choice becomes harder" for Grace when the townspeople start showing her a dark, hidden side, and even Chuck subtly blackmails her. Sexual harassment comes next, and further Bad Guys Close In when the police return. Things become nasty when, while she is hidden, Chuck brutally rapes her. To make things worse, Tom shows himself incapable of protecting her, so she has to endure the sheer rejection and aggression of some of the jealous women on her own. Following Tom's advice, Grace tries to flee from the village, but she is raped again on the way, and then brought back to the village, where everybody despises her for having tried to leave.

**All Is Lost:** Grace is chained by the neck to a heavy flywheel, which prevents her from trying to escape again. Yet she must still work for everyone as a slave.

**Dark Night of the Soul**: Grace laments her state, but things get worse when she realizes Tom has betrayed her, blaming her for the theft of the money that she used to escape. Autumn comes and almost every man in town periodically rapes her — except for Tom, who is not really more pure than the rest, but only wants her to accept his advances willingly.

**Break into Three**: Tom makes Grace publicly apologize to the whole village at the church to no avail; now people think she has brought "bitterness and troubles" to their lives. Later, *A and B Stories cross* when Tom tries to talk Grace into having sex, but after she cleverly rejects him once more, he decides to let it go and finds the phone number that the gangsters gave him in the Catalyst beat.

**Finale**:
1. Gathering the Team: No one bothers Grace the next morning — the village seems to have gathered to wait for someone. However, things look strange when they find out that a tree is blocking the road. Grace seems to suspect something; she is "gathering" her strength for the final decision.

2. Executing the Plan: Tom's "plan" of calling the mobsters is put into effect when they are welcomed into the town and Grace is handed to them, the inhabitants of Dogville expecting the reward. This could be viewed as her "plan" too, since she actually knows who is coming.

3. High Tower Surprise: The surprise for the citizens is clear to Grace, as the mobster's boss is her father (James Caan), come to take her home. Grace tries to defend the town's inhabitants: "Dogs only obey their own nature. Why shouldn't we forgive them?" But her father thinks that "dogs" should be disciplined by punishment.

4. Dig, Deep Down: Grace "digs, deep down" as she wonders what to do with Dogville's inhabitants. First she thinks she

would have done as they did with her... but then realizes that if that were the case, she would not be able to forgive herself. They still deserve punishment.

5. The Execution of the New Plan: Changed, Grace makes her "sacrifice" and decides to have the town burnt and everybody slain, as the world will be better off without Dogville. To show how much she has changed, she even kills Tom!

**Final Image:** Grace and the mobsters leave, and we behold the town again from above. Where once people lived, now there are only corpses in the ash, and all the chalk lines on the ground have been erased. The only living being that Grace spared... is a dog.

## GLENGARRY GLEN ROSS (1992)

The workplace and all the things that go with it — cubicles, reports, policies, pay cuts or layoffs — define the subgenre that is our "Business Institution." Aren't our jobs actually communities in themselves, in which we have to decide on a daily basis if we are "one of the guys"? There are consequences here for following "rules, ethics and bonds of loyalty."

Things get worse when the job itself sits on the thin Post-It-yellow line that separates honesty from crime. When our everyday tasks consist of tiptoeing on that boundary, making decisions and judgments about our companion's good or wrong doings, on which side of the line do we want to walk?

Such is the case of the main character of this wonderful film that depicts a day in the life of some real estate agents, and not just any random realtors! Stars like Jack Lemmon, Al Pacino, Alec Baldwin, Kevin Spacey, Alan Arkin and Ed Harris will fight each other with testosterone, profanity, mutual distrust and unforgettable dialogue — among the best ever written, in my humble opinion.

Based on master screenwriter David Mamet's stage play (which earned both the Pulitzer Prize and Tony Award), the film shows the contemporary nature of its characters, themes and situations in our personal world, where the "choice" between good and evil can be waiting at our desk every day.

I Type: Business Institution

I Cousins: *Margin Call*, *The Executioner* (*El Verdugo*), *Big Night*, *There Will Be Blood*, *Inside Job*

GLENGARRY GLEN ROSS
*Based on the play by* David Mamet
*Screenplay by* David Mamet
*Directed by* James Foley

**Opening Image**: Early '90s blue neon, jazz music and the passing subway introduce us to a hot and rainy night, and also to Shelley Levene (Jack Lemmon), an aging real estate agent in distress. Apparently, he has a daughter in the hospital who needs to be taken care of. Where will this "primal need" have taken him by the end?

**Set-Up**: Let us meet our "group." As is customary in films with an ensemble, it is best to introduce each character as early as possible, along with their trademark quirks and *things that need fixing*: angry Moss (Ed Harris), clueless Aaronow (Alan Arkin) and confident Ricky Roma (Al Pacino), the current top seller of the bunch. Apparently, all the real estate agents in the office are burdened with the same problem: they lack "good leads," people who may actually buy property. Without the leads, they are basically out of business, *Stasis=Death* for sure.

**B Story**: The thematic B Story focuses on Roma, who is quite the opposite of our main character. While Levene's glory days are fading and he is in a bad-luck streak, Roma is fueled by ambition, the desire to earn and glibness. Although their selling styles are very different, they have an eye on each other, because as we will understand at the end, they may end up working together.

**Theme Stated**: "Put that coffee down. Coffee is for closers only." A man who introduces himself as, "My name is F**k You" (Baldwin), has been sent by the owners of the company to shake things up at the office. With the new policy, mutual support is off the table — basic privileges are only for those who deliver, and the competition is on.

**Catalyst**: Blake (Baldwin's real name) "kicks the dogs" at the office, not only with his demeaning verbal abuse, but with the mission he has come to deliver: only the top two sellers will keep their jobs and will get a bonus, while the rest will be fired.

**Debate**: Obviously, such an outrageous measure is promptly protested (and Debated) by the agents: Isn't it crazy to give them a task like that on such short notice? Can they really meet their quotas with leads as bad as the ones they've been given? Soon we learn something else: the precious "Glengarry leads," easy and lucrative sales, await the closers. But for now, those will be locked in office manager and *Company Man* Williamson's (Spacey) desk.

**Break into Two**: "Those of you who are interested in a continuing job with this organization, get to work." The game is on, and every man in the office knows his livelihood, future and family are on the line. There is no turning back!

**Fun and Games**: Our *promise of the premise* is witnessing the literal workings of real estate agents in a high-pressure situation while also seeing the "pros and cons." They use techniques ranging from flattery to underhandedness to hook their prospective buyers... so our "choice" involves morality, if not legality. After some calls with no success, because the old leads are so weak, Levene tries to negotiate with Williamson to get some of the Glengarry leads to no avail. Even his futile attempt to bribe Williamson doesn't work out. Not even by personally (and rather bluntly) visiting his leads can Levene make the sale. At the same time, Moss and Aaronow discuss their bad luck, when a dark idea starts slipping into their conversation: "Someone should rob the office." For now, that seems like just a joke.

**Midpoint**: Moss and Aronson begin seriously discussing the idea of stealing the Glengarry leads to sell them to a competitor at another agency. Aronson wants no part of the plan, but Moss coerces him, *raising the stakes*. Levene is still unsuccessful, and he is about to make his "choice" between the company and himself. *A and B Stories cross* when we turn to confident Roma, who is about to make a sale to an unsuspecting customer — his personal *false victory*.

**Bad Guys Close In**: When triumphant Roma arrives at the office the next day, he is surprised to see that it has been broken into, and not only have the phones been stolen, but the Glengarry leads are missing, too. Also Bad Guys in the form of police officers Close In on whoever is the thief and start interrogating the agents, when Levene arrives in very high spirits. He has closed one of the tough leads, securing his job at the office and earning the admiration of all, among them, Roma. However, "the team starts disintegrating" when Moss does not take Levene's triumph well. And, even though Levine is proud, Williamson conjures up the Bad Guys of doubt and uncertainty when he points out that the sale may still be cancelled. Levene publicly humiliates Williamson, unknowingly bringing his boss's vengeance closer.

**All Is Lost**: All Is Lost, in this case, for Roma, when the man he sold property to the day before arrives to cancel the deal. Roma seeks Levene's help as they try to con the client, but to make matters worse, the client's wife has notified the attorney general.

**Dark Night of the Soul**: Roma "is beaten and he knows it," but he keeps trying, now lying straight to the client's face.

**Break into Three**: *A and B Stories cross* as Levene is called to be interrogated while Roma, alone, tries to make the deal stick by manipulating his client. But then, Williamson loudly and clearly contradicts Roma about the contract, causing the client to flee the room. "Company man!" shouts Roma to Williamson as an insult; he is not one of "them."

**Finale**:

1. Gathering the Team: Levene confronts a very embarrassed Williamson, ready to enjoy humiliating him.

2. Executing the Plan: Levene's "plan" consists of taking revenge upon Williamson, mocking him, his clumsiness, and pointing out his mistakes. "You are scum," Levene tells him.

3. High Tower Surprise: Levene says something that only the man who had broken into the office could possibly know. Williamson realizes Levene was the robber!

4. Dig, Deep Down: Levene "digs, deep down" while trying to use all his dirty tricks and techniques to lie and deny the truth he just let slip, but it doesn't work with Williamson.

5. The Execution of the New Plan: His "new plan" is to tell the truth: Moss asked him to steal the leads and sell them. Levene tries to bribe Williamson, who not only rejects the deal, but tells him that his sale will be rejected. Levene tries to plead in the name of his sick daughter, but Williamson turns his back on him.

**Final Image**: Roma leaves the office in high spirits and pays his compliments to Levene, asking him to be partners. But as we know, Levene is just waiting to be arrested. In our Opening Image, he was a free man with a "choice" that included honesty. Now, jail is all he has ahead — that is where his choice has taken him. The rest of his associates keep working as usual. How long until they have to make the same decision?

## CINEMA PARADISO (1988)

Seldom is a film both a critical and box-office success, let alone a true classic, but such is *Nuovo Cinema Paradiso*, our title in the original Italian. It is a wonderful film about film, a tale of nostalgia and an homage to the notion of doomed, impossible, yet true love.

It is also a film that seems to defy categorization and analysis, but we who are taught in the ways of the *Cat!*, can recognize a "Mentor Institution" film when we see one. In this subgenre, our protagonist is given a life lesson pertaining to a "group," a "choice" and a "sacrifice," so that he must decide between "I" and "them."

The mentor can be a "false teacher" to give us wrong lessons we must defy, or as in this case, a good man who, though blind, will help us see what is best for ourselves — even if it takes three decades and a dreaded return home! For the sake of this analysis, we chose the 2002 173-minute Director's Cut, which gives full meaning to the "choice."

Ironically, this version makes our analysis an even more interesting challenge, since the film is longer and the beats are more spaced out and subtle. Yet it's another example of how, no matter your format, our flexible tool can help us hold such a vast narrative together while letting us perfectly map our main character's transformation. Lights out, watch the film leader roll... and hush! Our favorite movie about the movies is about to start.

I Type: Mentor Institution

I Cousins: *The Last King of Scotland*, *Whiplash*, *Leon: The Professional* (*Léon the Professional*), *Apt Pupil*, *99 Homes*

CINEMA PARADISO (NUOVO CINEMA PARADISO)
*Story by* Giuseppe Tornatore
*Screenplay by* Giuseppe Tornatore and Vanna Paoli
*Directed by* Giuseppe Tornatore

**Opening Image:** Near the sea, an old woman tries to call her son, who has not been in his hometown village of Giancaldo for about 30 years. This man is Salvatore di Vita (Jaqcues Perrin), a successful filmmaker, who is given a piece of sad news by his much younger girlfriend: a man named Alfredo has died, and the funeral is the next day. Will Salvatore return? Our "choice" (in the past, to leave the village; in the present, to return) is introduced.

**Theme Stated:** "He won't even remember," says Salvatore's sister to his mom, who replies that he will remember well. As our story is a flashback, told through his memories, what *does* he remember after 30 years? Has he learned his teacher's lesson? And will he come back to the "group"?

**Set-Up:** A long flashback begins and introduces us to the many characters that inhabit the village of Giancaldo — they will be our "group," the society that Salvatore ultimately will have to decide if he belongs to, as different as he is. We meet him as a lively young kid nicknamed Totó, our *Naïf*, who is fascinated with the work of mentor-to-be projectionist Alfredo (Philipe Noiret), especially the splices of film he collects of kissing scenes censored by the church. Other characters are introduced, such as his class companions, the censor/village's priest, and Toto's young mother, who still waits for her husband to return from the war. In one way or another, all of them are related to the local Cinema Paradiso.

**Catalyst:** One night, after Salvatore has spent all his money at the movies, he is caught and punished by his mother in the street. Despite having kicked the kid out a few times from the projectionist's booth, Alfredo comes by and "Saves the Cat" by pretending the money was found on the floor — obviously, he cares about the boy.

**Debate:** Will they become mentor and mentee? Will Salvatore end up working with Alfredo, as is his wish? Can a boy like Salvatore grow up without a wise father figure in postwar Italy? After a child's burial, Alfredo and Salvatore hang out and talk about the child's father, furthering their bond and friendship. They will still have to wait for that, as Salvatore causes a fire that forces them apart again. After finding a way to spend time together again, the young boy asks to work with him, but Alfredo deems it too humble a job for the boy, showing that he has other plans for his pupil.

**Break into Two**: During an exam for the school certificate that both Salvatore and Alfredo are taking, Alfredo requests the help of his mentee-to-be. The kid takes advantage of the situation, demanding to become his helper at the cinema in exchange. Thus, Salvatore becomes Alfredo's "official" pupil.

**Fun and Games**: Our *promise of the premise* consists of seeing the inner workings of an old cinema and, of course, to see mentor Alfredo teaching the ropes to mentee Salvatore. The kid learns fast! Film history, village occurrences and life itself happens — Salvatore learns through cinema that his father is actually dead. Soon after, Alfredo has an accident in which film catches fire and the cinema burns. Salvatore saves him, but Alfredo loses his sight, and the movie palace has burnt to the ground. But the Cinema Paradiso reopens again, better than ever, and the entire village turns out to celebrate and watch a movie. Little Salvatore officially gets Alfredo's job, and when they reunite we see the affection they have for each other.

We jump forward in time to see Salvatore has grown into a handsome young man, still close friends with Alfredo, and still passionate about working at the Cinema Paradiso. Salvatore also gets a camera, starting to become what he will be at the end: a filmmaker.

**B Story**: Although late, here comes our B Story Character, *bellissima* Elena, a rich man's daughter who Salvatore immediately falls in love with. Their love story will tighten the second part of the film and will strengthen our "choice" and "sacrifice" elements.

**Midpoint**: Salvatore finds it difficult making Elena fall in love with him, in fact making a fool of himself every time he tries to speak with her. When he loses his temper at Alfredo in frustration, Alfredo tells Salvatore the story of "The Princess and the Soldier." It's a cryptic story that seems to give Salvatore the boost he needs to try once more with Elena... and this time, he wins her over.

**Bad Guys Close In:** Time itself (*ticking clock*) becomes a Bad Guy as it passes; although Elena declares her love for Salvatore, her father separates them. Even the advent of television is a menace for the old Cinema Paradiso. Salvatore is called to military service, and Elena fails to show up at their last date before he leaves for the army. He tries desperately to find her, and when he stops back at the Paradiso, Alfredo tells him Elena never showed up. Salvatore enters the army without seeing Elena, and throughout his enlistment, he never forgets about her. His attempts to get discharged so that he can return to her more quickly only backfire and earn him punishment.

**All Is Lost:** After his military service, Salvatore returns to Giancaldo and looks around as if he barely recognizes the place. He sees that his old job has been taken by another projectionist. He finds that Alfredo is housebound; he's seemingly lost all interest in interacting with anyone in the village. What's more, Alfredo hasn't seen Elena and doesn't know where to find her. When Salvatore says he finally understands the meaning of the story — that love is an illusion, and heartbreak is inevitable — Alfredo tells him to leave, and don't look back. "You have to go away... before you can come back and find your people." This is the "sacrifice" he must make — to leave his life, family and past behind.

**Dark Night of the Soul:** We now see present-day Salvatore returning to Giancaldo. He sees his mother and his old childhood home. When he sees Alfredo's widow (our *whiff of death*), she tells Salvatore that Alfredo always talked about him, and that he genuinely loved Salvatore. In a few beautiful moments, we can read on Salvatore's face the regret and the question that begins to form in his mind: did he do the right thing by leaving this place, and all of these people, behind?

**Break into Three**: At dinner with his family, Salvatore expresses he's not sure when, exactly, he'll be leaving. His "battle" in Act Three will be contending with his past, and deciding what his future holds. He visits the old Cinema Paradiso, now condemned and slated for demolition in a few days. Salvatore also glimpses a young woman he almost mistakes for Elena... but it can't be.

**Finale**:

1. Gathering the Team: Salvatore has a heart-to-heart with his mother — a first, he realizes — asking her why she never re-married. She explains that's just how she is — loyal — and that he's a lot like her. But, she tells him, he needs to let go. Here, there are "only ghosts."

2. Executing the Plan: Salvatore follows the young Elena look-alike, learning she is actually his former love's daughter. He manages to track down Elena, who at first refuses to see him. But they finally connect and and begin to catch up, politely filling each other in about their respective lives.

3. High Tower Surprise: When Salvatore can't take it anymore and, anguished, wants to know why Elena never showed up for their last date, the truth comes out: she did, but she was late. And instead of Salvatore, she found Alfredo at the cinema. He convinced her that it would be best for Salvatore if she let him go so that he could have a future. She agreed, then secretly left a note where Salvatore could find her. But Salvatore never saw the note. Having never made love in the past, they now share their first intimate night together.

4. Dig, Deep Down: Salvatore is hurt and confused as he visits Alfredo's widow to collect what she says Alfredo had left for him. But he can't be angry with Alfredo — the man only wanted Salvatore to have every happiness and opportunity in life. Salvatore returns to the old cinema, desperately searching for that note Elena claims to have left, as though he needs to

confirm it's the truth. And it does, as he finds it and reads her words to him.

5. The Execution of the New Plan: Salvatore calls Elena to discuss their future, but she tells him there is no future, only the past. Though clearly in pain, Salvatore accepts this. He cuts the last ties with his past when he sees the old Cinema Paradiso being demolished. He fulfills his "new plan" of going back to his life and his career, but he remembers Alfredo had something in store for him.

**Final Image:** In the dark projection room of a modern cinema, Salvatore watches his teacher's last life lesson: a montage of all the previously-censored passionate kisses he promised to save for young Salvatore. Moved, he cries, showing that, thanks to that last lesson, he has made peace with his past.

## PULP FICTION (1994)

Few films in the late 20th century have been more commented on, contested, quoted, studied, analyzed, criticized, lauded and — insert basically any past participle here — than Quentin Tarantino's masterpiece *Pulp Fiction*. Released in 1994, it established the director as a great filmmaker after his promising *Reservoir Dogs*, and made him the star-director he still is today. Of course, we had to include it in this book!

*Pulp Fiction* fits naturally in our "Institutionalized" genre, in which some characters decide if they want to be part of the "group" with its particular rules (in this case, a group of criminals) or take their own way, which always implies a "choice" (to act on one's own wishes or conform to the underworld code), and a "sacrifice," which of course, may involve death.

It is our chosen film for the "Issue Institution" subgenre, defined by Blake as one with an ensemble cast, several storylines and a theme, in this case, loyalty. As he reminded us, stories like this force the writer to compress and intensify every beat, so only the most relevant ones are shown and described.

As a result, this approach allows us to have not only one Beat Sheet, but *three* — one for each of the main characters: hitman Vincent Vega, fellow gunman Jules Winnfield and runaway boxer Butch Coolidge. Add a non-linear narrative, flashbacks, cool sexy music and fresh witty pop dialogue, and you'll realize just how flexible our favorite tool is when it's time to get creative!

I Type: Issue Institution

I Cousins: *Short Cuts, 21 Grams, Rashomon, Night on Earth, Happiness*

PULP FICTION
*Story by* Quentin Tarantino and Roger Avary
*Written by* Quentin Tarantino
*Directed by* Quentin Tarantino

**Opening Image / Theme Stated:** The Opening Image establishes tone and genre, and gives us a glimpse of who the three primary characters are in terms of loyalty, our theme. Vincent has his doubts about it, Jules is totally sure of his allegiance to Marcellus, and Butch is already planning his betrayal — quite different from whom they will be at the end! Also, the film opens with Pumpkin (Tim Roth) and Honey Bunny (Amanda Plummer) discussing whether or not to leave their criminal lives, stating, "They'll probably put us in a situation where it's us or them." Sounds a lot like our Institutionalized genre, doesn't it? So, will our characters choose "us" or "them"?

**Set-Up / Catalyst / Debate:** As in most Set-Ups, we meet each one of the characters to learn a little bit more about who they are: their pasts, their current situations, their motivations and the *things that need fixing* in their lives. Then a Catalyst (order, deal or occurrence) causes them to wonder (Debate) about who (our "group") they really owe their loyalties to.

Vincent Vega: Vincent (John Travolta) has just arrived from Amsterdam after three years working there for Marsellus Wallace (Ving Rhames), and once he is back in the gang, he gets a "call to adventure": taking his boss's wife Mia (Uma Thurman) for a night out. Sensing a probable sexual tension, Vincent Debates with Jules about the consequences of being disloyal to his boss, which will probably involve a very serious punishment.

Butch Coolidge: Butch (Bruce Willis) is a heavyweight boxer well past the heyday of his career, so Marsellus Wallace has an offer and a Catalyst for him: to take a dive in an upcoming match and get a lot of money out of it. But while he listens, Butch internally Debates what he is about to do instead — and it involves being disloyal to their deal.

Jules Winnfield: Jules (Samuel L. Jackson) and Vincent perform an easy job (to retrieve a briefcase for Marsellus), which involves coldly shooting some people and delivering an ominous Bible recitation, but his Catalyst moment arrives when a hail of bullets from a hidden shooter miraculously misses them. Jules openly Debates about it being a sign to abandon his until-now loyal thug life.

**Break into Two / Fun and Games**: Each of the characters "gets the case" with no possibility of turning back, so they move forward with their missions and goals, for now keeping the plot light, while still playing with theme.

Vincent Vega: Vincent Breaks into Two by finally taking Mia out. They have literal Fun and Games going for a dinner at Jackrabbit Slim's and performing their unforgettable swing dance. Their attraction is evident, and more so when they end up at home dancing together. Vincent knows it is a critical moment... can he "choose" to stay loyal?

Butch Coolidge: After a strange dream about his father's watch, Butch goes forward with his plan and wins the boxing match, killing his opponent and cementing his "choice" of disloyalty toward Marsellus. A strange taxi driver asks him how it feels to kill a man.

Jules Winnfield: Mulling about the miracle, Jules enters Act Two when Vincent accidentally shoots a man inside their vehicle. In danger of being caught, we witness the "pros and cons" of being a criminal, and they decide to go to his friend Jimmy's (Quentin Tarantino) to seek his help. Jules doesn't seem happy at all about it, until Winston "The Wolf" (Harvey Keitel) arrives to solve the "Bonnie situation."

**Midpoint / Bad Guys Close In / All Is Lost**: In these beats, after a brief *false victory* that makes them believe that their problems are over, *stakes are raised* when Bad Guys complicate each character's situation, making them reach a place where All Seems Lost.

Vincent Vega: Vincent enjoys a brief *false victory* when he decides to leave Marsellus's home without hooking up with Mia, although "the choice gets harder." *Stakes are raised* dramatically when she accidentally snorts heroin. Now Bad Guys Close In as she is overdosing, and he must find help to try to save her life.

Butch Coolidge: Our boxer enjoys a brief *false victory* with *Sex at 60* when he arrives at the motel to meet his girlfriend Fabienne. However, he discovers that she has left his important watch at home, so he must go back to get it, knowing Bad Guys will have Closed In. He kills Vincent and thinks he can finally go in peace, but after Marsellus finds him, they both are kidnapped by a couple of BDSM lunatics. All Is Lost for both of them.

Jules Winnfield: After "The Wolf" has sorted out their bloody, messy problem (AKA *false victory*), Jules and Vincent can relax and have a "Midpoint celebration" where he *publicly comes out* and says he is out of the gangster life for good. But Bad Guys Close In when two robbers hold up the restaurant; he will probably have to kill them, indicating that his new determination is "lost."

**Break into Three / Finale**: Our characters perform a very difficult decision which tests their strength and focuses on our movie's theme: loyalty. After that, loose ends are tied up and they can go on to live their new lives, however short or long they may be — that is their "choice."

> Vincent Vega: Vincent finally Breaks into Three by brutally injecting adrenaline into Mia's heart, bringing her back to life. He takes her home, and both can be happy — even though they like each other very much, they have kept their loyalty to Marsellus. Vincent has finally "chosen," and we will see where this takes him.

> Butch Coolidge: Butch Breaks into Three by managing to escape his ties and KO'ing the creepy Gimp, after which he decides to escape. In an unexpected twist, he gets a katana and frees Marsellus, "choosing" to show him respect and loyalty. Evening the score between them, he also secures that he and Fabienne will live.

> Jules Winnfield: For Jules, the easiest thing to do at the restaurant would be to shoot Pumpkin and Honey Bunny, but he has a new life ahead. So he "digs, deep down," performs his biblical monologue for the last time and "chooses" to let them go... alive.

**Final Image**: Every closing image shows the characters as very different individuals than they were at the beginning. Butch was an underestimated man who aimed to betray his employer and has gained respect by means of loyalty. Jules has kept that loyalty, bringing the suitcase to his boss while risking his life and his new determination, but his "choice" is to terminate his relationship with the "group," starting a new life. Finally, Vincent, the one who decided to keep that loyalty by living like a mobster... ends up dead.

The actress Mrs. Kendal visits John Merrick, who speaks of Romeo and Juliet in this touching Midpoint of *The Elephant Man*.

# 10  SUPERHERO

Let's say you are special. You have a certain set of talents, powers, a kind of inspiration, a dream for the future, a mission or a difference in you that can make the world a better place. You try to tell your fellow humans about it, hoping they will join you in your fight. After all, it's for the common good, isn't it? But instead...

Instead, you get *duh*-faces, disbelief, rejection, persecution and sometimes violence, torture and even death. Well, thanks, but no thanks! You just wanted to make their lives better! In a nutshell, these are the trials and tribulations that make up the foundation of our "Superhero" stories.

Judging from its name, you might automatically think about spandex-clad guys and gals with their undies on top, but despite well-known franchise superheroes like the ones who fight to conquer the box office each week (and that's an epic battle for sure), not everything in the hero-y world comes from the Marvel/DC realm. In fact, these are some of the oldest stories ever told!

The tale of the mysterious stranger — so different from "us" — who inspires awe and fear is as ancient as humanity, and demonstrates how we reject the good they bring simply because they are not like us. Thus, any "chosen one" will suffer from "our" rejection, and the system's too. In a way, as we will see, this repudiation balances their powers (and likability).

As always, we have five subgenres. First we have the **People's Superhero** in which someone as apparently normal as you or I discovers a "power within" that can make them "the chosen one" to defy power or meet a great challenge — even if only a small number of people accepts them. This is the story told in *The Big Blue*, *The Wrestler* and *The Insider*. The films don't have to begin their title with "The," though! Consider our chosen film, *Erin Brockovich*.

Then we have the **Real Life Superhero**, which usually encompasses epic biopics about leaders, artists or common people whose life is told in Superhero form. *Milk* (famous politician), *Che* (famous revolutionary), *Lenny* (famous comedian), *Control* (famous musician) tell these stories, whether the protagonist is famous or not!

There are two subgenres that speak for themselves. The first is the **Comic Book Superhero**, which features stories adapted for the screen whose source material comes from comic books. In our case, independent and European ones include *Akira*, *Tintin*, *V for Vendetta*, *Old Boy* or our own "chosen one," dark hero *The Crow*. The **Storybook Superhero** draws its choices from the literary and fairytale world, like Roald Dahl's *Fantastic Mr. Fox*, *The Adventures of Baron Munchausen*, *The Neverending Story* and so on.

Finally, we have our **Fantasy Superhero**, belonging to made-up worlds or pure adventure stories, such as noir-sci-fi fantasy *Brazil*, indie (yes it is!) sword-fighting epic *Highlander*, or Tim Burton's quirky dark musical comedy *The Nightmare Before Christmas*.

And what are the fundamental components to build a Superhero story? As in any of our genres, we need three main ingredients: a **power** or fundamental difference between the hero and the rest, a **Nemesis** or main antagonist who represents the opposition, and a **curse**, which is usually a consequence of the power, an Achilles heel that balances both.

When you think about a Superhero's power in the mainstream cinema world, those powers are pretty straightforward: super-strength, super-agility, super-stamina. In our indie realm, the heroes may be like this (like The Crow's invulnerability), but we will also count talents, a sense of inspiration, or a mission to "do the right thing" which makes him or her stand out, to be able to change our world... and which will inspire envy and rejection — like the natural hunting abilities of the *Fantastic Mr. Fox*, *The Elephant Man*'s gentleness and sensitivity, or *The Wrestler*'s and *Erin Brockovich*'s decisions to live their lives as they think fit, despite being frowned upon by those who do not understand their inspiration.

Ironically, this difference often brings the curse. Kryptonite is a cool visual device, but in our subtler world, curses are a consequence of power, such as the obsessive drive of many artists (*Pollock, Lenny, Frida*), the choice between family and work (*Erin Brockovich*), morality (*The People vs. Larry Flynt*) or sheer vengeance (*The Crow*). Our curses are fundamental because they are both an internal and external trial for our heroes, the price they pay for being special and a weapon to use against them by the Nemesis.

Speaking of which, who are the Lex Luthor-y guys and gals in our universe? As Blake said, our Nemesis opposes our hero's rise because it is a problem for them. The villains are usually self-made individuals with no true powers of their own, but they have gained privileges or abilities through money, genius or social class. They often represent The System, or The Man, relying on money, intelligence and brute force to oppose our gentler hero. For example, in many an artist's biopic (and in many a cinema auteur biography), the conservative academic establishment will be a worthy Nemesis, and in other cases we will have politicians (*Che*), businessmen (*Fantastic Mr. Fox*), crime bosses (*The Crow*), ministries (*Brazil*), or even entire corporations (*Erin Brockovich*) that stand in the way.

How can our "supers" defeat such powerful foes? There is something that all these self-made villains lack, and that is **faith**. Our hero knows he or she is doing the right thing, and thus holds to an absolute belief that their mission is worthy and their victory necessary — they represent universal, positive values of acceptance, freedom or change that the bad guy lacks. In turn, the villains usually only look after their own statuses and upholding the systems they represent. Most often, our hero surmounts the opposition, but sometimes he succumbs to it, as in *Brazil*.

If all this sounds a little familiar, check a couple of chapters back and you will realize how close our Fool Triumphant and Superhero genres are. But they have a crucial difference: in the former, the hero does not know he is special. Our Superheroes painfully know they are different, and this will weigh in their personal fights — they are too conscious that being different comes with a price! This is the reason why we will sometimes also find the **hero changes his name** beat: Eric Draven becomes The Crow with his newfound powers and The Elephant Man transfigures to John Merrick.

Another common element in Superhero films is the **Mascot**, the hero's helper famous for their loyalty, who is useful in showing the contrast between "us and them." Such is the case of Alfred for mainstream hero Batman, but also Sarah in *The Crow*, Kylie the opossum in *Fantastic Mr. Fox*, or Ed in *Erin Brockovich*.

In *Save the Cat!® Goes to the Movies*, Blake lamented the lack of female Superhero characters in this movie genre. And while it is true that in the mainstream world, women are usually forgotten by execs when matters like target audience and box-office earnings mix with the Superhero genre, in our indie world there is no such excuse. We write about characters who oppose a system to change it and get rid of the injustice and power imbalances — and history is filled with brave women who have made a difference doing exactly this.

We are sure that you will follow their lead, tell their tales and live your own super-story with your filmmaking powers. Are you *different* enough?

## SAVING THE WORLD, ONE GENRE AT THE TIME

A quick three-step guide on how to save the world, keep faith in yourself and defeat the bad guys, no matter if you come from real life or the pages of a comic book:

1. Remember to make your hero special by giving him a "power," even if it is just a mission to do the right thing, a talent to develop or a physical distinctness whose acceptance would make us better.

2. This power comes with a price, which we call the "curse," the downside of being special — it will make him different and bring rejection from "us."

3. The hero will have to fight the system, personified by a "Nemesis," an equally powerful individual or system representative who will try to kick the hero where it hurts most: through rejection.

Let's look at the five ways to be super — and try not to be defeated in the process.

## ERIN BROCKOVICH (2000)

"Real Life Superheroes" do not usually wear capes or masks, but they can still save the world. This subgenre encompasses biographies with determination, strength and bravery as their subjects' "powers," which allow them to fulfill a mission to make a better world for all of us, in small or great measure.

Such is the story of Kansas-born Erin Brockovich, who without formal education in the law, helped build a case against a large energy company in California whose wrongdoings had led to many people getting sick. Erin fought with valor and determination by caring about the victims and was instrumental in their victory.

Erin has a clear "mission" to do good, which is to build a case against PG&E, her "Nemesis." Not only is it a big company with unlimited means, but of course it lacks the "faith" in humanity that Erin will display, which will be her best weapon. But power comes with a "curse," in this case, having to distance herself from her family.

As pointed out in *Save the Cat!® Goes to the Movies*, the Superhero genre is known for having a dearth of female-driven stories, but the Real Life Superhero genre is probably the easiest to fulfill in this sense — just like Erin Brockovich, there are hundreds of female fighters waiting for their story to be told. "Will you be 'the one' to bring this change?" asked Blake.

SH Type: Real Life Superhero

SH Cousins: *La Vie en Rose, Trumbo, Frida, The Iron Lady, Lenny*

## ERIN BROCKOVICH
*Screenplay by* Susannah Grant
*Directed by* Steven Soderbergh

**Opening Image**: We meet Erin Brockovich (Julia Roberts) trying to find a job. Although she seems resolute, meritorious and talented, she doesn't have any formal qualifications, so she cannot find employment and she doesn't get respect. These are our first prerequisites for a story of triumph and sacrifice.

**Set-Up**: Erin is a middle-aged woman who, after two divorces, is raising three kids she's proud of — her resilience, talents and determination are her "powers." After getting hurt in a car accident, she seeks legal counsel in Ed Masry (Albert Finney), an older attorney, but when they go to court, straight-shooter Erin can't handle the tricky, ruthless legal maneuvers of the other side and blows the case. Soon, her domestic situation leads to a *Stasis=Death* situation, and she knows she must make a change.

**Theme Stated**: "You and me, we're gonna make him pay for it." Sounds promising coming from a lawyer, but for Ed, this is the usual rhetoric he tells clients to show he is caring for them, when in reality, he's not. However, Erin takes his word and together, they will make the Bad Guys pay for what they have done to other people. And in the process, she will teach Ed how to care for people.

**Catalyst**: Erin visits Ed again and essentially hires herself to make up for his lying to her about winning her case. If she isn't any good at the job, he can fire her.

**Debate**: Can she really make it? Isn't it crazy to think that someone without any legal qualifications or experience can work in a law firm? She steadily gets her work done although her lifestyle and clothing do not really fit in. This is her "curse": instead of having a "normal" life and appearance, she will defend her choices and identity, which will cause other coworkers to display hostility and reject her. Soon, Erin gets a *pro bono* case to file, and she becomes interested, as there seems to be more than meets the eye.

**B Story**: Our "love story" pertains to Erin and a biker named George (Aaron Eckhart). Just as people don't take her seriously because of her looks, his long hair and Harley-Davidson lifestyle ironically make her think *he* will not be up to the task. But by showing care, acceptance and respect, they will find comfort in each other.

**Break into Two**: Erin realizes that there is something fishy with the case she has been reviewing. Pacific Gas and Electric Company (PG&E) has been paying for residents' medical needs. Why? Erin "gets the case" when Ed allows her to further investigate. This will be her "mission."

**Fun and Games**: Erin uses her "powers," empathizing with people so that they tell her their troubles when they see how much she cares about them. She uses those same powers to convince a clerk at the regional Water Board to let her peruse the Board's files. She realizes PG&E has been polluting underground water with a carcinogenic product. However, she gets fired because her looks and demeanor made people assume she was not taking her job seriously enough. Ed confirms the information about the carcinogen and puts her back on the case, and new victims of PG&E seek her help.

**Midpoint**: *A and B Stories cross* when Erin has to rely more and more on George to take care of the kids. She and Ed attend a "Midpoint celebration" when they meet with the affected neighbors, and they have their *false victory* when the group decides to go ahead with the case. *Stakes are raised* when Erin realizes how many people could die if she does not help them and pushes her boss to sue PG&E.

**Bad Guys Close In**: All that "attention attraction" pays off when Bad Guys start harassing her with menacing calls. The "team starts disintegrating" when George tells her that maybe she should pursue another line of work. She realizes how much she is missing because of work (her "curse") when George tells her that her baby spoke her first words and how he is tempted to go on the road again with his motorcycle buddies. Things get even worse when Ed and Erin realize that PG&E knew about the contamination (which is difficult to prove) and some of the victims are developing lethal forms of cancer. They are offered money to settle, but they decline.

**All Is Lost**: Things reach the lowest point for Erin when George leaves her for neglecting their relationship, so she is "worse off than when she started."

**Dark Night of the Soul**: Erin drives the car with all her kids, a symbol of her having to juggle both lives. But can she? Ed hires a more experienced partner which, in a way, indicates that she is off the case.

**Break into Three**: *A and B Stories* briefly *cross* when Erin hears George's bike outside of her house and sees him leave again. New problems arise when the victims start losing their trust in Ed and the lawyers, who cannot empathize with them. Ed tells Erin, "I need you," and she is back in the case!

**Finale**:

1. Gathering the Team: Erin and Ed "gather" all the affected, but they need signatures from 90% of the claimants to allow a judge to rule on the case, with no jury.

2. Executing the Plan: Erin visits every one of the remaining victims door-to-door, seeking their signatures and showing that she cares about them. She gets the signatures. Now, is the case solid enough?

3. High Tower Surprise: A man whom Erin previously mistrusted, ironically because of his looks and demeanor, turns out to be a PG&E worker who was once asked to destroy documents... but he kept many of them.

4. Dig, Deep Down: Erin "digs, deep down" to earn the man's trust and respect, and gains access to the incriminating documents he's held.

5. The Execution of the New Plan: Erin and Ed use the new documents, proving her value. The case is settled and the affected will receive a substantial sum of money.

**Final Image:** At first, Erin was an unemployed single mother, but now she proudly works in a law firm that has grown greatly because of her talents. She was seeking a job but has received much more: respect... and a $2 million bonus!

## FANTASTIC MR. FOX (2009)

Wes Anderson stands out as one of the few filmmakers with a visual world so personal and powerful that a mere look at any of his autumn-tinted, vintage-spirited, mustard-and-chestnut colored shots makes his work instantly recognizable — even if the piece in question is a stop-motion animation film, the first he did in his career.

Based on Roald Dahl's family favorite book, the film fits right into our "Storybook Superhero" subgenre. The Superhero in question does not wear a cape, although his son does, underscoring our genre. Mr. Fox has the natural hunting and stealing "powers" of his species, but not using them is his "curse," the price he has to pay for being a family man.

Can he stand temptation when every day, in front of his newly-acquired home, he sees the richest farms in the country, well stocked with prey? Those farms are owned by our self-made "Nemesis" baddies, the really powerful, super-geniuses of farming and evil who lack the "faith" our hero has.

This faith comes not only from our hero and his powers, but also from his family and neighbors, who — despite their support — will also oppose many of his natural predatory instincts. Mr. Fox's arc is complete when he understands that the respect he seeks will not be given for using his "great powers" for his personal pride, but from the "great responsibility" he must show everyone. Haven't you heard those superhero-y words before?

SH Type: Storybook Superhero

SH Cousins: *Coraline*, *Kirikou and the Sorceress* (*Kirikou et la Sorcière*), *The Red Shoes*, *The Secret of Roan Inish*, *Tom Thumb*

## FANTASTIC MR. FOX
*Based on the book by* Roald Dahl
*Screenplay by* Wes Anderson & Noah Baumbach
*Directed by* Wes Anderson

**Opening Image**: Mr. Fox (voice: George Clooney) stands alone next to a tree — the polar opposite of how we will see him at the end. Watch this fast-paced film closely or you'll miss his "power" and his "curse": he wants to go hunting for squabs, which he does well naturally as a fox. Although he is very confidant in himself, he seldom listens to others (*a thing that certainly will need fixing*).

**Theme Stated**: About to be trapped, Mrs. Fox (voice: Meryl Streep) tells her husband that she is pregnant, adding this suggestion: "I want you to find another line of work." Which means he must stop hunting, a reasonable request if they are going to have a kid. But will he be able to suppress his natural instincts?

**Set-Up**: Twelve fox-years later, Mr. and Mrs. Fox live, well, in a fox-hole, and they have a teenage child, Ash (voice: Jason Schwartzman). Mr. Fox now works as a journalist, and Mrs. Fox is a stormy land-scape painter, while their son tends to be grumpy because he feels his athletic capabilities aren't up to his father's expectations. Mr. Fox has lived these past 12 years without using his "powers." But can that last? He feels "poor," which seems a lot like a *Stasis=Death*. How will he move on?

**B Story**: Our "relationship story" centers on the "fantastic" Mr. Fox and his ever-frustrated son Ash. In many ways, Ash will share our Superhero themes, as he feels "different," faces rejection from his father and even wears a self-made superhero suit, cape and all.

**Catalyst**: Mr. Fox decides to go upscale, purchasing a fancy treehouse that the family can barely afford. Also, something catches his eye: there are three farms in the distance. Isn't this a great temptation for a former chicken thief?

**Debate**: Mr. Fox Debates with his attorney Badger (voice: Bill Murray) about buying the treehouse, but unable to listen to good advice as always, ignores him and goes ahead with the purchase. What will be the consequences for the family? And will he keep his promise of not stealing again? Teenage cousin Kristofferson arrives, only causing more strain in the father-son relationship between Mr. Fox and Ash. Mr. Fox further Debates with Kylie the opossum (his Mascot) about his nature: "Who am I, and how can a fox ever be happy without a... chicken in his teeth?"

**Break into Two**: Mr. Fox starts devising a plan for performing "one last big job," which also implies lying to his wife and family.

**Fun and Games**: The day of the plan arrives and Mr. Fox and his band are about to storm the first of the farms. They belong to Boggis, Bunce and Bean, his Nemeses, self-made men who have the power and the will to oppose our hero's rise. Mr. Fox, full of inner "faith," has Fun and Games while he "shows off his powers" stealing from each one of them. *A and B Stories cross* with literal games, like the important "whack-bat" game that sets up the ending.

**Midpoint**: However sweet (or cider-flavored) this *false victory* tastes, Mrs. Fox finds out about the robberies and *stakes are raised* when Boggis, Bunce and Bean discover the animals' hideout. *Clocks start ticking* for all the animals!

**Bad Guys Close In**: The Nemeses Close In, Mr. Fox loses his tail and "the team starts disintegrating" when his wife tells him that he never listens to anyone, and that he broke his promise. As a sensible individual, she knows the "immutable laws of screenwriting physics" when she tells him, "In the end we all die… unless you change." The "team further disintegrates" as Ash and Kristofferson are unable to resolve their differences. The Bad Guys Close In even more when they nearly force Mr. Fox and the others out of their underground hideout with excavators and dynamite. Our Superhero faces more hostility when he meets the animals who have been forced from their homes by the farmers, and they blame him.

**All Is Lost**: Things seem "worse than ever before" when Kristofferson is caught by Bean's wife and locked in an apple crate, and the animals are forced by the farmers into the sewers. "Do you still think we beat them, Foxy?" his attorney asks.

**Dark Night of the Soul**: Mr. Fox seeks solace on an empty bridge (a typical location for our Dark Night of the Soul beat), and his wife arrives to comfort him. Mr. Fox acknowledges his wrongdoings and atones for his arrogance: "I think I need everyone to think I'm the greatest, the 'fantastic' Mr. Fox."

**Break into Three**: *A and B Stories cross* when Mr. Fox comforts his son: "It's not your fault, it's mine." He is about to turn himself in to his Nemeses, but a short duel with Rat (voice: Willem Dafoe) shows him how necessary his powers are for the rest.

**Finale**:
1. Gathering the Team: All the community "gathers" to listen to Mr. Fox's plan. And in a beautiful thematic turn, he uses the "differences" and talents of each species (Latin name and all) for the final attack (including having cool bandit hats).

2. Executing the Plan: Everybody in town awaits the "execution of the plan" like in a Sergio Leone western. The animals set

the town on fire, and Mr. Fox enters the farm to free Kristof-ferson. There, Ash apologizes and accepts himself: "I'm just different, apparently."

3. High Tower Surprise: They meet their surprise — the farmers are blocking the exit. How will they escape now?

4. Dig, Deep Down: Mr. Fox "digs, deep down" about his reasons to win, as does Ash. The latter uses his fast-running "powers" developed while playing "whack-bat" to open the door and let them out. "You're an athlete," says the proud dad.

5. The Execution of the New Plan: They execute their "new plan" by jumping from a stunt ramp and escaping. Our defeated Nemeses have a new plan, too: to wait until the animals get hungry to catch them again.

**Final Image**: However, the whole tribe of animals will be taken care of for years, as they have underground access to the groceries in the brand-new Boggis, Bunce and Bean supermarket. They dance together in victory and toast to their survival, thanks to a now more than ever, truly "fantastic" Mr. Fox.

## BRAZIL (1985)

Isn't it amazing how some fantasy films become more and more sim-ilar to the supposedly imaginary worlds they portray? *Brazil*, with its Big Brother-like government, paranoia-state mood, terrorist men-aces, small iPad-like screens and ducts (read: internet) invading each part of our private lives, seems more current than ever — except for, maybe, the slapstick humor!

In *Brazil*, Terry Gilliam — ex-Monty Python member and cre-ator of absurd-yet-plausible, humorous-yet-sad, violent-but-funny worlds with quirky characters (ask Jean-Pierre Jeunet, Alex Proyas, Tim Burton or Darren Aronofsky about his influence) — reached one of his creative summits with this fantastic tale about finding true love in a world deprived of it.

Thus, it is an example of our "Fantasy Superhero" in which protagonist Sam Lowry plays the part of a government official trying to go unnoticed. His rise through the ranks to find out more about his love will teach him that "power comes with a price." He does not belong to the oppressors, nor to the terrorists fighting the Man, and he knows it. So, he will pay for it.

Finally, as a "Nemesis," we have Jack, Sam's shadow-like reflection, a torturer doing the exact opposite: trying to be noticed so he can rise faster in the ranks. Oh! And please note that among the versions that exist of this film, we have chosen Gilliam's Director's Cut to beat out.

SH Type: Fantasy Superhero

SH Cousins: *Time Bandits*, *Pan's Labyrinth*, *Princess Mononoke*, *Highlander*, *The Dark Crystal*

## BRAZIL
*Screenplay by* Terry Gilliam & Tom Stoppard & Charles McKeown
*Directed by* Terry Gilliam

**Opening Image:** "Somewhere in the twentieth century," we behold a world in which terrorism, government control, bureaucracy, police forces and capitalism dominate the world and the lives of its oppressed citizens. Sound familiar? We also meet our hero, Sam Lowry (Jonathan Pryce), a low-level government official who seems quite satisfied with his unimportant job in a small ministerial department. Will he be just as happy at the end?

**Set-Up:** A bureaucratic mistake provokes the incarceration of a family man named "Buttle," when actually "Tuttle" was the man the authorities were looking for. Also, we get to know Sam a bit more — he has dreams in which he flies, is armor-clad and kisses a beautiful maiden (Kim Greist). Sam loves movies and is not what we would call a *Company Man*, taking his job a little less seriously. We behold his "powers," which involve having access to information. These powers come with a "curse": the more access he has, the more closely watched he will be. But he is happy where he is (*Stasis=Death*), so there's no problem for him... yet.

**Theme Stated**: "The truth shall make you free," we can read on a statue's plinth. But which truth? The government's? The truth we seek? The truth we imagine? This theme, along with issues of misinformation, mistaken identity and misuse of power will take us to the film's much-discussed ending.

**Catalyst**: At the Ministry's entrance Sam sees Jill, the woman who appears in his dreams. Then he discovers the Tuttle/Buttle mistake the system made and is notified that he is about to get a promotion. This is bad news for Sam, who just wants a tranquil life!

**Debate**: Sam visits his rich, plastic surgery-addicted mother, who is pulling strings for him to advance in his career. He wants to Debate about rejecting the promotion, and while they are having dinner in a restaurant, a terrorist attack happens, which does not seem to bother them, accustomed as they are to such events. In Sam's peaceful dreams, dark towers emerge, which seem like an inner Debate about a bad omen. He also meets the real Tuttle (Robert de Niro), who fixes his heating system but seems to be much more than that, possibly a terrorist?

**Break into Two**: Sam gets a new notice that the Tuttle/Buttle confusion must be fixed, so he is sent to the Buttles's home to take care of the affair. Unbeknownst to him, this is only the start of his adventure.

**B Story**: Our "Love Story" pertains to Jill, the mysterious girl who appears in Sam's dreams and who coincidentally seems to exist (but only with short hair) in the real world.

**Fun and Games**: Sam visits the slums in which the Tuttles live. The family there seems to still be in shock, and he is even more surprised when he sees Jill again. He tries to find her, but children pretending to be cops burn his car down! Sam then tries to find out more about Jill, fulfilling the *promise of the premise* of showing us the inner workings of the Ministry of Information. When his attempts to locate Jill are unsuccessful, Sam realizes the only way to find her will be to accept the previously-rejected promotion, which will give him access to classified information. Meanwhile, his apartment is seized by the official air-conditioning specialist of the Ministry, and his dreams become more unsettling: he loses his wings and has to fight a huge samurai warrior.

**Midpoint**: Sam attends his mother's "Midpoint celebration" and *A and B Stories cross* as he plans to accept the promotion. Finally, he gets his *false victory* when Deputy Minister Mr. Helpmann grants his promotion.

**Bad Guys Close In**: Sam attends his first day in his new position, not realizing he will now be subject to greater control, which of course means Bad Guys Close In. Asking Jack (Michael Palin) about Jill makes him appear more suspicious. He discovers Jill when she is being held at gunpoint but uses his position's influence to leave the Ministry with her, though she doesn't trust him. They flee together and survive a terrorist attack, but they are arrested by the police.

**All Is Lost**: Sam has lost Jill and learns that Jack believes she is connected with Tuttle. Also, he is drawing too much attention to himself — he is "worse off than when the story started."

**Dark Night of the Soul**: Sam gets out of the Ministry, crestfallen and sad...

**Break into Three**: ...and *A and B Stories cross* when Sam finds Jill in the street and is about to kiss her.  Sam thinks there is a way to save her and makes her appear as "dead" in the Ministry's files. They seek refuge at his mother's home and make love, trusting each other at last. But the next day, they are arrested again, and a gunshot is heard!

**Finale:**

1. Gathering the Team: Sam has been arrested and he is "gathered" not only with Ministry officials, but with a Santa-Claus dressed Mr. Helpmann too.

2. Executing the Plan: The "plan" is to have Sam's old friend Jack torture him to death!

3. High Tower Surprise: Fortunately, Tuttle and other terrorists break into the torturing "tower" and liberate Sam. They demolish the Ministry and flee until Tuttle is literally drowned in paperwork.

4. Dig, Deep Down: Sam "digs, deep down" to save Tuttle from the paperwork, but he has disappeared. What has happened? Sam can only keep fleeing. He seeks refuge with his mother, but she is attending a funeral... and now she even looks like Jill! Sam has only one option: to get inside the coffin, fall into the darkness and escape the nightmarish creatures that chase him. He finally opens a door.

5. The Execution of the New Plan: Sam finds himself in a truck driven by Jill! She drives them both out of the city, to the countryside, where they will be able to live the rest of their lives in peace, far from any control. Can they really find a place beyond the Ministry's reach?

**Final Image:** We suddenly go back to the torture room, and realize that ever since Sam was taken there, he has been hallucinating. He has lost his mind to the torture, and all has been a fantasy. His blank stare tells us the battle is over. He blandly smiles in a strange, deranged bliss, humming "Brazil."

## THE ELEPHANT MAN (1980)

Not many people would guess that comedy genius Mel Brooks produced David Lynch's second movie, so we can thank both for this masterpiece. Inspired by two books, the producers dared to give the author of *Eraserhead* a story in which he would be able to show his talent for darkness, madness and the deepest pits of the human heart and soul.

Don't let the "Man" in the title fool you either; as most of you know, this is not a story about any powerful Superhero, it belongs to our "People's Superhero" category. In this subgenre, a "civilian rising from the ranks" tale is told according to the guidelines of our primary genre, in which a very special, very "different" being must pay a price for being so.

The Elephant Man (real name: Joseph Merrick) must have been as scary as John Hurt portrays him in the movie. Unlike in Fool Triumphant tales, he certainly knows he is different (his "curse"), but as Blake points out, his "mission to be great" will push him to keep fighting to be himself — a gentle, generous, sweet human being, whose heart was never hardened by hate or rejection from "us."

And his "Nemesis" is not a small one! Mr. Bytes, the self-made owner of the freak circus where John is basically enslaved, will never accept him as a human being, lacking the "faith" that others will have in him. Fortunately, unlike Bytes, "we," inspired by John Merrick's candor, will not succumb to hatred either.

SH Type: People's Superhero

SH Cousins: *Che, Milk, Whale Rider, The Imitation Game, Amazing Grace*

THE ELEPHANT MAN
*Based on the books by* Frederick Treves and Ashley Montagu
*Screenplay by* Christopher de Vore & Eric Bergren & David Lynch
*Directed by* David Lynch

**Opening Image:** The film opens with disturbing, properly Lynchian images of a woman being assaulted by elephants. Narrative, or just a dream? The impression we get is one of distress, violence and pain — quite the opposite of what we will see at the end.

**Set-Up:** London, late nineteenth century. A certain doctor Treves (Anthony Hopkins) wanders in a fair in East London, when he notices something is happening at the freak show. It is being shut down by the police, apparently because a bizarre creature known as "The Elephant Man" is considered too much for the audience. Intrigued, Treves keeps investigating until he eventually finds a clue in the city's poorest neighborhoods.

**Theme Stated:** "He is a freak! How else will he live?" These words are uttered by Mr. Bytes (Freddie Jones), the creature's owner, when the show is cancelled. But is The Elephant Man really a freak? And can he live by other standards than those that make him appear to be just a monster? Doesn't he deserve respect, acceptance and a peaceful life? These are the questions that relate to our hero's re-jection by society.

**Catalyst:** Treves finally finds The Elephant Man (John Hurt) and offers Bytes money to see him. His wishes are granted and he beholds a terribly deformed individual, whose intelligence, on first sight, seems to be on a par with his disgraced body. The doctor cannot but cry. He requests the creature be sent to him for examination.

**B Story:** As we can guess, Treves is our B Story Character, the one who will act as "us" in his progressive acceptance of The Elephant Man. Their story of mutual respect and appreciation will be the embodiment of our theme, but another seemingly small role is noteworthy — that of Byte's boy, The Elephant Man's caretaker, another frightened version of "us" who will cross paths with our hero in key beats.

**Debate**: Can Treves really cure him? Will he be able to see the creature's humanity? Is The Elephant Man more than a "creature"? Things do not start well, as Treves basically performs another freak show with his colleagues, showing the "monster" for what he is (or seems to be): a deformed, illness-plagued being. Treves asks The Elephant Man several questions but does not receive a reply, so he just lets the creature go back with his master, saying, "I pray to God he's an idiot." For who could live sane in a body like that? Soon, Treves is called by Bytes to check on The Elephant Man's condition, and the doctor realizes that he has been severely beaten by his master.

**Break into Two**: Treves takes the "monster" to the hospital again, trying to do so in secrecy, but the hospital director, Mr. Carr-Gomm (John Gielgud) discovers him. However, The Elephant Man will be able to stay with them — for now.

**Fun and Games**: Our *promise of the premise* consists of seeing The Elephant Man's life in a new environment with different people; instead of drunks and lowlifes, he will be around cultured and well-meaning folks. But will they see his humanity? Bytes arrives to regain possession, and Treves manages to get Bytes off his back, but the chief nurse says, "He doesn't belong here." Seeing that he could lose The Elephant Man, Treves asks him to talk, realizing he not only can, but he is a gentle, Bible-knowing, good-mannered man named John Merrick. Behold our character's *change of name*! He was only too afraid to talk, a completely human reaction to the treatment he had been subjected to. He reveals how his disease began and that he must sleep standing up... or die of suffocation.

**Midpoint**: A long Midpoint beat begins with a *false victory*: John will be able to stay in the hospital indefinitely thanks to Treves (*A and B Stories cross*). *Stakes are raised* when Bytes's boy, working as a waiter, hears a night porter charging people to see the monster in the hospital — John is not yet safe. Meanwhile, John performs a *public coming out* dressed in an elegant suit and visiting the Treves's home. There is even a hint of "love at the Midpoint" when he plays a little bit of Romeo and Juliet with a theater actress, who tenderly kisses him. John cries out of happiness.

**Bad Guys Close In**: Our Bad Guys for now appear to be good-natured, since it becomes "in" amidst high society circles to meet John at the hospital. The chief nurse recognizes the situation, telling Treves, "They don't care anything about John." Treves realizes his error, his internal Bad Guys rearing their ugly heads as he acts like "Nemesis" Bytes, showing John off like a freak. They all dodge a new Bad Guys attack when the hospital's board members debate if they should keep John there, but royal intervention saves the day. However, Merrick is assaulted at night, not only by his nightmares, but by the night porter and the drunks this evil man brings to John's quarters to humiliate him. John almost chokes to death.

**All Is Lost**: Bytes steals John away from the hospital. Treves's now dear friend is nowhere to be found.

**Dark Night of the Soul**: Merrick is living his own long Dark Night of the Soul when he is taken to the continent and shown again like a freak. But this time, he is very sick and faints, a *whiff of death*. Angered, Bytes shoves him into the monkey's cage — John's lowest point. He was finally starting to be treated as a human, but now he is subjected to abuse like an animal.

**Break into Three**: *A and B Stories cross* when Bytes's son defies his father, taking John's clothes, including his hood and cape.

**Finale**:
1. Gathering the Team: The boy and the rest of the "freaks" free John so that he can escape.

2. Executing the Plan: Helped by his friends, John gets dressed with his hood and cap, and sets sail for England.

3. High Tower Surprise: Before he can leave the station, a flock of cruel children mock him, drawing the attention of a crowd that harasses him.

4. Dig, Deep Down: Cornered and unhooded, John "digs, deep down" to proclaim his humanity: "I am not an elephant! I am not an animal! I am a human being! I am... a man!"

5. The Execution of the New Plan: John returns to the hospital to be cared for by Treves and his friends. However, he is very sick and he will die soon. Luckily, he earns a last moment of appreciation when he is cheered and applauded in a theater like a human being. He fulfills his last "plan" and decides to "sleep like a normal person," although he knows this will kill him.

**Final Image:** While John dies, new surreal images mix with his dreams. Just like in the beginning, his mother appears, but whereas our Opening Image montage was creepy and bizarre, this one is calm, sweet, gentle and peaceful — similar to John himself. To the verses of "Nothing Will Die" by Tennyson, John finds his rest at last.

## THE CROW (1994)

If you were a teenager in the '90s (like me) and 90% of your ward-robe was black (like mine), chances are that you hold Alex's Proyas's piece dearly in your memories. It was a small film that became a sleeper hit and a cult movie, thanks to its immortal love story, dark ambience and, unfortunately, because of its star Brandon Lee's sad and untimely death.

It was hailed by Roger Ebert as "the best version of a comic book universe" he had seen, although this was said in pre-Marvel/DC franchise times, where independent comic books with great stories and characters (and not necessarily tights-clad heroes with names ending in -*man*) had a chance at the cinemas. Hopefully, it will happen again!

Though cape-less, Eric Draven AKA The Crow is an example of our "Comic Book Superhero," as he has both a "power" (he is invulnerable) and "a mission": to take revenge on his girlfriend's killers. For that, Eric will have to oppose a self-made "Nemesis" nicknamed Top Dollar, the crime boss of the city.

And of course, Eric has a "curse" — he will not be able to reunite with his lover in the afterworld until he has destroyed his enemies. He is "stuck" and does not belong to this world or to the next one. He is special and knows it, and so he has to pay a price for being our savior — which is what all Superhero stories are about in the end.

SH Type: Comic Book Superhero

SH Cousins: *Persepolis*, *Akira*, *Ghost World*, *Kick-Ass*, *Tank Girl*

THE CROW
*Based on the comic book by* James O'Barr
*Screenplay by* David J. Schow and John Shirley
*Directed by* Alex Proyas

**Opening Image:** Detroit, Devil's Night — the dark skies are illumi-nated only by the fires that mobsters have spread throughout the city.

At the end, this "system" will have changed. The man who started the fires will have died and will have paid for his wrongdoings. Also, a loving couple that has been separated by death will be united again.

**Theme Stated**: "Sometimes, if love proves real, two people who are meant to be together, nothing can keep them apart," says Sarah, our hero's *Mascot* in this film. Not even tragedy will be able to keep these two lovers apart, but there will have to be revenge.

**B Story**: Our love story, as it could not be any other way, revolves around Eric and Shelly, separated by a terrible tragedy and seeking to be together in the afterlife. She is his inspiration and his reason for coming back from the dead.

**Set-Up**: A beat cop, Albrecht (Ernie Hudson), investigates a sad crime — a soon-to-be-married couple has been savagely attacked because they tried to expose the mobsters that harassed them. Rock musician Eric Draven (Brandon Lee) has been killed, and his girl-friend Shelly (Sofia Shinas) dies soon after being raped and stabbed. After a year has passed, a strange black crow pecks on Eric's grave-stone, as if to wake him up. The ground opens, and a confused Eric rises from the grave.

**Catalyst**: Guided by the dark bird, Eric returns to his old, now dilapidated apartment, where he experiences a painful flashback that makes him remember what happened on that terrible night, seeing the faces of his attackers.

**Debate**: What must he do now? How is it possible that he is alive again? There can only be one answer, and that is to get revenge. Meanwhile, the criminals are preparing themselves for a new night of arson, in-toxication and aggression. At home, Eric paints his face like a mask and gets black clothes — this is our *hero changes his name beat*, where Eric accepts his destiny and turns into The Crow.

**Break into Two:** The Crow surveys the city, focusing on the gang territory where he is about to carry out his retribution.

**Fun and Games:** The Crow starts by killing, one by one, the mobsters who tortured Shelly to death, starting with knife-wielding Tin Tin. At the same time, we meet our Nemesis, gang lord, genius of evil, elegant arsonist Top Dollar (Michael Wincott) and his goth lover/sister Myca (Bai Ling). Unlike our hero, he has created himself and will crave the Crow's powers. But as we know, he will fail because of his lack of personal "faith." Meanwhile, The Crow gets back Shelly's engagement ring and kills another one of the mobsters, Funboy. He then helps Sarah's drug-addicted mother, prompting her to return to her daughter.

**Midpoint:** After his *false victory* of killing the second murderer, The Crow *publicly comes out* when he lets himself be seen by Top Dollar's minion Grange and when visiting Sergeant Albrecht at home. *Stakes are raised* when The Crow touches Albrecht's face and learns firsthand what happened to Shelly during her 30-hour agony, which cleverly sets up the ending. During this time, The Crow has earned the "attention attraction" of the villains, who now know who he is.

**Bad Guys Close In:** *Clocks start ticking* as there are only two of the killers still alive. The Crow finds T-Bird (David Patrick Kelly) and after a tense chase, makes him literally explode! But he must hurry — a new day rising tells us he only has a few hours left to carry out his revenge (more *ticking clocks*). The Crow finds the remaining baddie in Top Dollar's gang meeting and uses this occasion to dispose of a few more villains, making the Bad Guys really Close In on him with bullets and *jeet kune do* kicks. Soon, the police are chasing The Crow, but thankfully Albrecht finds him first and helps him escape. Now, all the Bad Guys *and* police in town (representing "us") are looking for our hero...

**All Is Lost**: Myca has figured out a way to destroy Eric! By killing the crow that is his link with this world — despite our hero's invulnerable powers, he could actually die!

**Dark Night of the Soul**: Eric walks towards the cemetery and meets a few playful boys and girls disguised for Halloween. He laughs, as his own *whiff of death* is a desired one.

**Break into Three**: Eric reaches Shelly's tomb, and *A and B Stories cross*. There, he can say goodbye to Sarah... but unbeknownst to him, as she exits the cemetery, she is kidnapped by Top Dollar and his minions! When Eric is about to touch the gravestone and rest forever with Shelly, he hears Sarah screaming.

**Finale**:

1. Gathering the Team: Behold our "castle," the gothic cathedral where the ending will take place. Here the mobsters are "gathered" with Sarah to wait for The Crow.

2. Executing the Plan: Our dark hero leaves the cemetery and enters the church to rescue Sarah.

3. High Tower Surprise: Surprisingly for him, they know about his "Achilles heel." They shoot the bird, injuring it, and they are about to kill Eric when Albrecht intervenes. Eric knows that he can die for real, but presses on anyway. Myca grabs the crow, but the bird pecks her eyes out, taking its own revenge.

4. Dig, Deep Down: Up on the cathedral's roof, The Crow and Top Dollar fight with swords among blasts of thunder and bolts of lightning. Top Dollar is about to kill Eric, when Eric "digs, deep down" in his memories and gives his Nemesis "30 hours of pain" all at once, causing him great agony and thus defeating him.

5. The Execution of the New Plan: Top Dollar falls to a gruesome death and Eric rescues both Sarah and Albrecht. As always, he leaves without saying goodbye.

**Final Image**: Eric returns to Shelly's tomb to die. Her spirit touches Eric and they, as our theme states, are reunited forever. The city has gotten rid of evil thanks to The Crow. And, thanks to his sacrifice, people like "us" will be able to live in peace.

# GLOSSARY

ALL STORIES ARE ABOUT TRANSFORMATION! This is not a Hollywood term... it is our motto! It should be printed out and put on top of our computers as a reminder of why we do this job. No story is worth telling unless change occurs in the hero — or in us, the audience. The bigger the growth, the more epic the tale.

ARC
This denotes the changes a character experiences as tracked from the beginning, through the middle, to the end of a screenplay.

BRANDO
The rebel found in stories of the Institutionalized kind. Named for Marlon Brando, who portrayed motorcycle tough Johnny in 1953's *The Wild One*, this is the radical who defies the system and doubts everything about the family, business or group that has stood the test of time.

CASE WITHIN A CASE
In a Whydunit, usually the initial or long-buried caper that for some reason is unresolved. By pursuing another case, the detective revisits the original — and cracks both.

COMPANY MAN
In an Institutionalized story, the one who has so bought into the establishment that he has sacrificed his humanity for it, e.g., General Mireau in *Paths of Glory* and Williamson in *Glengarry Glen Ross*.

COMPLICATION
The person, place or event that stops the lovers from being together in a romantic comedy or love story, e.g., the iceberg in *Titanic*, the short time together in *Before Sunrise*, and the secrecy in *The Reader*. Ironically, it is also the thing that keeps the lovers together — and is usually what your rom-com is "about."

CONFIDANT
In an Out-of-the-Bottle story, a person the hero can trust with the secret of his magic power — and sometimes the one who uses that information to harm the hero (so much for trust).

DOUBLE BUMP
This is Blake's magic getter-out-of-trouble when a plot with either a lot of "pipe" or a hero who must be pushed requires a couple of nudges to move into Act Two. Normally, only one "invitation" is required at Catalyst, something done to the hero. But if you need a second at Break into Two, bump away!

DOUBLE MUMBO JUMBO
In movies using "magic," the tendency of the writers to pile it on, or use several forms of it, and unwittingly make the story feel fuzzy or confusing. The rule is: We, the audience, are allowed to suspend disbelief once in a movie. You cannot be led to believe aliens and vampires exist in one world.

EXTERNAL AND INTERNAL
These are the twin skeins of action found in the Bad Guys Close In section of a script in which both external and internal pressure is applied to make our hero change — exactly what he is resisting! Having a sense of oncoming "death" in the All Is Lost moment, heroes resist both the external and internal, but cannot do so for long.

## EYE OF THE STORM

In a Dude-with-a-Problem film, the break from the fast-paced, confusing and dangerous situation our innocent hero suddenly finds himself in. It can be a friend or a love interest who also offer the hero a needed lesson.

## HALF MAN

In a Monster-in-the-House movie, the partial survivor who has had an interaction with the monster in his past and comes away damaged in some way because of it. This is the "false mentor" who can tell the hero — and us — the horror of what dealing with the monster will entail — and who is almost always sure to die!

## INSIDER

In a Fool Triumphant movie, the jealous one who realizes the "idiot" is wiser than everyone and seeks to stop him before others see this too, e.g., Doctor Lessing in *Life Is Beautiful* and Nola in *Match Point*.

## LIMP AND AN EYEPATCH

When characters lack character, that thing which gives them a unique identifying quirk or habit.

## MASCOT

In a Superhero tale, the loyal and very human underling who looks up to the title character but can never be him, e.g., Kylie the opossum in *Fantastic Mr. Fox* and Sarah in *The Crow*. Often used by the Nemesis to threaten the Superhero.

## MIDPOINT PARTY / PUBLIC COMING OUT / FALSE VICTORY / FALSE DEFEAT

When the hero has a *false victory* at the Midpoint, he thinks "he gets everything he wants." Sometimes, this manifests itself in the form of a celebration, while at other times, it's a *public coming out* as the hero declares a new identity or a new way of living. Sometimes, the hero has a *false defeat* where he "loses everything he thinks he wants." This, too, has a public aspect, as the hero's failure is often on display for others to see.

## MOMENT OF CLARITY, THE

Every hero has a period of collapse around All Is Lost. Boom. He's done. And in Dark Night of the Soul, since we've got his attention and he has nowhere else to go anyway, this is the moment when he says: "I get it!" The hero recognizes his flaws, and though it looks like he will never get a chance to capitalize on this... we know better.

## POPE IN THE POOL, THE

A distracting way to bury exposition, so called for a scene in a script where the pope swims in the Vatican pool while boring plot details are told to us. So if you have a lot of backstory to tell, try to divert the audience's attention while doing so.

## PRIMAL

What is basic about a story, a character's goal or a movie premise is its relation to our inner drives as human beings. Stories of survival, sex, hunger and revenge connote immediate interest on our part. We will stop and look when these themes are presented to us. We can't help it. We have to. It's primal. To you, the screenwriter, this means you must ground every action and story in its primal-ness. When characters are not acting like human beings, when they are not being driven primally, odds are you are testing the patience of the audience. To ask "Is it primal?" is to ask "Is this relevant to a caveman?" The answer must be: Yes!

## PROMISE OF THE PREMISE

The premise of a movie — its "What is it?" — can only be proven to be satisfying when we see it in action. What is fun, catchy or hooks our interest about a movie's poster must be paid off once we get inside the theater. If it is not paid off, we the audience will consider it to be a bad experience. We will feel cheated. The *promise of the premise* are those scenes or scene sequences that exploit the premise to its maximum and are usually found in the Fun and Games section of a screenplay. This is the point where we understand fully what this movie is about. This is why we bought our tickets.

## ROAD APPLE
In a Golden Fleece movie, this is the thing that stops the team from gaining the prize. It's the set-back, surprise backstab or bit of new information that makes the participants think they will never win the day, e.g., Alvin Straight's many obstacles in *The Straight Story*.

## RULES
The magic in an Out-of-the-Bottle story needs these parameters, guidelines or boundaries to keep what happens credible. State The Rules up front — and stick to them!

## SEX AT 60
Old-time Hollywood writers often put the first sex scene at page 60 of their normally 120-page scripts. Remarkably, this Midpoint rendezvous still occurs many times today, even in indie-world screenplays — though contemporary scripts tend to be shorter, so the Midpoint comes before 60.

## SIX THINGS THAT NEED FIXING
This is the list of a hero's minor character flaws, enemies and rivals that bully him, and a wish list that — if we like the hero enough, and think he deserves help — get "fixed" later in the film. We as an audience like to see the Six Things That Need Fixing get paid off later in the script — the more the merrier. It's thoroughly enjoyable to see those pay-offs. But you have to put the flaw in there in Act One to make the pay-off work.

## STAKES ARE RAISED
This is a term that is frequently heard in development meetings. Also known as the "ticking clock" or the "Midpoint bump," it means the raising of the level of tension. Suddenly from out of nowhere at the

Midpoint, some new thing — an even bigger and more unexpected thing than we've seen before, and one that seems insurmountable — becomes a problem for our hero. You must be sure the *stakes are raised* at the Midpoint to give the hero new challenges and lead him to his ultimate win.

## STASIS=DEATH

What's worse than going nowhere in life? Not much, and when we meet the hero during the Set-Up, this is where we find him. He's stuck in his current predicament, just "existing," but not truly living. If he doesn't do something, it's going to mean "death" for him, in some form or another. Luckily, there's a Catalyst just around the corner to jumpstart his journey.

## SYNTHESIS
a.k.a. Act One, Act Two and Act Three

*Thesis, antithesis* and *synthesis* describe the thematic progression of the hero's journey. In Act One, the hero's world is set up. In Act Two that world is turned on its head; it is the *upside-down version* of what he left behind. By mastering this surreal new world, the hero gains the knowledge to combine what was and its opposite to form a synthesis of everything he has learned. That synthesis occurs in Act Three. It is not enough for the hero to survive the journey; he must transform his world in order to truly be great.

## TANGIBLE AND THE SPIRITUAL, THE

There are two stories in every story: the thing that's happening on the surface, known as "plot," and the thing happening below the surface, known as "theme." The surface world is all material, tangible with concrete goals, obstacles, and consequences. The goals are all specific too, such as winning a trophy, a girl or a legal case. The below-the-surface world is the spiritual part; it is the lesson the hero learns from the plot — and the real story. Remember: A Story = plot = wants = tangible. And B Story = theme = needs = spiritual.

## TIME CLOCK
The "time clock" or "ticking clock" often occurs at the Midpoint as a way to let us know how much longer we've got — and to put pressure on the heroes to solve, get out of or triumph before it's too late. Examples are the pressure on Riggan to hire Shiner in *Birdman* and Minister Kempf demanding surveillance results from Wiesler in *The Lives of Others*.

## TWO-HANDER
A movie where we follow two characters, each has an arc, and each grows because of the other, e.g., *Before Sunrise*. *Three-hander* — A movie where we follow three stories, each with its own arc of growth, most often a love triangle. *Four-hander* — a movie where we follow four stories, most often a two-couple love story like *Closer* and *We Don't Live Here Anymore*.

## UPSIDE-DOWN WORLD
Once your protagonist enters Act Two, he steps into an upside-down version of life as he knew it. It's a mirror reflection of Act One, an *antithesis*. Things might be the opposite of before, but his problems still follow him. Because of this, it forces the hero to confront new challenges head-on and to grow.

## WHIFF OF DEATH
The added extra bonus found in the All Is Lost beat of a well-structured screenplay is that very special moment where something dies — actually or metaphorically. The All Is Lost point is rife with the *whiff of death* because it marks the end of the world as is and the beginning of a new world the hero will create from this seeming end.

**SALVA RUBIO**

# ABOUT THE AUTHOR

Salva Rubio, born in Madrid, Spain in 1978, is a screenwriter and "The Indie Analyst."

For 10 years he worked for Spain's foremost independent distribution, exhibition and production company, Alta Films. There, he analyzed scripts by Eric Rohmer, Gus Van Sant, Walter Salles, Jane Campion, the Coen Brothers, Christopher Hampton, Amos Gitai, John Turturro, Marjane Satrapi, Larry Clark and David Cronenberg, among others. He has also analyzed scripts for Spain's Ministry of Culture (ICAA), Instituto Cervantes, Fundación Carolina and Casa de América.

He is a professional writer, working in several media. As a feature film screenwriter, he co-wrote the animated movie *Deep* (2017) and has been hired to work on three more feature films plus several animated series and shorts.

As a graphic novel writer, he works in the French-Belgian market (Le Lombard Editeur), having published such projects as *Monet*, *Nomad of Light* and the novel *Zingara: Searching for Jim Morrison*, and is currently writing the novelization of the successful Spanish TV series *El Príncipe*.

He is a *Licenciado* in Arts History (Universidad Complutense de Madrid) and has a Master's Degree in Film and TV Screenwriting (Universiddad Carlos III de Madrid). He teaches screenwriting and narrative in a few selected schools.

He also likes to draw, paint, play guitar and recently has somehow found time to take up the trumpet.

Check him out at
*www.salvarubio.info*

and contact him at
*salva@salvarubio.info*

# SOFTWARE
# BOOKS
# WORKSHOPS

---

# SAVE THE CAT!®

www.savethecat.com